THE PEOPLE'S REPUBLIC OF CHINA

The People's Republic of China

A Concise Political History

WITOLD RODZINSKI

THE FREE PRESS
A Division of Macmillan, Inc.
New York

The Free Press
A Division of Macmillan, Inc.
866 Third Avenue, New York, N. Y. 10022

First American Edition 1988

Printed in the United States of America

printing number

1 2 3 4 5 6 7 8 9 10

Library of Congress Cataloging-in-Publication Data

Rodzinski, Witold.
    The People's Republic of China.

    Bibliography: p.
    Includes index.
    1. China—Politics and government—1949—
I. Title.
DS777.75.R63 1988   951.05   87-33183
ISBN 0-02-926871-0
ISBN 0-02-926872-9 (pbk.)

Contents

Author's Note

*Part One The Pioneering Years of People's China
1949–66*

1	The Establishment and Consolidation of the People's Republic, 1949–52	13
2	Economic Reconstruction, 1953–7	31
3	The Great Leap Forward, 1958–9	55
4	The Great Economic Crisis, 1960–1	77
5	Respite Before the Storm, 1962–5	90
6	Preparing the 'Cultural Revolution', January 1965–May 1966	106

Part Two The 'Cultural Revolution' 1966–76

7	The First Stage, May 1966–April 1969	117
8	The Intermediate Period, April 1969–August 1973	179
9	The Last Years, August 1973–September 1976	189

Part Three Seek Truth from Facts 1976–86

10	Facing Up to the Past, September 1976–December 1978	207
11	The Establishment of New Guidelines, 1979–82	236
12	The 'Second Revolution': Socialism with Chinese Characteristics, 1982–6	265

Select Bibliography	285
Index	297

Author's Note

The main aim of this work is to present and discuss some of the principal problems relating to the political development of the People's Republic of China. For this reason attention has been focused primarily on the history of the Chinese Communist Party, the key force in shaping the country's destiny. It has not been possible in this volume to deal with all the issues; for example, the interesting question of policies towards the national minorities is not touched upon. And art and literature deserve a full independent study; they are beyond the scope of a political history and have been omitted.

These reflections are largely the result of almost five decades of much interest in and concern with the events occurring in the Chinese political arena, enhanced by lengthy sojourns in China during the 1950s and 1960s. Some of them have been expressed earlier, in much briefer form, in the last two chapters of *The Walled Kingdom*, while the historical background of the PRC era also constituted the subject of the two volumes of *A History of China*. As in the case of these earlier works, the present one has been written in English. This time, however, the 'pinyin' transcription has been used throughout with a few exceptions.

I would like to take this opportunity to express my gratitude to the Faculty Board of Oriental Studies of the University of Cambridge. Its oft repeated hospitality has done much to facilitate the preparation of this work. Similarly the Chinese Academy of Social Sciences enabled me to revisit the People's Republic in 1983 and 1986, and to benefit greatly from a series of fruitful discussions concerning my earlier works and problems connected with the present volume.

WARSAW
February 1987

PART ONE

The Pioneering Years of People's China

1949–66

CHAPTER ONE

The Establishment and Consolidation of the People's Republic, 1949–52

The proclamation of the People's Republic on 1 October 1949 not only marked the victory of the Chinese communists, one of the most momentous events in twentieth-century history, but constituted as well the first step in the series of profound transformations which were to affect dramatically the world's most populous country. The significance of the victory was eloquently expressed in Mao Zedong's speech on 21 September 1949: 'The Chinese have always been a great, courageous and industrious nation; it is only in modern times that they have fallen behind. And that was due entirely to oppression and exploitation by foreign imperialism and domestic reactionary government . . . ours will no longer be a nation subject to insult and humiliation. We have stood up.'

A multitude of tasks still faced the Chinese Communist Party (CCP); its armed forces had to complete their operations against the sizeable remnants of the Guomindang troops and, most important of all, a truly effective government capable of administering the entire country and undertaking the restoration of the economy had to be established. For the accomplishment of these aims the communist leadership had at its disposal basically two closely interlinked forces: the Party itself, about four million strong by May 1949, and the People's Liberation Army (PLA).

A long and tortuous road had led to the CCP's triumph from its foundation some thirty years earlier. Its real roots rested in the May Fourth Movement of 1919 – China's intellectual rebirth – in which an attempt was made to find answers to the overwhelming problems facing the backward, semi-colonial and semi-feudal country.

During the course of this search, which entailed much confusion as to the proper choice of modern and, almost inevitably, Western concepts that could prove to be useful for dealing with China's difficulties, two of the most active participants of the May Fourth Movement, Chen Duxiu (1879–1942) and Li Dazhao (1889–1927) took the lead in turning to Marxian socialism becoming thereby also the two principal founders of the Chinese communist movement. They were soon to be joined in this pursuit by a relatively small number of still younger intellectuals who constituted the Party's first generation.

The new philosophy of Marxism, propagated primarily in its Leninist form due to the victory of the October Revolution, seemed to promise answers to the questions which preyed most on the minds of those intellectuals who were stirred into action by the May Fourth Movement. Marxism–Leninism, with its critique of capitalism and imperialism, appeared to be quite different from other Western concepts: it seemed not merely appropriate for China but actually capable of providing the key to the solution of the country's basic problems. Its adherents regarded it from the outset as a monolithic world view which could furnish them with all the necessary guiding principles for carrying out what they conceived to be the primary tasks facing them – the modernization of China and her re-emergence as a great and powerful country – a status to which, they ardently believed, China was fully entitled on the basis of her former splendid civilization and four millennia of culture. Moreover, Marxism–Leninism offered them a programme for a consistent struggle against imperialism and warlord rule – the two principal forces oppressing and degrading the country – based on the setting into motion of a social revolution making full use of the vast potential strength of the Chinese masses, particularly the peasantry.

It was the vitality and topicality of these concepts which enabled Marxism–Leninism to make an ultimately decisive impact on the shaping of modern Chinese history. However, the first two decades of the Chinese communist movement showed that the proper utilization of Marxism–Leninism and its adaptation to Chinese circumstances was a supremely difficult task. The tragedy of the 1925–7 revolution and the equally significant setbacks suffered during the retreat from the south also meant that the great majority of those who had joined the Party in its formative years had perished. It was the survivors of the legendary Long March, sheltering in a remote and backward area in the north-west, who were to preside over a new, basically different stage in the history of the CCP and of Marxism–Leninism in China.

The most crucial period in the Party's development was the War of Resistance (1937–45), for the successful struggle against Japanese imperialism transformed it in many essential aspects. Its ability to pursue the course of national liberation attracted to it tens of thousands of young peasants and intellectuals, and during these years the CCP grew in size immensely, from about 40,000 in 1937 to over 1,210,000 in the spring of 1945. It is the survivors of this Yan'an generation who make up the bulk of the present leadership of China. During the war with Japan the leadership of the CCP was able to shape the Party into a truly independent and self-reliant force, developing its own ideology by the complex process of adapting the basic tenets of Marxism–Leninism to Chinese conditions.

At the end of the War of Resistance, the CCP was still headed by the surviving members of its first generation, and its political leadership was composed of such outstanding individuals as Mao Zedong, Liu Shaoqi, Zhou Enlai, Chen Yun and Deng Xiaoping. Those who commanded the Party's armed forces – the key to its success and victory – included Chen Yi, He Long, Li Xiannian, Lin Biao, Liu Bocheng, Nie Rongzhen, Peng Dehuai, Xu Xiangjian and Ye Jianying, as well as Zhu De. The line separating the political and military leaders is, in this case, largely fictitious, since all of those mentioned had worked together from 1927 for a political cause – the establishment of socialism in a free and independent China. Under Chinese conditions, this could be pursued only by means of military struggle. In the twenty-year period since 1927 these men had achieved a rare degree of unity of thought and action and had accumulated invaluable experience in the conduct of political and military operations, especially during the war with Japan. The high calibre of the leadership, as well as its independence and self-reliance, made it possible for the CCP to face with relative composure and confidence, in spite of immense odds against it, the challenge of the civil war imposed upon it in 1946 by the Guomindang. It could afford also to disregard Stalin's advice not to fight, and thus continue the struggle to its victorious conclusion. In bringing about the triumph of the Chinese Revolution, the Chinese communists demonstrated not only their military valour and superior strategic skill but, above all, their political acumen and ability to rally all the forces hostile to the Guomindang regime.

The final preparations for the establishment of the People's Republic were completed during the session of the Chinese People's Political Consultative Conference (CPPCC) – the united front organization comprising the CCP and the eight small parties co-operating with it – held in Beijing on 21–30 September 1949. On 23 September this body adopted the Common Programme, actually a provisional constitution. The fundamental purpose of the Common Programme was to complete the tasks of the bourgeois democratic revolution and create a united, independent Chinese state. This state was defined, in theory, as a 'people's democratic dictatorship' consisting of a coalition of four classes – the working class, peasantry, urban petty bourgeoisie, and the national bourgeoisie – which together constituted over 90 per cent of the people. It was also clearly stipulated that in this new state, democracy would apply to the four classes while dictatorship would be enforced over the landlords and the bureaucratic bourgeoisie. All the elements of the people's democratic dictatorship were based on concepts evolved and put into practice by the CCP during the War of Resistance, which were given a final, succinct formulation by

16

Mao Zedong in his essay 'On the People's Democratic Dictatorship', published in June 1949.

The CPPCC also promulgated the Organic Law of the People's Republic of China (PRC) and established the Central People's Government. The Central Government Council was designated as the supreme state authority and Mao Zedong was chosen as its chairman. The State Administrative Council formed the actual governmental structure in the shape of ministries, and Zhou Enlai was nominated its premier. Thus the first steps were taken in the construction of a continuously expanding and complex state apparatus.

The military operations were concluded without any particular difficulties. The PLA entered Guangzhou (Canton) on 14 October and Urumgi on the 20th. By the end of December the campaign in Sichuan had been concluded with the liberation of Chengdu. In April 1950, PLA units successfully took control of Hainan Island. Only the width of the Taiwan Straits and the communists' lack of naval forces prevented the liberation of Taiwan during the same period and made it possible for Chiang Kai-shek and his last followers to remain on Chinese soil. The conclusion in May 1951 of an accord between the PRC and the Tibetan authorities completed the process of extending the sway of the new government over the entire mainland. The termination of military operations also signified that a considerable part of the CCP cadres working in the PLA could now be transferred to the task of building the civilian administration.

The whole country was divided into six large administrative areas under the supervision of special regional bureaus of the CCP but directed in all important respects centrally from Beijing by the communist leadership in its dual character as head of the Party and the new government. This united front strategy had proved eminently successful earlier, particularly in the 1945–9 period, for rallying all the anti-Guomindang forces, and hence was considered by the CCP as one of the three main weapons which had defeated the enemy. A large number of non-communists received posts in the central government, but the dominant and decisive role of the CCP was apparent from the outset. Ultimately all fundamental policy and decision-making rested in the hands of the Party's Political Bureau.

Within three years the communists succeeded in creating a viable administrative structure, the first truly unified government in modern Chinese history, while simultaneously extending the functioning of the Party to the entire country, in most cases down to village level. This was an outstanding achievement in view of the country's vast size, immense population of well over 500 million and great regional diversity, reflected in basic differences in the form of the spoken language. Furthermore, the new administration was scrupulously honest, which was a striking contrast and break with the Guomindang past. This was a continuation of the practices established in the Liberated Areas during the war against Japan.

The CCP established its rule under extremely unfavourable and difficult conditions. The backward economy, suffering from the effects of twelve years of war, was a shambles. Industrial production in 1949 was barely half the pre-war level. In any case, China's industrial base (heavy industry 30 per cent, light industry 70 per cent) was woefully inadequate. Modern heavy industry was restricted primarily to the north-east, and what remained of it was located in a few coastal areas. Light industry, mostly textile and food processing, was somewhat more developed but its technical level was also low and its distribution faulty. Total production of modern industry, transport and mining amounted in the pre-war era to only 10 per cent of the national output, while the modern working class numbered little more than 2 million.

In spite of the great traditional skill of the Chinese farmers, agricultural production remained low due to both economic and social factors, primarily landlordism. Agriculture, in which 80 per cent of the total population was still engaged, continued to be characterized by chronic poverty and instability, with the threat of famine ever present. In 1949, grain production amounted to a disastrously low figure of 113 million tons.

Military operations had also contributed to wrecking a major part of the country's completely inadequate transport network, especially the railways which in 1949 had only 18,000 kilometres of track, with less than half in operation.

The generally parlous state of the economy was aggravated still further by the hyperinflation created by the KMT regime which reduced the financial system to chaos.

By a series of brilliantly conceived and energetically implemented measures the new PRC authorities succeeded in resolving the current problems with remarkable speed. At the end of 1952 the gross output of industry and agriculture was 77.5 per cent higher than in 1949; coal production had been raised to 63.5 million tons, steel to 1.3 million. Grain production amounted to between 152 and 154 million tons, 10 per cent higher than in 1936, the best pre-war year. The railway system had been restored even earlier and by 1952 the construction of new lines had raised the total track length to 24,000 kilometres. Inflation was largely brought under control and a number of ingenious methods, such as tying wage levels to a basket of commodities, as well as the fact that the government kept its budget balanced and refrained from using the printing press, helped to keep the newly introduced PRC currency stable. These achievements undoubtedly contributed to a marked increase in political stability as well. At the same time, they constituted the groundwork which enabled the new government to proceed to the implementation of its plans for a fundamental reconstruction of the economy.

In May 1946, when it became apparent that the Guomindang was determined to embark upon civil war, the CCP replaced the limited rent and interest reduction policies it had pursued during the War of Resistance and launched a new land reform movement. It was implemented in a series of profoundly dramatic campaigns in practically all of the old Liberated Areas and succeeded in gaining the backing of the majority of the peasants, particularly the poor and landless, who made up about 70 per cent of the rural population. This consolidation of social and political support for the communist-led government constituted probably the most important single factor in making the victory of the CCP possible.

During the course of the military operations land reform was not extended to the new, rapidly expanding liberated territory and thus in 1949 the old agrarian order was still intact in almost four-fifths of the country. In this situation the CCP was convinced, for a number of reasons, that it was absolutely necessary to carry out the agrarian revolution to its fullest extent. Ideologically, it was felt that land reform was a fundamental part of the bourgeois democratic revolution, since it would bring about the elimination of all the remnants of semi-feudalism in Chinese society. Politically, it would deprive the landlords, potentially the most hostile class, of their economic position and strength, removing them from the political arena, while increasing the support of the peasants for the new government. Economically, it was seen as a means of solving the crucial problem of restoring and increasing agricultural production. This was 'the indispensable condition' for implementing the Common Programme, whose aim was 'the development of the productive forces and the industrialization of the nation'.

On 28 June 1950, the Agrarian Reform Law was enacted and an immense campaign was initiated against the peasants' erstwhile exploiters and oppressors. With the aid of hundreds of thousands of Party, government and PLA cadres sent down to the countryside in work teams, the entire peasantry was systematically mobilized, village by village, primarily by means of creating peasants' associations and through intense propaganda.

Apart from large areas in south-west and north-west China inhabited mostly by the national minorities, which were scheduled for land reform later on, the programme was basically completed by the end of 1952. About 46 million hectares, nearly half of all the cultivated land, changed hands, involving more than 300 million peasants. Draught animals, farm implements and housing were also subject to confiscation and redistribution. The former landlords were left with just enough land to carry on as individual farmers in the poor peasant category. Thus the rural gentry as a class was eliminated after more than two millennia of dominance in the Chinese countryside.

The elimination of the landlords was pursued relentlessly,

20

leading to physical extermination in a number of cases, as was confirmed by information obtained in the 1950s from the participants in the campaign. It is difficult to estimate the number of those who perished. At present, Chinese historians are inclined to minimize the losses, maintaining that a distinction should be made between the campaigns held before 1949 in the Liberated Areas, which were more severe, and the countrywide post-liberation reform. This is a valid point, but the fact remains that even if only one person per village was killed during the latter, then the total number of those who died is in the hundreds of thousands. It is likely that the general movement to suppress counter-revolutionaries contributed to the ruthlessness of the land reform, which was further exacerbated from October 1950 on by the Korean War. It does seem that in this respect the land reform left a heritage of dubious value, as demonstrated by the propensity for violence revealed later on during the tragic decade of the 1966–76 'cultural revolution'. All this does not alter its significance as one the most far-reaching social revolutions in the history not just of China but of the world.

The agrarian reform, while satisfying in part the demand of the peasants for land, was not in itself considered sufficient to form the basis for the development and modernization of agriculture. It is clear that the CCP leadership envisaged, even then, a relatively rapid transition to co-operativization and collectivization. However, at the time of the completion of the land reform no firm decisions had been taken regarding the speed with which this process should be promoted and the priority it should receive in general economic planning. In June 1950 Mao Zedong himself had maintained that the time for socializing agriculture 'is still very far off'. One of the basic issues involved was whether the achievement of a relatively high level of mechanization of agriculture (and hence of industrial growth) was to be considered as an indispensable prerequisite of the implementation of co-operativization. It seems certain that in the early 1950s there was no unanimity of views on this problem among the top communist policy makers.

The total bankruptcy of the Guomindang regime had created

21

a situation in which the establishment of the new communist government was greeted with relief by a good part of the urban population which had been longing for so many years for peace and stability. According to reliable eye-witness accounts the entry of the PLA into the major cities had been welcomed with considerable warmth. The most enthusiastic response came from educated youth, which had been particularly active in the struggle against the KMT in the years immediately preceding the establishment of the PRC. The most important of the increasing number of youth organizations was the New Democratic Youth League (NDYL), which in 1957 became the Communist Youth League. NDYL membership increased rapidly, from 200,000 in April 1949 to 3 million at the end of 1950 and 9 million in 1953, and it served as the primary recruiting ground for the CCP itself. In 1949 and 1950 tens of thousands of students were enlisted for training as new cadres for the growing Party and government bureaucracy.

Although the CCP had considerable experience in administering the countryside and dealing with the peasants, the task of ruling the cities and operating industry posed a number of serious problems. In the initial period of reconstruction, nationalization was limited to the largest enterprises, which in most cases had been under the control of bureaucratic capitalism, especially of the notorious Four Families of the Guomindang oligarchy. Hence, in 1949, the private sector accounted for 63.3 per cent of the total industrial output, while 85 per cent of trade still remained in private hands. Only the banking system was placed under total state control from the very outset. However, by a number of measures, such as the provision of raw materials and purchase of products, the state quickly increased its control over the private sector industries. By 1952, state-owned industry accounted for 56 per cent of total output, joint state/private enterprises for 26.9 per cent, while private enterprises for only 17.1 per cent. The new measures made full use of the limited number of existing trained personnel.

It can be assumed that, as in the case of the further transformation of the rural economy, there was a lack of clarity and consensus within the communist leadership regarding how long this multi-structured industry and commerce was to be tolerated and the initial relatively moderate policies towards the national bourgeoisie pursued. Nonetheless, there was no disagreement as to the basic aim of ultimately eliminating capitalist ownership in these two domains.

It is unlikely that the capitalists harboured any illusions as to their future position, since the fundamental policies of the government were never disguised. From the outset the CCP regarded the capitalist sector as a potential source of debilitation and corruption from which the 'sugar-coated bullets' of the bourgeoisie would spread to demoralize the Party and state apparatus. It was largely for this reason that the first of two campaigns, the San-fan (three-anti) campaign against corruption, waste and bureaucracy, was launched in the urban areas in late 1951, first in the north-east and then on a national scale. None of these three 'evils' was a new phenomenon and the last one, in particular, had deep historical roots. The public was mobilized to criticize and ultimately remove or demote cadres whose behaviour was deemed to be unsatisfactory.

The Wu-fan (five-anti) campaign against bribery, tax evasion, fraud, theft of government property and stealing state economic secrets was waged with even more intensity from February to June 1952 in the main urban centres, especially Shanghai. It showed clearly that not only was the government determined to exercise strict control over the privately owned enterprises but also that the process of extending state ownership to all of industry would be speedily completed.

The new PRC authorities also lost little time in facing up to the vast social evils of the urban areas they now ruled. Opium addiction, alcoholism, gambling and prostitution were all rife here, especially in Shanghai. These activities were most often wholly in the grip of the secret societies, especially the notorious Green Gang which also had great influence in industry through its control of labour. By 1952, the leadership of the Green Gang had been dealt with drastically and effectively, while prostitution and opium addiction were eradicated by comprehensive

23

methods of reform and rehabilitation. In the mid-1950s, one could wander safely around Shanghai and notice almost nothing which would be reminiscent of the city's earlier notoriety.

Effective government administration was built up in the towns through neighbourhood committees and in the countryside through natural villages. Other types of mass organization also played an important role in strengthening the influence of the new authorities and implementing the new social policies being introduced. The Women's Federation, for example, was assigned the additional task of giving practical effect to the very significant Marriage Law passed on 30 April 1950. This had the basic, far-reaching programmatic aim of putting an end to the inferior position, upheld by many centuries of tradition, of half of the country's population. With its prohibition of child marriage, polygamy and concubinage, the Marriage Law constituted the first step on the long and difficult road leading to the emancipation of Chinese women. Other organizations, such as the trade unions, were used primarily to disseminate the Party's programme and ideology. Complete control of all the media, which existed from the outset, facilitated this task, but the sad legacy of the past, and especially the shockingly high illiteracy rate (over 80 per cent), presented great problems and necessitated a programme of mass education. Considerable progress was achieved almost immediately in enlarging school attendance. The figures for those attending primary schools increased from 24.4 million in 1949 to 51.1 million in 1952–3, while the number of those attending secondary schools increased from 1.27 million in 1949–50 to 3.13 million in 1952–3. In both cases the rate of increase continued to climb in subsequent years. To achieve its goal of ideological and political indoctrination of the country as a whole the CCP paid special attention to what was called the remoulding of the intellectuals, probably the most difficult task of all.

The intellectuals were said to number around 4 million, and thus included almost everyone who had completed secondary education; of these, around 100,000 were classified as 'higher' intellectuals. The vital importance of this small but crucial stratum of Chinese society was fully recognized by the Chinese communists, and a series of ideological campaigns was waged for the purpose of inducing the intellectuals, some of whom were Western-educated, to be favourably disposed towards the new order. It should be pointed out that the majority of Western-educated intellectuals stayed in China when the communists took power and were willing to help in rebuilding the country; some eminent scholars who were abroad at the time of the establishment of the PRC returned home for the same purpose. In a number of cases, as for example that of the noted rocket specialist Qian Xuesen, they had to overcome considerable difficulties before they could achieve their aim.

The cardinal question of what foreign policy would be pursued by the new government in Beijing was elucidated by Mao Zedong even before the establishment of the PRC. It would 'lean to one side' in the international arena by allying itself with the Soviet Union at a time when the 'cold war' was becoming more intense. The decision was, at least in part, ideological, for the Chinese communists did at that time regard the Soviet Union as a socialist state which could and should offer China much needed political and economic support and serve as a model for building socialism. Nonetheless, there is no reason to assume that the Chinese communist leadership had any particular illusions as to the actual attitude of Stalin towards China, since this emerged very clearly from the policies he had pursued quite consistently in the 1930s and 1940s, and especially during the crucial period of the War of Liberation (1946–9). Stalin's principal aim had always been to subordinate the CCP and its struggle to the interests of the Soviet Union as he conceived them. The Chinese communists had to fight strenuously to assert their independence in order to bring victory to the Chinese Revolution. Although their struggle was often disguised by esoteric language, such basic CCP documents as the 'Resolution on Party History', passed in 1945, served precisely this goal. The severe criticism of the mistakes committed by the Wang Ming faction, which had faithfully followed Comintern instructions, was, in reality, directed against Stalin.

When the Chiang Kai-shek regime launched civil war in 1946, Stalin, who had never disguised his disdainful view of the CCP, rated the Chinese communists' chances of winning as insignificant and advised them to come to terms. The Chinese listened politely, probably expressed complete agreement with his views, and then, after returning to China, did exactly the opposite of what he proposed.

The amount of aid the Chinese communists received from the Soviet Union during this crucial period was, as could be expected, meagre. It was limited to some of the military equipment which the Soviet army had taken from the Japanese forces in the north-east; this was much less than what the Guomindang had acquired in other parts of the country and the unstinting aid it received from the United States.

As the victory of the Chinese Revolution drew closer in the spring of 1949, Stalin's negative approach remained unaltered. It is reported that he sought to persuade the Chinese leadership to refrain from having the PLA cross the Yangtse and complete the military annihilation of Chiang Kai-shek's regime. This may have been due to Stalin's apprehension about a possible conflict with the United States. It is also possible that his reluctance to see the Chinese communists gain complete power was partially the result of the Soviet break with Yugoslavia, which had taken place the preceding year and had markedly increased Stalin's pathological suspiciousness of the independent-minded Chinese. Mao Zedong had stated in 1962 that before the Korean War Stalin viewed him as a potential Tito.

It was against this background that within a few months of the establishment of the PRC, recognized immediately by the Soviet Union, high-level talks were initiated between the two governments. Mao Zedong travelled to Moscow on 16 December 1949 for what was said to be his first official meeting with Stalin. Although fêted royally, he was kept cooling his heels, probably to cut him down to size and make him more malleable in the forthcoming negotiations. Mao's reaction to this peculiar treatment was characteristic of his perception of his own place in history and of the significance of the victory of the Chinese

Revolution. He expressed his displeasure in pithy and earthy Hunanese peasant fashion and stressed his determination to return home immediately unless things changed. The gambit worked; negotiations, lengthy and arduous, did begin, culminating in the signing on 18 February 1950 of a thirty-year Sino-Soviet Treaty of Friendship, Alliance and Mutual Assistance. It provided also for what resembled a restoration of Tsarist Russia's position in the north-east before its defeat in the Russo-Japanese War of 1905. Thus, in separate agreements, joint control of the Changqun railway line (the old Chinese Eastern which the Soviet Union had in fact sold to the Japanese in 1935) was established, while a Soviet military base was set up in the Port Arthur-Dalien area.

Simultaneously, separate economic talks were conducted, which concluded with the granting by the Soviet government to China of credits worth US $300 million (50 cents per capita of the Chinese population). In passing, it might be noted that the value of the industrial equipment (mostly modern and selectively chosen) shipped out by the Soviet military from the north-east in 1946-7 as 'war booty' has been estimated at between $600 and $800 million.

The formation of the Sino-Soviet alliance seemed to indicate a notable increase in the strength of what was then referred to by some as the socialist camp. The Soviet Union had gained, with barely any effort on its part, a potentially invaluable ally, and the international balance of forces was thereby radically altered. It is open to question, however, whether the Soviet leadership, either then or later, fully appreciated the significance of what had been presented to them on a silver platter, and in particular whether they grasped the fundamental distinction between the PRC and, for example, Bulgaria.

One of the factors which inclined the CCP to favour the conclusion of an alliance with the Soviet Union was the hostility with which its victory and the establishment of the PRC was regarded by the United States. The US administration had done everything in its power to save the moribund Chiang regime; it had lavished about $6 billion of aid, primarily military, in its efforts to prop up the Guomindang, only to see the PLA drive triumphantly into Beijing in American jeeps and trucks. The 'loss' of China, as the Americans viewed the situation although the country was not theirs to lose, became an acutely controversial issue in American domestic politics, with the Republicans attacking and berating the Democratic administration for its supposed weakness and lack of determination. In these circumstances, no steps were envisaged to acknowledge the *fait accompli* and recognize the new government in Beijing, as Great Britain did in January 1950. Instead, the Truman administration chose to wash its hands of Chinese affairs. In August 1949 it issued the fatuous White Paper on US–China policy which was supposed to demonstrate that the results of the civil war were the product of internal Chinese forces which the United States had tried to influence with unstinting effort but could not. This admission of total political impotence was followed by the adoption of a policy of 'waiting for the dust to settle'. In reality this amounted to hoping that the Chinese communists would prove unable to master the vast problems of ruling a ruined country and incapable of consolidating their new government. The American refusal to recognize the new government also blocked China's entry into the United Nations.

Although resentment at American intervention in the civil war had been well-nigh boundless, the Chinese communists were not averse to normalizing relations with the United States if it should show itself willing to treat the new Chinese government as the sole representative of the entire country. This meant that the Americans would refrain from offering further assistance to their erstwhile client Chiang Kai-shek, now ensconced in his new refuge in Taiwan. However, eight months after the founding of the PRC, the war in Korea put paid to any attempt to achieve Sino-American détente.

All the endeavours of the new government in Beijing were vitally affected by the outbreak in June 1950 of the war in Korea. Whatever the origins of this conflict, the one thing that can be ascertained with complete certainty is that the Chinese communists did not initiate it. In view of their immense and complex domestic tasks it can also be safely assumed that they were not at all eager to participate in it. Nonetheless, a number of factors did induce the Chinese leadership to decide for intervention. When, after the Inchon landing, American forces advanced to the Yalu River, Zhou Enlai repeatedly cautioned them against approaching the Chinese border. His warnings were contemptuously dismissed by MacArthur and, from the Chinese point of view, the danger to the north-east became imminent. In addition, the Chinese leadership took into account the distinct possibility that the Americans might assist the Guomindang in renewing civil war on the mainland, for on 27 June Truman had ordered the Seventh Fleet into action to 'neutralize' the Taiwan Straits. This was tantamount to establishing a United States military protectorate over Taiwan and the Guomindang regime.

By the second half of October 1950 the dies was cast. PLA units, 400,000 strong, having sewed on their uniforms a small oblong patch with the inscription 'Chinese People's Volunteers' (CPV), crossed the Yalu unperceived, and in a series of rapid offensives, starting in November, pushed the Americans back across the 38th parallel, capturing Seoul in January 1951. However, the overwhelming technical superiority of the enemy, particularly in the air, brought about the loss of Seoul in March, and the conflict settled down to a long, bitter and costly seesaw struggle on the 38th parallel in which the Chinese People's Volunteers, ably commanded by Peng Dehuai, proved themselves a match for the world's strongest military power. The price in casualties was considerable and among those who fell was Mao Anying, Mao Zedong's eldest son. But it demonstrated that the China of the Opium Wars and the I He Tuan era had truly receded into a remote past. It was, in the apt phrase of a French historian, a brilliant revenge after a century of powerlessness and humiliation. Having fought the Americans to a standstill, the Chinese agreed in July 1951 to begin negotiations, finally concluded in July 1953 with the signing of an armistice.

The domestic consequences of the Korean War were extensive. The campaign for the suppression of counter-revolutionaries, which became intensive from February 1951 on, was probably launched largely due to the involvement in the Korean conflict. Its severity, especially during the first half of 1951, when thousands of people were executed, was clearly exacerbated by the general political tension induced by the war.

It should be noted that the campaign against counter-revolutionaries also involved what the Chinese termed a 'settling of accounts' for crimes committed in the past. In 1955 a club room for retired railway workers in Wuhan displayed a series of photographs illustrating the trial in 1953 of a former top official of the Beijing–Hankou railroad. He was accused and found guilty of collaborating with the military in suppressing the famous February 1923 strike which had ended with the massacre of close to forty of its participants. The last picture showed the man in question being driven off in an open lorry to his execution. The comment of the old workers, who had themselves taken part in the strike, was characteristic: 'We had to wait a long time – thirty years – but justice was finally done.'

After the entry of the CPV into Korea, the Beijing authorities organized an immense political mobilization campaign under the slogan 'Help Korea, Resist American Imperialism', which continued throughout the war and reached almost the whole population of the country. It was probably one of the most successful political campaigns to be waged in the PRC, for its appeal to Chinese patriotism found a strong response among practically every sector of Chinese society.

It is difficult to estimate the economic cost of the Chinese involvement in the Korean conflict. The CPV rose to around 700,000 strong, with most of the PRC's armed forces seeing action in Korea due to systematic rotation. The maintenance of such a sizeable force must have been a considerable financial burden and it is clear that valuable resources, not least in human terms, were devoted to the war instead of being concentrated on economic recovery. The PRC did receive fairly substantial military assistance from the Soviet Union during the years of combat in Korea, particularly in building up its almost non-existent air force, but this too had to be paid for, down to the last bullet.

CHAPTER TWO

Economic Reconstruction,
1953–7

The successful completion by the end of 1952 of basic economic rehabilitation enabled the CCP leadership to begin the transition to socialism through a far-reaching programme of reconstruction. The fundamental aim was to achieve, as quickly as possible, comprehensive modernization of the backward country. In this endeavour the Chinese looked to the Soviet Union as a model to be followed in almost every respect, as they had ever since the establishment of the PRC. The Soviet Union was the one major country which had attempted to build socialism, and had also successfully industrialized a backward country. China, however, was still more backward economically and socially than Tsarist Russia had been. The level of industry in China in 1949 was less than half of that in Russia in 1917, and by 1952 Chinese industry amounted to only 25 per cent of the Soviet level for 1927. Agricultural production per capita in China in 1952 amounted to only 20 per cent of that in the Soviet Union in 1927. Thus, the economic conditions for building socialism, or for that matter for carrying out any appreciable modernization of the country, were far less favourable in China. Nonetheless, the Chinese leadership was adamantly determined to tackle the transition to socialism almost as soon as economic recovery had been completed. One of the basic reasons for this desire rested in the fact that the Chinese leaders were now in their fifties and sixties, and they wanted to see these tasks accomplished in their own lifetimes.

In September 1953 the principles of the First Five-Year Plan, covering 1953–7, were published, though a final version was not adopted until April 1955. Since it was taken as axiomatic that socialism could not be built without an appropriate expansion of the economy and hence that industrialization was absolutely crucial, this was where the main emphasis of the plan lay, with priority being given to the development of heavy industry. The principal aim was to double industrial production within the period of the plan. Fifty-eight per cent of the money to be invested was designated for industry, of which 88.8 per cent was assigned to heavy industry, 11.2 per cent to light industry. By contrast, only 7.6 per cent of investments was earmarked for agriculture.

The basic premises of the First Five-Year Plan were modelled almost entirely on Soviet experience and were drawn up with the participation of Soviet experts and advisers. Their assistance played a considerable role during this period, especially in the establishment of previously non-existent sectors of industry, in machine building, electronics, steel and oil industries. Close to 10,000 Soviet experts worked in China during these years, as did hundreds of engineers from East European countries; and thousands of Chinese technicians were trained in the Soviet Union. Direct assistance in the furnishing of industrial equipment was also significant, with 147 key plants being provided by the Soviet Union.

The programme of industrialization was, however, based on the assumption that it would have to be financed primarily by China herself. The total value of Soviet assistance amounted to only 3 per cent of the overall sum assigned for the fulfilment of the Five-Year Plan. However it was valuable because the possibility of obtaining aid from the West was minimal, largely due to American hostility. Agriculture would have to provide the main funds required for China's industrialization. This factor was reflected in the urgency with which the reconstruction of agriculture was embarked upon in 1955.

The nationalization of industry and commerce was completed by the beginning of 1956. In the process a whole series of measures were applied step by step with much ingenuity, which represented various transitional forms of state capitalism, end-

ing with entire branches of industry and commerce being oper-
ated on a joint state–private basis. Ultimately, the capitalists
were bought out, receiving, up to 1967, fixed interest payments
of 5 per cent on the shares they had held. A number of them also
continued to be employed in the administration of the enterprises they had previously owned. It is now officially admitted
that a 'proper job in employing and handling some of the former
industrialists and businessmen' was not done. It is also accepted
that the reorganization of private industry and trade was both
premature and too hasty, resulting in a shrinkage of the com-
mercial network and a decrease in the variety and quantity of
goods and services available.

The costs of industrialization were borne primarily by the
peasants who paid for it in two ways: a relatively high agricultural tax was imposed and, perhaps even more important, the
compulsory sale of grain to the state was introduced. The prices
fixed were low while at the same time the prices of goods bought
by the peasants, particularly industrial products, were set at
high levels. In November 1953 state monopoly of the grain
trade was established.

The economic results of the land reform had not been up to
expectations as far as increasing production was concerned; the
growth of the total grain crop in 1953 and 1954 was very meagre.
Furthermore, some of the communist leaders, Mao Zedong in
particular, envisaged the possibility that in the post-reform
period the peasants would polarize into those getting richer and
those getting poorer and thus create the danger of a further
growth in rural capitalism. Actually, the rich and upper middle
peasants were not in a position to be a serious threat, either
economically or politically, although it was of course true that a
considerable number of them would have preferred the situation in the countryside to remain as it had been established after
the agrarian reform.

Probably the most important single motive guiding the thinking of some of the communist leaders was simply the somewhat
doctrinaire and dogmatic view, expressed in July 1953 by Li
Fuchun, one of the top economic policy makers, that 'socialism

cannot be built up on the basis of a small peasant economy; it can be built up only on the basis of large collective industrial or agricultural undertakings'. This view undoubtedly reflected the tendency then prevalent of regarding the Soviet model and experience as binding and obligatory.

Thus the initial decision to put the matter of agricultural co-operatives on the agenda, made in December 1951, was not surprising. What did turn out to be astounding was the speed with which the development took place from 1955 on. It is possible that there was an unspoken desire not to let the peasants get too accustomed to the post-land reform situation and to regard it, as many would have wanted to – since their attachment to the land, both the old and the newly acquired, was intense – as something eternal and unalterable. It is also likely that the CCP wanted to take full advantage of the authority and prestige that had accrued to it among the peasants for having initiated and carried out successfully the agrarian reform. Of decisive importance, as well, was the belief, firmly held by the majority of the Chinese communist leaders, that the co-operativization of agriculture should and would lead to a sizeable increase in production and would also make the overall management of agriculture by the state authorities appreciably easier.

In the simplest form of co-operation, that of mutual aid teams, steady progress had been achieved; by early 1955 around 65 per cent of peasant households participated in them. However, in the next level, that of 'lower' co-operatives, in which remuneration was based on the contribution of land, tools and animals, as well as the labour expended, not very much had been accomplished, since by December 1953 only around 14,000 of these co-operatives had been established. It was against this background that on 16 December 1953 the Central Committee of the CCP passed a new resolution on the development of agricultural producers' co-operatives, which can be considered the launch of the basic campaign to implement co-operativization. By the end of 1954, the number of co-operatives had increased to 100,000, incorporating 7 per cent of the total number of peasant households and 8 per cent of the land. The intensity of the

34

campaign was then increased, with the result that by June 1955, 650,000 co-operatives had been set up, embracing 16.9 million households out of a total of 110 million. According to the provisions of the First Five-Year Plan, this number was to increase to 1 million co-operatives (one-third of all households) by the end of 1957.

In the summer of 1955, however, the whole question of agricultural co-operation took on a completely new aspect as a result of the drastic personal intervention of Mao Zedong. The opinions and advice of many CCP officials directly concerned with rural development, such as the able and experienced Deng Zihui (1896–1972), then head of the Central Committee's Rural Work Department, who favoured continuing a moderate step-by-step approach, were disregarded by Mao. He advocated an immediate speeding up of the process of co-operativization which, according to him, was to be completed by the spring of 1958. His speech on this topic, delivered on 31 July 1955, is a good illustration of his impatience and desire for hasty progress, which was to become more and more pronounced. Mao presented his own views as if they were those of the peasants, supposedly more eager for a rapid advance than many of the CCP cadres. He berated the latter, who complained of excessive speed, as tottering women with bound feet. At the same time, Mao reversed his previous stand that full collectivization of agriculture would have to wait for industrialization to develop to a level that would assure appropriate mechanization. By throwing his immense prestige and authority on the scales, Mao put an end, as the outspoken Chen Yi caustically observed, to the debate on this topic, which had been going on since 1949, if not earlier.

There was one aspect in his momentous speech which, in retrospect, appears ironic and tragic. Mao reminded his audience that the CCP's celebrated slogan during the revolutionary wars was 'fight no battle unprepared, fight no battle you are not sure of winning', stating that it could be applied to the work of building socialism as well. But his decision to rush forward to full collectivization turned out to be but the first of many examples of his own failure to adhere to this wise adage.

35

On the basis of Mao Zedong's views, the Central Committee passed on 17 October 1955 a resolution on problems of agricultural co-operation, setting April 1958 as the date by which full co-operativization should be achieved. In reality, the pressure exerted by the Party apparatus, and especially by the rural cadres eager to prove their worthiness, was so great that by December 1955 more than 70 million households (over 60 per cent of the total) had joined the co-operatives, which now numbered 1.9 million. By December 1956, the figure had gone up to 88 per cent of the peasant families, and by the end of 1957 the entire population of the countryside had been supposedly incorporated into co-operatives. These were then reorganized into 'higher' socialist co-operatives, in which only the labour expended and not the land contributed constituted the basis for remuneration. In the process of this reorganization the units were enlarged and ultimately 485,000 collective farms were formed.

The initial collectivization of agriculture in the PRC, although carried out at such a rapid pace, did not entail as calamitous a disorganization and loss of production as had been the case in the Soviet Union, nor did it bring with it comparable hardship and suffering for the majority of those involved. One can assume that the awareness of the Chinese communists of what had really happened in the Soviet Union during collectivization had been one of the basic reasons for the care and moderation exercised until 1955. It is also quite possible that they wished to show that with their superior knowledge and much richer experience of working with the peasants they could carry out collectivization without the disastrous consequences felt in the Soviet Union. This did not prevent Mao Zedong from hypocritically praising Stalin's collectivization, and stating that 'the Soviet Union's experience is our model'. However, whatever lessons the Chinese had drawn from the negative example of the Soviet Union were soon forgotten when within two years the commune movement was launched. Nevertheless it is true that, as Mao claimed, the successful completion of collectivization – 'the high tide of socialism', in his words – did denote a fundamental change in the country's political and socio-economic situation, signifying that 'the victory of socialism will be practically assured'.

It is almost impossible to ascertain how willing the Chinese peasants were to join the co-operatives in 1956 and 1957. If there was resistance, then it was clearly on a much smaller scale than in the case of the Soviet peasants; there are no reports of the slaughter of cattle in such immense numbers nor, more important, of such ghastly losses of human lives. But, with the wisdom of hindsight, it is now clear that the speed with which collectivization was implemented gave rise to very serious divergences within the Party's leadership, with dire consequences for its future. However, at the time, these divisions were very successfully concealed; inner-Party debates were shrouded in far-reaching secrecy and the myth of complete unity within the CCP leadership continued to be maintained and skilfully propagated. It might be noted, in passing, that it was precisely this facade of unity which impressed Marxists and progressives so favourably all over the world, not excluding the countries of Eastern Europe and the Soviet Union. This was particularly true during the dire and terrible last five years of Stalin's life, which corresponded with the first years of the PRC. The contrast with People's China was a heartening one; it seemed to many that the Chinese could and would prove that revolution does not have to devour its makers, and that a group of brilliant leaders could work together for their common cause and not repeat the folly and horrors of the Stalinist purges.

By the end of 1951 the successes achieved in the rehabilitation of the economy and in the political consolidation of the new authorities made it possible to prepare for the transition from provisional government, adopted in 1949, to a more permanent administration. In November 1952, work on the draft of the new constitution was begun; the pace followed was rather leisurely, for the final version was not completed until June 1954. It was adopted on 22 September 1954 during the first session of the new formal government body, the National People's Congress.

A greater degree of centralization now prevailed: the great administrative areas were abolished in June, while the regional CCP bureaus came to an end in December 1954. Apart from this the new government and constitution did not give rise to significant changes. The great majority of the incumbent ministers and officials, led by Zhou Enlai (premier from 1949 until his death in 1976) continued to hold their previous posts and, as before, all the fundamental policy-making decisions rested till 1966 in the hands of the CCP Political Bureau. The creation of a new government machine did lead, however, to a further expansion of both the state and Party apparatus, for which a detailed system of hierarchical ranks was established in 1955. It was possible to note a distinct tendency to overstaffing, while the style of work of this costly and overblown officialdom was clearly becoming more and more bureaucratic.

A somewhat similar trend of development also affected the People's Liberation Army which, after the Korean War, and partly as its result, was slowly becoming a more professional army. In 1955, new military ranks and uniforms were introduced, both modelled on those of the Soviet Union. This produced a curious phenomenon since it meant that the Chinese communist military, who had won their own revolution, wore Tsarist epaulettes, which had been reintroduced in the Soviet Union during the war with Nazi Germany. If at that time one questioned the suitability of these ornaments, the straight-faced answer was that they served to emphasize the solidarity of the socialist camp.

After the end of the Korean War, which in itself greatly strengthened its position, the PRC became increasingly active in international affairs. In the spring and summer of 1954 China participated in two conferences in Geneva devoted to the Korean and Indochinese questions. While the first of these, held from 26 April to 15 June, produced no results whatsoever, it did provide an excellent opportunity for Zhou Enlai to display to the world his remarkable diplomatic talents. Until February 1958 he held the portfolio of foreign minister in addition to his principal office of premier. Zhou's experience in the diplomatic field was already considerable, dating back at least to the famous Xi'an Incident of 1936. It included as well his years in Chongqing during the war against Japan and his conduct of negotiations with the Guomindang and the United States in 1945-6 on the eve of the War of Liberation. During the conference on Indochina (8 May–21 July), which did have some results although only very temporary ones, Zhou's skilful advocacy of a moderate policy made a strong impression, especially when contrasted with the icy, rigid hostility displayed by the Americans, in particular John Foster Dulles.

Still more significant successes were gained by the Chinese, and by Zhou Enlai personally, at the Bandung Conference on 18-24 April 1955 attended by twenty-nine Asian and African states. Zhou's enthusiastic and adroit support for the Five Principles of Peaceful Co-existence (mutual respect for territorial integrity and sovereignty, non-aggression, non-interference, mutual equality and benefit, peaceful co-existence) greatly enhanced the stature of the PRC, significantly increased its prestige in the international arena and also facilitated an intensification of its activities in the Third World. The Five Principles are now once again, after the vagaries of the 1960s and 1970s, at the centre of Chinese foreign policy.

It was also during this period that the first serious dissension within the communist leadership was revealed in connection with the accusations cast upon two prominent officials, Gao Gang and Rao Shushi. Gao Gang (1902–54), a CCP member since 1926, had been the leader of the peasant and guerrilla movement in his native province of Shaanxi and one of the founders of the revolutionary base in north Shaanxi, which served as a refuge in 1935 for Mao Zedong and the other survivors of the legendary Long March. Having held high positions in the Party during the War of Resistance, he assumed, in 1945, the post of top representative of the CCP in the north-east where, together with Lin Biao, he succeeded in extending the sway of the Party to all parts of this crucial region. In 1952, already a Political Bureau member, he was transferred to Beijing to become chairman of the State Planning Commission. In February 1954 he was accused at a plenum of the Central Committee of having created for himself an 'independent kingdom' in the north-east. With Rao Shushi (1903–75), the former political commissar of the New Fourth Army and the Third Field Army, head of the East China Regional Bureau and from 1952 chief of the key Organizational Department of the Central Committee, Gao Gang was also accused of conspiring to form an 'anti-Party alliance' with the aim of 'splitting the Party and assuming supreme power in the Party and the State'. Both men, and some of their associates, were expelled from the Party and removed from all posts; Gao Gang is said to have committed suicide.

Over a year later, in March 1955, when a National Conference of the CCP approved the measures taken earlier against Gao and Rao, the affair was made public. There is little possibility of determining the validity of the charges against the two men, but it should be noted that some of those who were accused of being Gao Gang's 'accomplices' were restored in the 1980s to high Party positions. A factor which further complicates an assessment of this affair is that some of the individuals actively engaged in condemning Gao and Rao hold at the present moment the most prominent positions in the CCP leadership. In any case, the incident was, and still is today, presented as purely a factional, unprincipled struggle for power. There are some indications that Gao Gang's 'independent kingdom' in the north-east was in fact an attempt to increase Soviet influence and control in that vital area. In view of the close relations between Stalin and Gao Gang, and the former's penchant for seeking to recruit at least some leaders of other ruling communist parties as his own agents, such a possibility cannot be excluded.

Relations between the PRC and the Soviet Union altered after Stalin's death in March 1953. The struggle for succession in Moscow automatically strengthened Beijing's position. When the Khrushchev group finally emerged victorious, it showed a willingness to depart from Stalin's distrustful and niggardly attitude and policies towards China. In September 1954, Khrushchev and Bulganin went to Beijing for the celebration of the

PRC's fifth anniversary. During their visit the question of the restoration of Port Arthur was resolved, the four Sino-Soviet companies set up to exploit the natural resources of Xinjiang and the north-east – a prime example of Stalin's colonialist policies, detested by the Chinese communists – were liquidated, and agreements regarding further Soviet economic assistance in connection with China's industrialization programme were concluded. The period between March 1953 and the 20th Congress of the Communist Party of the Soviet Union in 1956 was probably the most harmonious in the entire history of post-1949 Sino-Soviet relations.

From the very outset, the CCP had been adamant in its efforts to bring about a complete remoulding of the thinking of the country's intellectuals, seeking their total conformity with the Party's ideology. A seemingly endless number of campaigns had been launched with this aim in mind. Most of the intellectuals had been subjected to various forms of indoctrination including the tedious and interminable meetings devoted to criticism and self-criticism so characteristic of the Chinese communists' style of work and propaganda. As the social and economic transformation in the mid-1950s increased in scope, the growing intensity of ideological struggle also became more apparent. In 1955 it took on a particularly ominous character with the raucous campaign launched against the well-known literary critic Hu Feng (1903–85), a former close collaborator of the famed writer Lu Xun. Hu Feng considered himself an independent Marxist and had already clashed with the official literary establishment in Shanghai in the years immediately preceding the war with Japan. In 1954, Hu and his followers challenged the rigidity of the Party's line and policies in the field of the arts, literature in particular, questioning its right to be the sole arbiter and demanding more freedom for individual artists. A co-ordinated onslaught against Hu Feng was speedily set into motion and in May 1955 he was accused of heading a 'counter-revolutionary clique' which had the aim of 'overthrowing the PRC and restoring imperialist and Guomindang rule'. Hu's accuser was no less an authority than Mao Zedong himself. Hu Feng was imprisoned, perhaps to serve as a warning to others in line with the Chinese saying 'Kill the rooster to frighten the monkey'.

In 1980 it was confirmed that the charges against Hu Feng had been completely groundless. It is difficult to ascertain at present whether Mao had been misled by false reports or whether, as is quite likely, this incident was one of the earlier instances of his excessive suspiciousness and over-reaction to what was, in reality, an insignificant challenge to his own authority. The volume of selected works published under Hua Guofeng's official editorship included Mao's writings on the Hu Feng affair, and make sorry reading indeed.

As well as seeking to suppress any overt criticism or opposition, the PRC authorities were endeavouring to induce the country's top intellectuals to engage more directly in the vast and ambitious programme of transformation. It was for this purpose primarily that a special session of the Chinese Academy of Science was held in Beijing in June 1955 to begin discussion of the long-term plan of its scientific research. The meeting was attended by Zhou Enlai, whose participation was an illuminating illustration of his capability. During a long, wearisome exposition delivered by Lu Dingyi (b. 1906), then head of the Central Committee Propaganda Department, in his thick Shanghai accent, to which the audience of 200-odd of the best brains in the country listened impassively and expressionlessly, Zhou could be seen jotting down notes. He then delivered extemporaneously a one-and-a-half-hour-long lucid, cogently argued speech on the tasks of science and scientists in China.

There was no one better suited than Zhou Enlai for pouring oil on troubled waters and for speaking a language which the intellectuals could understand and appreciate. He returned to the fundamental subject of the CCP's approach towards the intelligentsia in a policy-setting speech delivered on 14 January 1956 at a special conference of the Central Committee. It reflected also a new tendency towards liberalization, partly derived from the satisfactory results achieved in the collectivization of agriculture and the nationalization of industry and trade, which had markedly increased the self-confidence of the communist leadership, a quality of which they were never particularly short.

Stressing the vital role of the intellectuals in the country's development, and repeating much of the argument he had employed during the meeting with the Academy of Science six months earlier, Zhou Enlai told the intellectuals that the Party would spare no effort to mobilize them for the current tasks of socialist construction, treating them with trust and generally improving their work and living conditions. He told them that, regardless of their social origin, the overwhelming majority should now be regarded as constituting part of the working class. In return, Zhou stressed that the Party expected the intellectuals to continue the process of remoulding their ideology.

Few events in the history of the international communist movement were as dramatic and far-reaching in their consequences as the 20th Congress of the Communist Party of the Soviet Union held on 14–25 February 1956. The issues raised there by Khrushchev's speech reverberated like the shock waves from an earthquake, especially among the other ruling communist parties. They were also instrumental in bringing out into the open for the first time significant divergences between the Soviet and Chinese parties.

It was clear from the outset that the Chinese communist leadership, and Mao Zedong in particular, found Khrushchev's revelation of Stalin's crimes, although it was only partial at most, completely unacceptable. Hence, a proper assessment of Stalin's role and place in history, and with it the problem of the 'personality cult', was soon to become an ever more serious source of contention between the two parties. The disagreements on this subject were initially exacerbated by the resentment felt by the Chinese communists for not having been consulted about Khrushchev's speech before it was delivered like a bombshell. But this resentment was not, of course, felt only by the Chinese.

On 5 April 1956 the CCP published its own evaluation of some of the issues raised by Khrushchev's speech in an article entitled 'On the Historical Experiences of the Dictatorship of the Proletariat'. It was written by some of the best pens – or rather brushes – in the Party, and became the first salvo of a long and increasingly bitter polemic.

Although their own experiences with Stalin had not been the easiest, to say the least, the Chinese communist leaders, and especially Mao Zedong himself, refused to accept Khrushchev's indictment of him, although it had revealed only an infinitesimal part of the Soviet people's sufferings during his reign. Instead, the Chinese leadership continued to present Stalin as an 'outstanding Marxist–Leninist fighter' who had, however, committed some serious mistakes. These included, among other things, the 'broadening of the scope of the suppression of counter-revolution'. The entire problem of Stalinist terror and of the millions of its innocent victims was thus cavalierly disposed of with this one phrase, which must be the understatement of the century.

The CCP took the view that most of the problems raised in Khrushchev's speech, especially the question of the personality cult, did not apply to the Chinese party as it had supposedly adhered to practising democratic centralism and collective leadership. In particular, the employment of the 'mass line', i.e. maintaining constant contact with the masses, had prevented the emergence in China of negative phenomena similar to those existing, by implication, in the Soviet Union. These claims, only partially true to the period up to 1956, were to be made almost completely untenable within only three years.

In criticizing Khrushchev for his simplistic approach, the Chinese communists were guilty of the same fault. They did not analyse the historical roots and structural faults of the Soviet system which had made the authoritarian tyranny known as Stalinism possible and rendered the claim that socialism had been built in the Soviet Union so very specious. The fundamental reason for this lack of analysis was that the political and socio-economic order in the USSR resembled that of the PRC to a discomfiting degree. Moreover, the legacy of Tsarist Russia, shaped by Byzantine autocracy and Mongol despotism, which influenced the shaping of the Soviet state so profoundly, was but a parvenu in comparison with the Middle Kingdom's heritage of almost four millennia of monarchic rule and over 2000 years of a centralized, absolutist state. In both countries, the absence of a thoroughgoing bourgeois revolution and of an extensive period of capitalism made the building of socialism on democratic principles – the only truly feasible basis – that much more difficult. In the case of China, where the effects of the long despotic-bureaucratic past were even more tenacious and tangibly present, the failure to face up to these problems was to prove extremely costly ten years later when Mao launched his disastrous 'cultural revolution'.

In April 1956, Mao simply dismissed the entire problem of Stalinism and Stalin; employing the ingrained Chinese habit of numerical comparisons, he portrayed Stalin's achievements as outweighing his mistakes in a ratio of 7 to 3. It should be noted, however, that in the speech in which he repeated and expanded this assessment of Stalin ('On the Ten Major Relationships', delivered on 25 April 1956, but not published until 1977), Mao was by no means uncritical of the Soviet Union. On the contrary, he pointed to a number of serious errors and defects in Soviet development, which the PRC would do well to avoid repeating. Primarily, though, Mao was concerned with discussing some fundamental political and economic problems facing China, and he dealt with them in a generally realistic and balanced fashion. This perhaps explains why the work is currently considered an outstanding example of the intellectual ability he could still display, and an illustration of his role as one of the CCP's leading, if not most eminent, theorists.

With the intention, more than likely, of opposing the prevalent tendency of blindly and thoughtlessly emulating everything Soviet, Mao maintained that the Soviet practice of excessively squeezing the peasants as a method of capital accumulation was a grave mistake since it 'dampened their enthusiasm in production'. Other features of the Soviet system which he considered to be negative included the 'over-concentration of everything in the hands of the central authorities' and the abnormal relations between the Russians and the minority nationalities. Mao also noted that 'many people in the Soviet Union are conceited and very arrogant', an observation presumably based exclusively on the behaviour of the only individuals he had had contact with – members of the Soviet leadership.

A further reflection of the far-reaching repercussions in China of the 20th Congress of the CPSU, and intimately connected with the eternally perturbing problem of the intellectuals, was revealed in the slogan 'Let a Hundred Flowers Bloom, Let a Hundred Schools Contend', contained in a speech delivered by Mao on 2 May 1956. The speech has never been made public, but it can be assumed that its general tenor was faithfully reproduced by Lu Dingyi in his address on 26 May. Explaining that the Hundred Flowers referred to the arts and the Hundred Schools to the sciences, Lu maintained that a policy was needed to encourage these domains to flourish, for this would make possible independent thinking, debate and creative work. He stressed that the natural sciences in particular had no class nature as such. As in the case of Zhou Enlai's speech of January 1956, the main political purpose of the 'Double Hundred' policy was to facilitate the mobilization of the intellectuals, and it was with this in mind that Lu Dingyi emphasized the danger of doctrinairism, dogmatism and sectarianism. This was in line with the general tendency, mentioned earlier, towards a degree of liberalization in the period leading up to the Eighth Party Congress. The reaction of the intellectuals was restrained and cautious, which is not surprising in view of their experiences during the assorted ideological campaigns of the previous seven years. In any case, the CCP did relatively little to implement the policy on a large scale before the spring of 1957.

On 15–19 September 1956 the CCP held its Eighth Party Congress. In the eleven years that had elapsed since the previous Congress the situation in the country and the position of the Party had altered radically. Seven years had already passed since the Chinese communists had brought about the victory of the Chinese Revolution and now, as a party in power, their aim was to sum up their experiences and determine the main features of China's road to the future.

At the time of the Seventh Congress, the CCP had a membership of 1.2 million. By September 1956 it had grown almost tenfold to 10.7 million members, of whom around 90 per cent had joined the Party since 1945, and 60 per cent after 1949. These figures highlighted a problem which was by no means specifically Chinese – that of motivation. While it is clear that those who joined the CCP before its victory in 1949 did so mostly for selfless and idealistic reasons, the motives of the post-1949 generation are more open to question. Party membership became an almost indispensable requirement for advancement in many fields, particularly in the state bureaucracy, with the result that the gates of the Party had been opened to a growing influx of opportunist and careerist elements. There was an awareness of this dilemma among the CCP leadership but, apart from seeking to recruit new members selectively, no easy solution was found, either then or since. A partial answer rested in the fact that the bulk of the really important positions in the Party and state apparatus were systematically reserved for and assigned to veteran revolutionaries only.

The criteria for judging a Party member's worth included adherence to the Party's ideology and programme, fulfilment of duties, and discipline, but not social origin. A census conducted in June 1953 showed that over 80 per cent of China's 583 million lived in rural areas, which was reflected in the composition of the CCP membership: 69 per cent were peasants, 14 per cent were workers and 12 per cent intellectuals. Nonetheless, the CCP continued to proclaim itself, as it had all along, a proletarian party, a claim almost wholly based on the nature of the ideology it sought to profess.

The deliberations of the Eighth Congress were well prepared in advance, with the main reports and the voices in discussion vetted beforehand. It was devoted to a pragmatic and realistic appraisal of the achievements of the post-1949 period. This was particularly true of the principal political report of the Central Committee, delivered by Liu Shaoqi. In passing, it should be

47

noted that the Eighth Congress was the only one in the Party's history since 1921 to the present for which almost complete documentation is available. The report made by Zhou Enlai concerning the Second Five-Year Plan, scheduled for the years 1958–62, was of a similar nature. The plan was realistic and feasible, though the goals set in it were quite ambitious. Its basic premises were similar to its predecessor's, with emphasis again placed primarily on heavy industry as the indispensable foundation for general industrialization, and modernization, and an escape from the backwardness and poverty still prevalent in the country.

The principal reports presented to the Congress and the resolutions adopted emphasized that the socialist system had been basically established in China, and that the principal task now was to close the gap between the demands of the people for rapid economic and cultural development and the country's ability to supply their needs. All efforts were to be concentrated on developing the nation's productive forces.

Some attempts were made, albeit limited in scope and ultimately completely ineffective, to face up to the problems of the personality cult and stress the need for collective leadership. Thus, while Mao Zedong remained chairman of the Central Committee, a Standing Committee of the Political Bureau was nominated, whose membership included, apart from Mao, the four vice chairmen – Liu Shaoqi, Zhou Enlai, Zhu De and Chen Yun – as well as Deng Xiaoping, appointed to the newly restored important post of general secretary. And the reference to Mao Zedong Thought contained in the 1945 Party constitution was deleted in the new constitution adopted by the Congress.

Deng's report on the draft of the new constitution included measures intended to promote democracy within the Party, providing in particular for the systematic convening of Party congresses, especially on the national level. The measures were never put into effect, however, primarily due to the increasing political struggle within the ranks of the top CCP leadership.

Some of the CCP leaders already had quite definite views on the question of the personality cult. Deng Xiaoping stressed that the CCP 'has always held that no political party and no individual is free from flaws and mistakes in their activities . . . and it abhors the deification of the individual'. Liu Shaoqi had expressed this view even earlier in a pithy and pungent fashion when he said that 'there is no such thing as a perfect leader, either in the past or the present, either in China or elsewhere. If there is one, he is only pretending, like a pig inserting scallions into his nose in an effort to look like an elephant.'

It is not by chance that the post-1978 leadership of the CCP evaluates the Eighth Party Congress as highly successful, deeming its political line to be correct; in many respects its own policies are a direct continuation – with a lacuna of twenty years which contains the Great Leap Forward and the 'cultural revolution' – of those advocated in 1956.

The Eighth Party Congress is looked back upon by many Chinese communists who were politically active at that time as the culmination of the initial period – the 'golden years' of People's China, an era of spirited hopes and unbounded optimism. In their view, in spite of the turbulence of the land reform and the campaign to suppress counter-revolutionaries, the successes and achievements in practically every domain outweighed by far the errors and shortcomings, most of which were derived from a mechanical emulation of the Soviet model. The promise that a new China was being built seemed real, and this goal was worth almost any sacrifice. It is a view with which the present writer sympathizes and shares to a considerable degree. The story of how these great expectations were frustrated and negated, step by step, during the next two decades is one of the saddest, even in the long and often tragic history of the Chinese.

In the late autumn of 1956, almost immediately after the conclusion of the Eighth Party Congress, events in Poland and Hungary gave the CCP leadership much food for thought, not least on the crucial question of how to exercise power. The Chinese communists were compelled to take a stand on the issues evolving in Eastern Europe. When at the historic Eighth Plenum on 19–21 October the Polish Party, as a symbol of its determination to struggle for greater autonomy, made Gomulka its princi-

pal leader, the CCP strongly supported the action (as it had inti-
mated it would). It made its views about Soviet interference in
Polish domestic affairs well known in Moscow, which contributed significantly to the Soviet government's decision to put an
end to the military undertakings it had begun. Although it was
not publicized at the time, the Chinese communists regarded
the policies pursued by the Soviet Union towards the Eastern
European countries as a classic demonstration of great-nation
chauvinism, a trait which they admitted Stalin had shown as
well.

Towards Hungary the CCP maintained a position close to
objective neutrality until the fateful moment on 1 November
when Imre Nagy announced Hungary's withdrawal from the
Warsaw Pact. This proposed departure of a member country
from the socialist camp caused the Chinese communist leadership to disregard the reservations they had and give full public
support to the ensuing Soviet intervention.

Within a few months of the outbreak of the crisis in Eastern
Europe, Zhou Enlai paid a visit to Warsaw on 11–16 January
1957, stopping in Moscow on his way there and back. The main
purpose of the trip was to acquaint himself personally with the
new Polish leadership. He had been briefed very accurately on
the situation in Poland by some of the highly talented officials
in the Chinese Foreign Ministry, a number of whom had been
his closest associates in Chongqing. His talks with the Poles
confirmed that Gomulka and his colleagues, while wishing to
place relations between Poland and the Soviet Union on a more
equal footing, had not the slightest intention of taking their
country out of the Warsaw Pact, nor of abandoning the further
building of socialism as they understood it. For Zhou, this vindi-
cated the CCP's support of the Poles in October.

Zhou presumably reported the situation in Poland as it actually was, which may have alleviated the sceptical and rather distrustful attitude of Mao Zedong to the Gomulka group, to
which he had given expression as late as 18 January when he
berated it for its supposedly excessively anti-Stalinist position.
With his innate caution and moderation, Zhou no doubt took

care to couch his report in terms that did not run directly counter to any of Mao's strongly held, preconceived notions.

It is abundantly clear that the developments in Eastern Europe and the critical situation in the international communist movement which they revealed gave rise to some of the ideas put forth in Mao Zedong's very significant speech 'On the Correct Handling of Contradictions Among the People'. It was delivered on 27 February 1957, but published in a substantially altered version only on 19 June. Distinguishing between antagonistic and non-antagonistic contradictions, Mao stressed the non-antagonistic nature of the contradictions in Chinese society, including the principal one – between the rulers and the ruled – maintaining that they could and should be resolved by non-coercive political means. In spite of the fact that the bourgeoisie no longer held any real economic or political influence, Mao advanced the concept that the class struggle between them and the proletariat still persisted, especially in the ideological field where it would be 'protracted and tortuous and at times even very sharp'. It was this thesis which, in an exaggerated and distorted form, later served as the theoretical foundation of the 1966–76 'cultural revolution'.

In the spring of 1957, however, the main concern was to reduce tension by creating the means for expressing legitimate criticism of prevailing conditions. With this in mind, Mao renewed on 12 March his 'Double Hundred' appeal, combining it with the inauguration of a new Party rectification movement. It was directed against the 'three evils' in work – bureaucratism, sectarianism and subjectivism – and was to be conducted in a manner similar to a 'gentle breeze and mild rain'. The novelty was that non-Party people were to participate in it and contribute their criticisms. It is generally held that the CCP leadership was divided as to the wisdom of launching the rectification movement and, in particular, of having non-Party people participate in it.

Within a few weeks, the flowers really did begin to bloom. Although the authorities sought carefully to restrict the movement to the urban intelligentsia, sharp and penetrating criticism of the fashion in which the CCP had been running the country for the past seven years became ever more widespread, encouraged in fact by some of the Central Committee's own departments. The main charge was that the communists were busily transforming themselves into a ruling elite as contemptuous of and remote from the people as the Guomindang or the imperial scholar officials had ever been. They were accused of seeking material gains and every conceivable privilege for themselves and their families; in other words, of becoming a Djilas-like 'new class'.

The ferment was particularly noticeable in May among the students, and the campuses of the main higher schools in Beijing were the scenes of endless meetings, the walls plastered with hundreds of big-character posters. This was particularly true of the famous Beijing University (Beida), noted for its tradition of participating in the historic student movements of 4 May 1919 and 9 December 1935. There was a distinct possibility that the unrest at Beida, which was well known to outsiders due to the presence of foreign students there, would spread to a number of other cities as well, and thus create a situation which the authorities might regard as uncontrollable.

Some of the leaders of the small, numerically and politically insignificant 'democratic parties' which had aided the CCP in establishing the PRC in 1949 joined in the fray, taking advantage of this opportunity to express the frustrations and resentment that had been accumulating in their minds. Their trenchant criticisms dealt, above all, with the way in which the communists had shoved them aside and, by completely monopolizing political power, reduced their participation in the government to a meaningless farce. It should be noted that most of the criticism was not directed against socialism or Marxism as such but against the abuses of the CCP bureaucracy and against the reputed failure of the Chinese communists to live up to their proclaimed slogan of serving the people.

By the beginning of June, a sharp frost nipped the blossoms before they could unfold further. Some of the communist leaders felt that the dominant role of the CCP was being seriously challenged. Although there was no real evidence to substantiate this fear, they now tended to regard the blossoms not as potential fragrant flowers, but as poisonous weeds to be uprooted as quickly as possible.

On 8 June the Party press announced the immediate termination of the Hundred Flowers campaign. It was promptly succeeded by a vociferous drive against alleged rightists – i.e. those Party and non-Party members who, having believed in the CCP's sincerity, had had the temerity to voice the critical views which the authorities had been asking for.

The Anti-Rightist Campaign was continued well into 1958 and was directed, above all, against the intellectuals. In many places, especially the universities, it became a vicious witch hunt with the number of rightists who had to be discovered, unmasked and properly punished being determined by quota. Many of those who had been outspoken in the spring months of 1957 were compelled to go through the humiliating ritual of public recantation.

Ultimately, the anti-rightist drive affected the lives of hundreds of thousands of individuals, in many cases for the next two decades, as well as of their families who had to bear the stigma of being relatives of 'enemies of the people'. The victims of this campaign, many of whom were to undergo still more drastic suffering during the ill-fated 'cultural revolution', included some of the country's ablest and most dedicated intellectuals. They were thus deprived of the opportunity to make any further contribution to the cause of Chinese socialism, to which many had devoted their entire lives.

In line with the ever-present tendency to seek to preserve the image of the Party's infallibility, some CCP officials maintained that during the Hundred Flowers episode criticism had been encouraged in order to bring the enemies of the new order out into the open and facilitate their identification and political annihilation. This cheap, pseudo-Machiavellian line of reasoning shocked and distressed many of the non-Chinese Marxists to whom it was also peddled at the time. It was quite false; the fact was that the Chinese communist leaders had simply not expected that the rule of the CCP, with so very many undoubted achievements to its credit, should give rise to as much resentment and disaffection as the criticism in the spring of 1957 revealed.

In the 1981 Resolution on Party History – a significant document which will be referred to often and discussed separately – in which the present leadership offers its own interpretation of CCP history, it is admitted that the scope of the Anti-Rightist Campaign 'was made far too broad' and that a number of people 'were unjustifiably labelled "rightist" with unfortunate consequences'. However, it is still maintained, without any proof provided, that some of those who voiced their criticism during the Hundred Flowers were 'engaged in an attempt to replace the leadership of the Communist Party'. Hence, 'it was therefore entirely correct and necessary to launch a resolute counter-attack'. This assertion is an unfortunate echo of the mode of thinking which was responsible for bringing untold calamities upon the country, especially in the 1966–76 decade. It seems to originate in a nagging feeling of insecurity among a number of the communist leaders, who view any criticism, no matter how valid, as a danger to the Party's power and authority, and thus consistently over-react to it. The final fruit of the Anti-Rightist Campaign was the absurd stand to be taken by Mao Zedong himself, who began to regard any opposition to or criticism of his policies as the work of enemies within the Party. One is forcibly reminded of Engels' penetrating analysis of the essence of Jacobin terror; it was, in his pungent phrase, 'the work of *hosenscheissenden Spiessbürger*' (overwhelmed by fear).

CHAPTER THREE

The Great Leap Forward, 1958–9

The intensive efforts exerted during the First Five-Year Plan, which was fulfilled successfully and ahead of schedule in some fields, had produced substantial results in building up a modern, albeit still limited industrial base, including the development of a number of new branches of manufacturing. This was only the first step on the road to China's modernization, but it did signify that Mao Zedong's taunt at the country's backwardness, uttered in June 1954, that 'We can't make a single motor car, plane, tank or tractor' was no longer quite so apt.

During the period of the First Five-Year Plan, industrial production increased in value from 3.4 billion to 7.8 billion yuan, i.e. 128 per cent, an annual increase of 18 per cent. Steel production had grown from 1.3 million tons in 1952 to 5.3 million in 1957; output of coal from 66 million tons to 131 million; electrical power had increased from 7.2 billion kilowatts in 1952 to 19.3 billion in 1957. The industrial working class had grown proportionately, increasing from 4.9 million in 1952 to 9 million in 1957. Labour productivity rose at an annual rate of 8.7 per cent while wages in industry increased by 7.4 per cent per annum, thus markedly improving the standard of living of at least the Chinese working class.

However, the development of agriculture lagged considerably behind that of industry during this same period, increasing by only 20 per cent, an annual growth rate of less than 4 per cent. Collectivization had not resulted in the really significant increase in production that some of the Chinese leaders had expected. Grain production rose from 150 million tons in 1952 to 185 million in 1957, cotton production from 1.3 million tons to 1.6 million in the same period. The most serious aspect of this was that the increase in agricultural production barely kept up with the rapid growth in population which reached an estimated 656 million in 1957 compared to 583 million in 1953. This increase was concentrated in the cities; the agriculturally non-productive urban population had grown from 58 million in 1949 to 92 million in 1957.

The population growth was perhaps one of the most important problems facing the PRC authorities from the very outset. The annual rate of natural increase in the early 1950s worked out at around 2 per cent, and if this rate was maintained, the population would double in the next thirty-five years (which in fact it almost did). Up to 1953 the demographic problem was almost completely ignored, and any talk of introducing population control was dismissed and severely criticized as reactionary Malthusianism. However, the data provided by the 1953 census, which at last furnished some relatively reliable figures on the population situation, helped to bring about a more thoughtful approach and from 1954 to 1958 the authorities started to promote birth control policies. But, when the new economic strategy was introduced in 1958, the official view reverted to ignoring the demographic problem. The voices of such consistent advocates of population control as, for example, the eminent economist Ma Yinchu (1882–1980), president of Beida, were ignored. Ma continued to express his views and in 1960 he was removed from his post.

It was against this background that a part of the Chinese leadership, and Mao Zedong in particular, began to question increasingly the validity of the economic strategy pursued up to 1957, which had been largely based on a faithful and unduly mechanical copying of the Soviet model.

Dissatisfaction with the emulation of Soviet experiences did not appear to lead to any deterioration of relations between the PRC and the Soviet Union; they were still relatively good during this period. The disagreements over Eastern Europe in the autumn of 1956 had been largely papered over, and when in

April 1957 Voroshilov, the formal Soviet head of state, arrived in China for a prolonged official visit, his reception was marked with the most correct outward forms of great friendship and cordiality. Nonetheless, a small incident illustrated that differences could arise even in superficial matters. After ending his speech at the arrival ceremony, filled with all the proper platitudes on Sino-Soviet friendship and unity, the diminutive Voroshilov embraced Mao Zedong in the customary Russian bear hug. The sight of Mao's utter shock was unforgettable. After delivering his own welcoming speech of trite generalities, Mao kept his guest at a proper distance with a firm handshake.

In November of the same year, Mao paid a long visit to the Soviet Union on the occasion of the fortieth anniversary of the October Revolution. Two conferences were held, one attended by the leaders of only the ruling communist parties, with the exception of Yugoslavia, the other by representatives of all sixty-four parties. There is little doubt that at the gathering of all the leaders of the international communist movement, Mao Zedong was the most prestigious personality present. During his many meetings with those attending the ceremonies and in the speeches he delivered he took the opportunity to express the principal views of the CCP on the international situation and the tasks facing the world communist movement. His interpretation of the balance of forces in the international arena was influenced to a considerable degree by such Soviet successes as the launching of the first intercontinental ballistic missile and the Sputnik. From these events Mao drew, or professed to draw, the somewhat hasty and unsubstantiated conclusion that the socialist bloc had achieved a position militarily and politically superior to that of the capitalist world; this was essentially the meaning of the colourful phrase he employed that 'The east wind prevails over the west wind'. From this Mao sought to establish that the socialist camp could afford to pursue a bolder policy in its confrontation with imperialism, not least by granting greater support to anti-colonialist and national liberation struggles.

In his characteristically diffuse and rambling speech, Mao

went on to speculate on the possibility of a future nuclear war. He was said to view the prospect with amazing equanimity, maintaining that even if half of the world's population were to be annihilated, this would at least signify the end of imperialism and hence the victory of socialism, while the population loss would be compensated for within a few generations. This was actually a paraphrase of Mao's contention that the atom bomb was a paper tiger, a weapon which one should not be frightened of, especially since it had ceased to be the monopoly of the United States.

It was clear that the PRC was quite determined to become an atomic power itself. Under the Sino-Soviet agreement concluded in October 1957, the Soviet Union promised assistance to China in the development of atomic technology including, almost surely, the provision of sample atomic weapons. The agreement was considered one of the cornerstones of future relations between the two countries.

While stressing the indispensable need for maintaining the unity of all the socialist countries, Mao Zedong also propagated the thesis that the Soviet Union was and had to be the leader of the socialist camp, due to its size, obvious economic superiority, as well as its historical place as the first socialist country. However, this leadership was to be exercised on the basis of equality between the socialist states, as the CCP had maintained earlier, notably during the 1956 crisis in Eastern Europe. What the CCP was in fact seeking to obtain was an equal partnership with the CPSU in determining the general political line of the international communist movement, a status which the Soviet leadership was certainly not prepared to grant, then or at any other time later. It should be noted that there was much more unanimity among the Chinese communist leaders on this subject and other issues concerning Sino-Soviet relations than on numerous domestic Chinese problems. Attempts by Western writers to distinguish between so-called pro- and anti-Soviet factions within the Chinese leadership are on the whole quite groundless.

As well as the differences that had already arisen between the

CCP and the CPSU, primarily in connection with Khrushchev's denunciation of Stalin, the Chinese communists also had private reservations about other propositions put forth by Khrushchev, particularly those pertaining to the possibility of a peaceful transition to socialism in a capitalist world. During the Moscow conferences this issue became a major bone of contention, finally resolved by a compromise, as were other points of disagreement. It was also during these conferences that the CCP leadership began to stress its opposition to revisionism, which it claimed presented the greatest danger to the international communist movement, taking a particularly strong position against the activities and stand of the Yugoslav leaders. Thus the Chinese began to assert their self-proclaimed role as the principal guardians and defenders of the purity of what they claimed to be orthodox Marxism–Leninism. These bids for leadership were received unenthusiastically by both the ruling and non-ruling parties. In spite of the high regard for the achievements of the CCP, the past experiences of the international communist movement were not conducive to recognizing a new source of authoritative proclamations and interpretations of doctrine. In the case of the Soviet party, it was unlikely to be willing to cede what it considered to be its primacy and practical monopoly in this domain.

In a number of speeches made at the beginning of 1958, Mao Zedong unveiled a fundamentally new and different approach to the problems of economic construction, based more on political and ideological assumptions than on a realistic assessment of economic factors. The key element in his thinking was the desire to harness the one resource that China had in great abundance, the labour force represented by its vast population, especially its 500 million peasants, whose potential was only partially being utilized. It could be directed into at least two domains: large-scale water conservation and irrigation projects (where much had been accomplished since 1949 but an immense amount remained to be done); and the development of small-scale industrial production in the countryside, to be undertaken in parallel with the continued further expansion of large-scale urban industry. This was one aspect of the policy known as 'walking on two legs'.

The above tasks were to be achieved by the political and ideological mobilization of the entire nation. It was assumed that this would result in rapid and equal progress in all branches of the economy, industry as well as agriculture, and eliminate the dangers inherent in the widening gap between the development of the cities and the rural areas.

Already in January 1956 the initial draft of a Twelve-Year Plan for the development of agriculture had been prepared. It was ambitious, calling for large increases in grain and cotton production, as well as a comprehensive scheme for water conservation. Its forty points also included such items as an appeal to eliminate illiteracy completely within the time span of the plan, and a call to combat the Four Pests (flies, mosquitoes, rats and sparrows). This gave rise to an immense, nationwide campaign which greatly reduced the pests. However, and this was characteristic both of this campaign and others similar to it, what had been forgotten was that sparrows not only consume great quantities of grain, which is why the authorities considered them a pest, they play a very useful role in the elimination of insects of every kind. It was only when the insect population increased dangerously that realization dawned on the authorities; the lives of the remaining sparrows were preserved, and bedbugs substituted as the fourth pest.

In the event, serious reservations about the overly ambitious aspects of the Twelve-Year Plan among the majority of the CCP leadership caused it to be shelved; the excessive speed of collectivization had created quite enough problems in the countryside. Nonetheless Mao Zedong and some of his followers still pressed for its adoption as quickly as possible.

The plans for total mobilization of the nation were derived from the hope that a single, vast, supreme effort could break China out of the vicious circle of backwardness and impel her along the road to self-sustaining growth. Economic self-reliance should match her political independence, since one thing seemed quite certain: the Chinese communists had not fought for decades for the victory of the Chinese Revolution to have their country become the obedient, servile client of any other state. There was nothing intrinsically at fault with these concepts as such, but the expectation of achievable results was both exaggerated and unrealistic, and, as the future was soon to show, implementation was to be carried out in a disorganized and unco-ordinated fashion.

Mao Zedong's vision of the Chinese road to socialism was also partially derived from his belief in the necessity of regarding the revolution as a permanent phenomenon in which 'one revolution must follow the other, the revolution must continuously advance'. Certainly the course of events in the 1949–56 period, especially the rapidity with which total collectivization and nationalization of industry and trade had been carried out, resembled such permanent revolution to a remarkable degree. The considerable successes achieved, the price of which he tended to disregard, encouraged Mao in his advocacy of continuing such a course.

It has become customary to refer to Mao Zedong's concepts as voluntaristic, with the implication that in their application insufficient attention was paid to objective factors; stress was placed, above all, on the decisive role of human consciousness. But the entire history of the Chinese Revolution from 1927 to 1949 derived from precisely this emphasis; its victory had certainly not been brought about by objective causes, but by a supreme exertion of human will and intelligence. The very backwardness of China and the compelling desire to do away with most of its features as quickly as possible only served to reinforce the tendency towards a voluntaristic approach, and fuelled the overwhelming impatience that was demonstrated time and time again when dealing with objective difficulties.

It would seem advisable, when examining the motivation of the Chinese communist leaders in the mid-1950s, to pose the question whether the victories they gained both before and after 1949 did not give rise among some of them to a feeling of hubristic self-confidence and a belief in the almost infinite possibilities of manipulating the Chinese people in line with their own intentions. In April 1958, Mao Zedong stated that 'China's 600 million people have two remarkable peculiarities, they are, first of all, poor, and secondly blank. That may seem like a bad thing, but it is really a good thing . . . a clear sheet of paper has no blotches and so the newest and most beautiful words can be written on it, the newest and most beautiful pictures can be painted on it.' This essentially contemptuous attitude towards the Chinese people suggests that the answer to the question may well be in the affirmative.

It was in these circumstances that the Chinese people were impelled into what proved to be one of the most painful episodes in their long history – the Great Leap Forward. The initial decisions regarding this venture were taken at the Third Plenum of the Central Committee which took place from 20 September to 3 October 1957, when the Twelve-Year Plan was taken off the shelf and endorsed as the fundamental guideline for the future. During the first stage of the Great Leap Forward, from the autumn and winter of 1957 to the spring of 1958, tens of millions of peasants were mobilized to participate in a gigantic programme of water conservation and other public works. All of this was very much in the Chinese tradition, since the employment of 'millions of people with teaspoons' had been going on for over two millennia. But the scale of the mobilization in 1957–8 was unprecedented; by March and April, a shortage of labour for the spring planting became evident. This was partly compensated for by the much greater employment of women in agriculture. A further source of labour was provided by increasing the number of urban groups sent into the countryside, a practice first initiated early on in the life of the PRC.

An unrelenting propaganda campaign of unparalleled intensity, even by Chinese standards, called on the nation to engage in three years of hard work in line with the slogan 'more, better, faster and more economical', to be followed by a thousand years of happiness. It was claimed that agricultural production would double in 1958, and then double again in 1959, thus leading to a solution once and for all of the food problem which had been present in China since the dawn of history. The aim was also to catch up and surpass the industrial level of Great Britain in many fields within fifteen years. Economic decision-making was to be largely decentralized, mainly to the provincial level, while the Second Five-Year Plan, which was due to start in January 1958 and had been modelled on its predecessor, was to be set aside and much higher targets established. The original targets had already been sufficiently ambitious, calling for an annual increase of industrial production of 14 to 15 per cent, but they would have been feasible if carried out with the prudence advocated by the pragmatic Chen Yun. Chen was the top economic expert in the ranks of the Chinese leadership and had been in charge of the economy during the successful rehabilitation drive of 1949–52. Born in 1905 near Shanghai, a typesetter by trade, Chen was one of the few principal leaders of the CCP who had himself been a worker. A Party member since 1924, he had participated in the labour movement during the 1925–7 revolution. He was later active in the Central Soviet area, becoming a Political Bureau member in 1934. His responsibility for economic affairs dated from the War of Resistance.

The programme for the Great Leap Forward received its official blessing during the second session of the CCP's Eighth Congress on 5–23 May 1958. Its single most important element was the further transformation of agriculture and the countryside by the establishment of the people's communes. Rural communes were to be created by the fusion of existing production co-operatives. Their primary purpose was to facilitate an increase in production, at a time when it was still impossible for industry to furnish all the equipment required for mechanization. They were to embrace, according to the original concept, every aspect of peasant life, including especially the participation of the villagers in the people's militia. In fact, from the outset, a military style of work permeated the activities of the Great Leap Forward, constituting a purposive harkening back to the Yan'an period. The communes were intended to become the basic level of rural administration, and were soon proclaimed to be the fundamental solution to all the problems arising from China's backwardness.

The first commune was organized on an experimental basis in Henan. During the summer, after Mao Zedong had expressed his enthusiastic support for the Henan venture, the entire Party apparatus, and especially the rural cadres, concentrated practically all their efforts on establishing rural communes throughout the country. By the end of the year the 740,000 production co-operatives, embracing over 123 million peasant households, had been reorganized into slightly over 26,000 communes. The establishment of the communes and regulations concerning them were formally approved, *post hoc*, in a resolution passed by the Political Bureau in August 1958. In a spirit of total euphoria, this document stated that 'it seems that the attainment of Communism in China is no longer a remote future event'. The utopianism of this statement requires no comment.

A number of Western authors are inclined to view the formation of the communes as largely spontaneous expressions of the enthusiasm supposedly felt by the peasants. This view, based mainly on the reading of Chinese press material which was nearly always propagandistic in its aim, does not seem to be justified. It would be more logical to assume that the Chinese peasants, with their centuries-long heritage of dealing with domineering officialdom, adhered to the old adage of behaving like the grain which they raised, and swayed with the wind. In any case, the relentless pressure exerted by the rural cadres, anxious to carry out the instructions of high authority and thereby prove their political reliability, left the peasants with no other choice but to accede to the extreme measures being taken. In the frenetic process of establishing the communes, many of the peasants' meagre personal possessions and, most important, their private plots on which they raised their vegetables, poultry and pigs were also converted into communal property, which must have given rise to much heart-searching in the villages.

Simultaneously, in the autumn of 1958 another immense campaign was launched. Around 90 million people all over the country were mobilized to engage in local, small-scale steel-smelting operations. With backbreaking, endless labour, over 600,000 back-yard furnaces were built in both urban and rural areas. The campaign was supposed to result in the doubling of steel production within one year, raising it to 10.7 million tons. Subsequently, according to Mao Zedong's airy prediction, it would increase to 30 million tons in 1959 and 60 million tons in 1960. The question of where the iron ore, coal and transport facilities were to come from for this gigantic increase remained blithely unanswered. Mao was not far off when in August 1959 he stated, 'I understand nothing about industrial planning.'

The steel campaign was undoubtedly the most hare-brained aspect of the Great Leap. Since the source of the raw material had not been adequately determined, an immense, countrywide hunt for scrap metal ensued, consuming untold quantities of pots and pans, and fixtures of every description. Only a limited number of the smelting furnaces built were to be retained in the future. The steel drive ended dismally in the spring of 1959, having cost over 2 billion yuan in subsidies and another 2 billion in work costs – a great catastrophe, in Mao's own words.

The campaign had been part of the general aim to decentralize industry. Fundamentally, the idea to reduce the excessive centralization, which was characteristic of the First Five-Year Plan, was not unsound, especially in view of the country's size, but its implementation was so inept and inadequately prepared that it resulted in a chaotic disorganization of industrial production.

In the autumn of 1958 the Chinese media were putting forth grandiose statements of colossal achievements in all fields; under the impact of the Great Leap, both agricultural and industrial production were said to have almost doubled. Within less than a year it became increasingly apparent that all these claims were spurious. The mechanism for this falsification was relatively simple. When the higher-level Party authorities set astronomical goals and demanded immediate results, the lower-level cadres felt compelled, for a number of reasons, including careerist ones, to provide appropriately inflated data, and competition ensued to see who could perform this best. The top leadership, influenced by its wishful thinking, were willing participants in this grand act of self-deception. In the meantime, the central statistical system, established with so much effort after 1949, was brought to a point of almost complete collapse.

Luckily for the Chinese, exceptionally favourable weather conditions did result in a bumper crop of between 200 and 210 million tons of grain for 1958, though this was much less than the 375 million tons claimed. But in 1959 grain production was to plummet to between 160 and 170 million tons, partly because the weather was average, but primarily because that year at least 70 million people were assigned to the steel-smelting campaign and water conservation projects, creating an acute shortage of labour. A contributing factor was the total disarray brought about by the organization of the communes and the policy applied there of 'distributing according to need'. The self-deception continued, with official claims at the beginning of 1960 that grain production in 1959 had amounted to 270 million tons.

Although by the end of 1958 it was already apparent that the country was approaching a severe and largely self-inflicted crisis, the Sixth Plenum of the Central Committee held in Wuhan from 28 November to 10 December 1958 endorsed completely false economic results. As well as the inflated figures for grain, cotton production was supposed to have increased from 1.6 million to 3.3 million tons, coal output from 130 million to 270 million tons, and steel production from 5.3 million to 11 million tons. On this basis, equally unrealistic targets were set for 1959. Steel production was to increase to 18 million tons, coal output to 380 million tons, cotton to 5 million tons, while grain production was to jump to a fantastic 525 million tons (the highest figure achieved in this field up to the present was 407 million tons in 1984). Later these figures were reduced slightly, but they were still unrealizable.

During the Sixth Plenum an attempt was made to curb some of the excesses of the commune movement, and to introduce a modicum of rationality into their organization and functioning. The transfer to the commune of the peasants' household goods, pigs and poultry was revoked and the first steps taken towards restoring the private plots to peasant ownership.

At the same time, it was announced that Mao Zedong would no longer hold the office of PRC chairman, though he would retain the infinitely more important post of chairman of the CCP Central Committee. This decision came into effect in April 1959, when Liu Shaoqi assumed the largely ceremonial post of head of state. It is difficult to ascertain to what degree this move resulted from the factional dissension which was soon to surface in the CCP leadership. It is more than likely that the reason given then, and repeated on other occasions by Mao himself, was largely true. The aim was to make it possible for Mao to concentrate on basic problems of policy, while assigning day-to-day operations to other members of the leadership. However, this move did mark the beginning of the process by which fundamental policy-making decisions were partially taken out of Mao's hands, though full outward reverence for his role as the Party's paramount leader was maintained. Mao himself is said to have stated that henceforth he was 'treated with respect as a dead parent at his own funeral'.

In the spring of 1959 the signs of an oncoming economic crisis were obvious and undeniable, although claims of gigantic successes were still being trumpeted. The faults of the Great Leap Forward programme were many; the present leadership of the CCP maintains that these errors arose primarily from 'a lack of experience in socialist construction and inadequate understanding of the laws of economic development and of the basic economic conditions in China'. This in turn accounted partially for the dominant ultra-leftist tendencies manifesting themselves in the excessive targets set and the arbitrary direction of the Great Leap campaign. But perhaps the principal error rested in the mechanical application of political and ideological mobilization, which had proved so successful in attaining victory by 1949, to a quite different set of problems and circumstances. It would seem that many of the communist leaders, and Mao Zedong in particular, became so smug about the considerable and very real successes achieved earlier that they forgot some of the basic elements of their previously applied strategy, especially the need to prepare a campaign with the utmost care and with full appreciation of all the factors involved. In 1957 and 1958 their actions were characterized by an overwhelming impatience, psychologically comprehensible but no less harmful, derived from their intense and legitimate desire to drag China out of the mire of poverty and backwardness during their own lifetimes. It was this subjective approach which led them to cherish totally unrealistic expectations and to formulate grandiose, badly planned and clumsily implemented schemes, which heaped immense, insupportable burdens on the Chinese people.

In the last months of 1959, although the Chinese media were still full of overblown pronouncements on the subject, the Great Leap Forward started to fade into nothingness. Within a year it disappeared completely from the Chinese historical arena, although its termination was never announced publicly. It did not end with a whimper (even if at least two authors have been unable to resist the temptation of invoking T. S. Eliot) but in an utter catastrophe, since it ushered in and was the primary cause of the great economic crisis of 1960–1. The clean sheet of paper, so highly valued by Mao Zedong, had been inscribed not with a most beautiful picture but with an ugly distorted daub.

With the exception of main addresses delivered at such gala occasions as the Eighth Party Congress, the Chinese communists do not publish political speeches, still less the stenographic records of discussions at such vital gatherings as the plenary sessions of the Central Committee. It goes without saying that the records of the most important meetings of all, those of the Political Bureau, are also unavailable for a historian's perusal. As a result it is very difficult to reconstruct a true picture of the debates of the communist leaders on all the really crucial issues in the post-1949 period. However, during the first years of the 'cultural revolution' a certain amount of material, often doctored and distorted, was leaked on purpose, usually for quite reprehensible reasons. It was eagerly pounced upon by Western *soi-disant* China experts, who treated it as priceless and revelatory. Unfortunately, it is these publications, whose authenticity and reliability are obviously open to question, which also constitute the main source of data on the inner-Party disputes in connection with the Great Leap Forward.

The chief protagonists in these debates were Mao Zedong and Peng Dehuai, and the open confrontation between these two equally tough and stubborn Hunanese peasants began during the Seventh Plenum, held in April 1959.

Peng Dehuai (1898–1974) came from a poor peasant family in Hunan. As a youth he joined the local military, primarily to escape from poverty. Having participated in the 1925–7 revolution he clandestinely joined the Communist Party while he was still a regimental commander in the Guomindang army. In 1929, together with other secret CCP members, he organized a revolt of the troops under his command and took his forces to join Mao Zedong and Zhu De in the famous redoubt of Jinggangshan. He was soon to become one of the principal leaders of the Chinese Red Army and participated in the Long March. In the War of Resistance Peng was the deputy commander-in-chief of the Eighth Route Army, and during the War of Liberation he led the PLA troops in north-west China, whose tasks included the defence of Mao Zedong and Party headquarters. Peng had been a member of the Political Bureau since 1945, and was renowned both for his uprightness and outspokenness. His courage was legendary.

Peng Dehuai's critical attitude towards the Great Leap Forward had been confirmed by his inspection trip to Gansu and a visit to his native village where the peasants recounted to him the true extent of the disastrous consequences of the policies pursued by the authorities since the summer of 1958 and the privations they were suffering.

Peng was by no means the only prominent communist leader critical of the excesses of the Great Leap Forward; his views were shared by a number of others, including Zhang Wentian (1900–76). One of the most talented surviving intellectuals of the Party's first generation, Zhang had held in the early 1930s, under the name of Luo Fu, the highest posts in the CCP. During the first stage of the Long March he had played a decisive role at the crucial Tsunyi meeting in January 1935 in supporting Mao Zedong, thus enabling Mao to establish his dominant position within the Party leadership. Although Zhang was re-elected to the Political Bureau in 1945, he ceased to be one of the top CCP leaders and in 1956 was demoted to alternate membership in the Bureau. However, he continued to be admired by those who had worked with him for his modesty, humaneness and selfless dedication. His reputation as a staunch and indefatigable life-long seeker for truth was well deserved.

Increasingly aware of the acute nature of the problems created by the Great Leap, the CCP leadership gathered together for an enlarged meeting of the Political Bureau in Lushan during most of July 1959. The original intention was to examine the situation and work out appropriate solutions so as to avoid a further deepening of the crisis. Both Peng Dehuai and Zhang Wentian took part in the meeting and openly expressed their views. On 14 July Peng submitted a Letter of Opinion to Mao Zedong in which he listed some of the negative features of the Great Leap Forward which it was imperative to correct. These included bad, unbalanced planning, the initiation of too many industrial projects, gross exaggeration of production results which undermined the Party's credibility, and the fundamental error of ceasing to adhere to the Party's long-established and well-tested principle of seeking truth from facts. All these failures were largely derived from 'petty bourgeois fanaticism' and were a sign that 'left' tendencies were now paramount in the Party's political line and activities.

Peng's letter was very moderate in tone, and no attempt was made in it to charge Mao Zedong with the primary responsibility for what had happened. It could not be construed as a direct challenge to his authority and leadership, but Mao interpreted it as just that. Also moderate and non-accusatory was Zhang's speech made on 21 July in which he presented a carefully balanced and thorough twelve-point analysis of the critical economic and political situation created by the Great Leap Forward policies. On 23 July, however, Mao launched a counter-attack against Peng and those who had expressed similar views. In a long, rambling speech Mao accused them of being rightist opportunists and of having formed an anti-Party clique. Subsequently, on the last day of the dramatic and turbulent Eighth Plenum held on 2–16 August, Mao, using the full weight of his prestige and authority, railroaded through a resolution castigating Peng Dehuai, Zhang Wentian and a number of others. Although they were not expelled from the Party, their political careers came to an end. A month later Peng Dehuai was removed from his post of minister of defence and replaced by Lin Biao. Those who had supported Peng also lost their Party and government positions.

Many of those who voted in favour of Mao's resolution agreed inwardly with most of the criticisms raised by Peng, Zhang and the others, but Mao had turned the issue into one that challenged his position as the acknowledged supreme Party leader. This gambit proved effective, especially when combined with a threat to create a new Red Army and restart the revolution if the PLA did not remain faithful to him. Those present, most of them veterans of the Long March and all the subsequent struggles, had to stand up and be counted; the overwhelming majority chose to support Mao, probably primarily for the sake of preserving the Party's unity. However, the consequences were far-reaching and harmful, for the Lushan meeting put paid, once and for all, to any possibility of freely airing different views or openly criticizing policies which Mao Zedong was known to favour; it removed all semblance of democracy in the Party's supreme policy- and decision-making body. The tendency towards autocracy within the CCP leadership was enhanced and reflected in the style of work of the entire Party and state apparatus. In 1981 the Lushan decisions were declared to be 'entirely wrong', but in the meantime immense damage was done.

It is instructive to note the fate of Peng Dehuai and Zhang Wentian. Zhang sank into almost total obscurity. Removed in 1959 from his post as first vice minister of foreign affairs, he was not permitted to do any work until 1961 when his request for an assignment was finally granted and he became a special

71

researcher in the Institute of Economics of the Academy of Science. Thus, he made at least some use of his vast erudition and talent, as shown by the essays he wrote up to 1966.

The 'cultural revolution' spelled utter disaster for Zhang Wentian. His actions at Lushan were swiftly recalled and he became one of the most fiercely persecuted veteran leaders, subjected to unceasing maltreatment and humiliation. In her deeply moving reminiscences, Zhang's widow, Liu Ying – a participant of the Long March and a communist activist of long standing in her own right – has described some of the torments inflicted on her husband, including the fierce beatings at a 'struggle session' against him and Peng Dehuai held in the ill-famed Beijing Aeronautical Institute.

For his courageous stand in 1967, when he took upon himself the responsibility for making the decision in the 'Case of the 61' (see page 154) thus refusing to incriminate Liu Shaoqi, he was soon jailed. Subsequently, in 1969 Zhang and his wife were exiled to a remote area in Guangdong where they lived under military supervision until 1975. His health deteriorating badly, Zhang appealed to Mao to be permitted to return to Beijing for proper medical treatment. The appeal was rejected; instead he and Liu Ying were transferred to Wuxi in Jiangsu, where Zhang, worn down by his sufferings, passed away in July 1976. He died incognito, as he had been since 1969, so that his widow could not even place his real name on the memorial wreath.

Until the last months of his life Zhang Wentian, his face perhaps still wreathed with the gentle smile for which he was famous, kept his trembling hand busy writing. His essays, some of which have miraculously survived, showed that there were people capable of conceiving other paths of development and other modes of action, more rational and humane than those pursued with such disastrous results by the Great Helmsman. Zhang was fully rehabilitated only in 1978, two years after his death; in 1981 his proper place in the history of the CCP as one of its 'outstanding leaders' was finally and formally recognized.

The case of Peng Dehuai was still more tragic. In December 1966 he was arrested and imprisoned for the rest of his life. His jailers charged him with being a counter-revolutionary who had committed the most serious, heinous crime of 'opposing Chairman Mao all his life'. Faithful to his nature as a true revolutionary, Peng refused to admit to any crime. According to the authors of the introduction to Peng's memoirs, his infuriated interrogators 'kicked him until his ribs were fractured and lungs injured. Beating sent him unconscious to the floor.' Peng shouted, 'I fear nothing; you can shoot me.' He was interrogated until he was bedridden. 'He was deprived of the right to sit, to rise up, to drink water, to go to the toilet or to turn over in his bed.' By the time he suffered 'a martyr's death' on 29 November 1974, 'he had gone through 130 interrogations'. Feudal fascism? Yes, indeed.

In December 1978, the record was put straight; Peng Dehuai was completely rehabilitated. In 1981, his stature as an 'outstanding leader' was restored. However, there is no information as to whether any of the surviving CCP leaders, his closest comrades in arms for almost four decades, sought to help him in any way during his terrible last eight years. There is also no way of knowing what, if anything, has happened to his tormentors.

Although during Mao Zedong's stay in Moscow in November 1957 relations between the CCP and CPSU appeared outwardly still proper, and much stress was placed on the unshakable and unbreakable unity of the socialist camp, the first important cracks on the facade of this supposedly monolithic structure were to appear in the subsequent two years. The divergence was caused by a large number of issues, of which the assessment of the correct strategy to pursue in international affairs assumed particular importance. The ultra-leftist tendencies which the Chinese communists demonstrated in their domestic policies were evident in this domain as well. For example, the Chinese sought to pressure the Soviet leadership into taking a stronger position against the independent, non-aligned policies pursued by Yugoslavia. To Moscow's considerable embarrassment and annoyance, Beijing launched in May and June 1958 a virulent and long-running propaganda campaign against Tito and his associates, accusing them of the heinous crime of revisionism.

Direct contact between the Chinese and Soviet leadership was still being maintained and at the end of July 1958 talks were held in Beijing between Khrushchev and Mao Zedong during which problems of economic co-operation were mainly discussed. The Chinese maintain that at this time the Soviet leader also proposed some forms of military co-operation (among them the building of a Soviet radio station on Chinese territory) which were interpreted as an infringement of Chinese sovereignty.

In pursuing their forward policy, the CCP leaders sought to test the possibility of eliminating the Guomindang hold on some coastal islands, Quemoy in particular. The shelling of these positions began on 23 August and the ensuing two months are referred to as the Taiwan Straits Crisis, which involved much brinkmanship on the part of both the Chinese and American governments. During this period, the Chinese came to the conclusion that the reliability of Soviet support for their confrontation with the Americans was open to serious doubt. This impression was drawn from the fact that Khrushchev came out firmly on the side of the PRC only after the Chinese themselves had already made the moves necessary to bring about a relaxation of the crisis.

The question of further Soviet aid to China was raised again in negotiations between the two governments in the first months of 1959, and on 7 February new agreements were signed, but they were never put into effect. One of the issues involved was the Chinese attitude towards the scale of Soviet aid being granted to countries outside the socialist camp, especially to India. Although the CCP's resentment was never expressed publicly, one can safely assume that the Chinese believed at this time that the limited amount of economic aid which the Soviet Union could afford to provide to the outside world should be granted primarily to its ideological and political allies, and not to the dubiously non-aligned governments of the Third World.

One of the prime factors which led to a worsening of CCP–CPSU relations was the critical attitude of the Soviet leadership

to the domestic developments in the PRC during the Great Leap
Forward. In addition, Khrushchev and other Soviet leaders did
not conceal their dismay at the ideological pretensions of the
Chinese to the effect that the policies being implemented in
China, and the establishment of the communes in particular,
signified an innovative step in the development of Marxism–
Leninism and, most important, indicated that the PRC would
be able to effectuate the transition to communism relatively
quickly. One can assume that these reservations had been
expressed during direct talks between the Chinese and Soviet
leaders. However, an exchange of views between 'fraternal'
parties was one thing, expressing carping criticism to outsiders
was quite another. Yet this was precisely what Khrushchev did
when in December 1958 he outlined his critical views of what
the Chinese were doing to the American Senator, Hubert
Humphrey.

The issue of the Soviet attitude towards domestic developments in China became much more serious in July during the
dramatic confrontation which took place at Lushan between
Mao Zedong and Peng Dehuai. Mao maintained that Peng's
actions had been encouraged by the Soviet leadership (Peng had
been on a visit to the Soviet Union and a number of Eastern
European countries in April–June, during which he had met
Khrushchev). In effect Mao accused his opponent of acting in
collusion with a foreign power, unnamed at the time. No evidence was ever presented to support this accusation, but the
clumsy efforts made later by Khrushchev to defend Peng
Dehuai were interpreted by the Chinese as a sign of interference
by the Soviet leaders in Chinese domestic affairs. Even during
the Lushan conference itself, Khrushchev publicly criticized the
commune movement in a speech delivered in Poznan on 18
July.

An even more significant event, which can be regarded as a
milestone in the deterioration of Sino-Soviet relations, was the
decision of the Soviet government to scrap the accord on co-
operation in the field of atomic technology. The Chinese maintain that on 20 June 1959 the Soviet authorities announced that

they would not honour the October 1957 agreement, and would not provide the Chinese with either the sample atomic weapons or the technology necessary for their production, as had been promised. There is no doubt that the Chinese communist leaders considered this move to be of crucial significance. In the early 1960s, when the Chinese Party discussed Sino-Soviet relations with leaders of West European communist parties, it was customary to have two separate dossiers on hand. One pertained to the exchange of views between the Chinese and Soviet parties on a large number of political issues, the other was wholly devoted to one subject – the Soviet refusal to furnish the Chinese with atomic weapons and know-how.

By the time that Khrushchev visited Beijing once again on 1 October 1959, for the celebration of the tenth anniversary of the PRC, the accumulation of grievances and irritations was quite considerable. It was aggravated further by the divergent views on Soviet policy towards the United States, since Khrushchev had just completed his meeting with Eisenhower, and was full of enthusiastic praise for the spirit of Camp David. Also, only a few weeks before his arrival, the Soviet government had announced its 'neutral' stand towards the sharpening border dispute between China and India. It is quite logical to conclude that the talks held between Mao and Khrushchev ended in complete deadlock, for not even a face-saving communiqué was issued. It can also be assumed, although this factor is often disregarded, especially by Chinese and Soviet authors, that a growing personal animosity between the two leaders helped to poison the atmosphere and make a reconciliation of ever more divergent views increasingly difficult, if not impossible.

CHAPTER FOUR

The Great Economic Crisis, 1960–1

In the winter of 1959–60 the economic situation had already reached a critical stage, but worse was still to come. During the harvest of 1960 drought and floods, many of them caused by faulty and erratic irrigation works, affected close to 60 per cent of the cultivated areas, and grain production, already in disarray due to the commune movement, fell to a catastrophic 150 million tons, according to Mao Zedong himself. The Chinese economy was on the verge of collapse.

As recently as four years ago the present writer, when dealing with this topic, maintained that the Chinese authorities had succeeded, in spite of the prevailing near famine conditions, in preventing a disaster on a scale similar to that of the 1930s. However, on the basis of newly released Chinese source material (according to recent official figures, for example, grain production in 1960 was in fact as low as 147.5 million tons) this conclusion can no longer be upheld. Famine on an immense scale affected vast areas of the country, and millions of Chinese died, either directly from starvation, or prematurely from diseases caused by malnutrition. According to the eminent Chinese economist Sun Yefang, the mortality rate increased from 1.08 per cent in 1957 to 2.54 per cent in 1960. This would signify, assuming a population of around 700 million, the additional death of over 10 million people in 1960 alone. Proportionally many more deaths occurred in the countryside than the cities, for in their desire to feed the urban population, however inadequately, the authorities did not lower the grain procurement quotas; in fact they had raised them earlier on the basis of false estimates of future production results. The government's proud claim that it could keep the population nourished on a relatively adequate and equitable level became demonstrably untenable. The strict rationing of food functioned quite effectively, but by September 1961 the rations probably amounted at most to only 1500 calories per person a day. Such was the 'price of blood' (the phrase is Sun Yefang's) which the Chinese people paid for the megalomania of the Great Leap.

While Liu Shaoqi had many times spoken in support of the Great Leap policies, he had also been in the forefront of those who, from the end of 1959 on, sought to remedy its errors. In 1960, his sister informed him about the drastic conditions in their native Hunan; in the spring of 1961 he spent six weeks visiting various parts of the province including his own village. Liu Shaoqi, Party builder and organization man *par excellence*, selfless, modest, taciturn and reserved, was aghast at the devastation caused by the Great Leap and the obvious suffering of the peasants. The experience affected his views profoundly. Later on, in a bitter speech in January 1962, Liu claimed that the food crisis had been 70 per cent man-made; natural calamities accounted for the remainder.

There was little doubt as to who had been the principal author of the Great Leap. Mao Zedong partially admitted his responsibility, but already at the Lushan meeting in 1959 and subsequently in a number of speeches delivered in 1960–1 he sought to shift the major part of the blame on others in the CCP leadership and especially on the lower echelon Party cadres whose blind enthusiasm had, he claimed, been instrumental in wrecking the economy. Liu Shaoqi, on the other hand, began to play a leading role in the formulation and implementation of new policies aimed at bringing the country out of the crisis. The different positions adopted by the two men at this time rest at the roots of the intensifying conflict between them. Mao's hostility towards the policies pursued by Liu and his associates, which he regarded increasingly as a challenge and threat to his own authority, turned into growing distrust, resentment and personal enmity. Only this can explain, at least partially, Mao's willingness to have Liu denounced within a few years as the number one enemy of the Party.

At the cost of prodigious effort, especially on the part of the peasants, and with the aid of a number of emergency measures, the food crisis was gradually alleviated. Grain production rose to an estimated 160–165 million tons in 1961 and probably to around 170 million in 1962. From 1961 sizeable quantities of grain were also imported, both for current consumption and to build up the almost totally depleted reserves. In 1961 close to 6 million tons of grain, mostly wheat, were brought in from Australia and Canada at a cost of around $350 million. This expense constituted a serious strain on the country's limited reserves of foreign exchange.

A series of important top-level Party meetings were held to deal with the problems of agriculture. A Central Committee Work Conference, held in July–August 1960, established guidelines for a new economic policy, in which agriculture was proclaimed the foundation of the economy, and industry its leading factor; in other words, industry must furnish agriculture with the necessary means for its further development, such as chemical fertilizers and farm equipment. New Central Committee directives on rural work (the Twelve Articles), issued in November 1960, reorganized the rural communes into smaller, more viable units, increasing the number from the original 26,000 to 74,000. Most of the initial far-fetched and unpractical projects, such as the commune canteens, were eliminated. Gradually, production teams comprising groups of twenty to thirty households became the basic unit for accounting and determining production plans. Private plots, the litmus test of agrarian policies, and always anathema to Mao Zedong and a constant bone of contention among the CCP leaders, were finally restored on a firm basis and thus could once again play their role in enlarging production and raising the peasants' living standards. Free rural markets, in which the peasants could sell their surplus production after completing deliveries to the state, were also reopened and contributed significantly to an improvement

in the economic situation. By and large, agriculture was successfully stabilized by the end of 1962 and henceforth grain production continued to rise.

It should be noted that in the years 1959–76 the PRC
authorities published only very fragmentary statistics, and for
almost two decades most of the information pertaining to this
period derived from foreign estimates, mostly quite far-fetched
and very often wrong. Fortunately, since 1978 this situation has
undergone a radical change and substantial statistical data are
now available from Chinese sources, not only for the last fifteen
years but also for the 1950s and 1960s. In 1983 official figures
were published showing that the total output value of agriculture in 1958 amounted to 55 billion yuan. In 1959 it fell to 47.5
billion (−13.6 per cent); in 1960, to 41.5 billion (−12.6 per cent);
in 1961 to 40.5 billion (−2.4 per cent). It rose in 1967 to 43 billion yuan.

In 1958 and 1959 industrial production increased, in most
cases very sharply due to the lavish and wasteful use of additional labour power. The number of those employed in industrial enterprises grew during these years by supposedly as much
as 30 million. However, the effects of excessive decentralization,
mismanagement, the general chaos of the Great Leap, and
especially of the agricultural crisis, soon brought about a slump
whose dimensions were almost as calamitous as those of the
agrarian sector. The authorities were forced to reduce investment in industry and close down countless new enterprises that
had sprung up during the Great Leap. The resulting large-scale
unemployment in the urban areas was dealt with by sending the
redundant workers, many of them peasants who had flocked to
the cities earlier, into the hungry countryside. By the spring of
1962 probably close to 20 million people had been affected by
this policy. At the same time, a concerted effort was made to
restore central economic planning and to reintroduce material
incentives in order to stimulate production. By the end of 1962,
industry too had regained considerable stability.

The formulation and implementation of the new economic
policy was largely in the hands of four senior CCP leaders – Liu

Shaoqi, Zhou Enlai, Deng Xiaoping and Chen Yun. The work of the last, noted for his moderation and realism, was of particular importance. To refer to the years 1960–5, in which these leaders sought to formulate and put into effect their sane, pragmatic policies, as a period of Thermidorean reaction, as has been done by the author of a readable and on the whole sensible history of the PRC, is quite preposterous.

The critical state of the Chinese economy was further exacerbated in July 1960 by the abrupt withdrawal of nearly all the 1400 Soviet experts who had been engaged on 257 key projects, mostly large and crucial installations in various stages of completion. The surprise move was as much of a shock to the Chinese as it was to the Soviet personnel involved, who were also instructed to take back with them the blueprints of the enterprises they were working on. In 1964 the Chinese, who customarily refer to the Soviet withdrawal as 'perfidious', described its results as having 'disrupted China's original national economic plan and inflicted enormous losses upon China's socialist construction'. The question arises as to what prompted the Soviet action. It would seem most likely that the intention was to bring the insubordinate CCP leadership to heel; the same motivation had been displayed the previous year when the accord on atomic co-operation was scrapped. It was as subtle as using a heavy hobnailed boot to step on feet shod in Chinese-style cotton shoes. In view of the hypersensitivity of the Chinese communists to questions of national sovereignty – a legacy of China's one hundred years of humiliation – the move was a monumental blunder. The results were exactly the opposite of what had been intended, and propelled Sino–Soviet relations into yet deeper discord.

The ignominious collapse of the Great Leap Forward undoubtedly constituted a severe political setback for Mao Zedong. It is clear that from 1960 on, one of his main concerns was to strengthen his influence and control over the PLA. No one was better able to appreciate the role which the PLA had played in gaining power for the CCP, or its significance in maintaining this power. In spite of his apparent victory over Peng

Dehuai at the Lushan meeting, it was obvious to Mao that Peng's views were shared by many of the top military commanders; hence he saw a need to eradicate Peng's influence in the PLA. To accomplish this Mao availed himself of the eager assistance of Lin Biao, whose willingness to extol Mao and his thoughts was constantly being demonstrated.

Lin Biao (1907–71) came from a bankrupt gentry family in Hubei. He was already a member of the Socialist Youth League when he joined the famous Whampoa Military Academy in 1924, becoming a member of the CCP the next year. He took part in the march to the Yangtse and participated in the famous Nanchang Uprising in August 1927, celebrated as the foundation of the Chinese Red Army. Together with the survivors of this ultimately unsuccessful revolt, Lin Biao joined the forces of Mao Zedong and Zhu De. His military talents quickly brought him high command, and during the Long March he led its advance unit. At the outset of the war with Japan, Lin Biao became famous nationally for the victory won by his troops at the Battle of Pingxingguan. By now he already had the reputation among his comrades of being the most expert and original tactician of all the communist military leaders. In the final struggle, the War of Liberation, it was the troops under his command, ultimately called the Fourth Field Army and the largest and best equipped of all the communist-led forces, which, after the liberation of the north-east, marched triumphantly all the way down to Canton. In September 1955, Lin Biao was one of the ten top military men to be granted the baton of a marshal; in the same year he became a member of the Political Bureau. By May 1958 he had reached the very highest level of CCP leadership, becoming a member of the Political Bureau's Standing Committee.

In September 1959, after Lin Biao had taken over the position of minister of defence from Peng Dehuai, a far-reaching series of personnel changes was made in the top posts of the PLA, with six new deputy ministers being appointed. Simultaneously, a thorough reorganization of the General Headquarters was carried out. Lin utilized the occasion to promote to leading posts some of his closest associates from the Fourth Field Army, and the dominance of this group was to continue until 1971. Nonetheless, while the importance of past ties and loyalties of PLA commanders certainly explains some of the phenomena of the Chinese political scene, it has been simplistically over-emphasized by a number of American writers, who see in it the basic, if not the sole, key to interpreting Chinese politics.

One of the tasks which Lin Biao set himself was to build up the organizational network of the CCP within the armed forces, and a marked increase in new Party membership did take place in 1960 and 1961, especially among the officer corps. The main emphasis, however, was on strengthening the political indoctrination of the PLA, in line with Lin Biao's slogan that every member of it should become a 'good soldier of Mao Zedong'. In parallel with Mao Zedong's advocacy of placing politics in command, Lin also advanced the goal of stressing the primacy of man over weapons, of political work over any other work, of ideological work over routine work, of living ideology over bookish study. These points were referred to as the 'Four Firsts'. An attempt was also made to revert to the conditions prevailing in the armed forces during the Yan'an period, especially to restore close relations between officers and men; for this purpose the practice was introduced of having officers serve as rank-and-file soldiers for one month each year.

The principal aim of all these measures was to assure the complete, unconditional loyalty of the PLA to Mao Zedong, and perhaps equally well to Lin Biao, who was being constantly presented as 'the foremost exponent of Mao Zedong Thought'. Thus, a seemingly solid and assured political base was being created for both men, with the PLA being groomed to play a decisive role in this process, whose true nature was to be revealed fully only in 1966.

Another extremely significant figure in the ideological elaboration and dissemination of the Mao Zedong cult was Chen Boda (b. 1904). Born into a poor peasant family in Fujian, Chen became a member of the CCP in 1927. He worked in the Party underground in north China during the early 1930s, while lecturing at one of the universities in Beijing. During the War of Resistance he spent almost the entire time in Yan'an, serving also as Mao Zedong's political secretary. It was during this period that the co-operation between the two men became very close and intimate. Chen served not so much as Mao's amanuensis as his ghost writer, and it is maintained that he learned Mao's style so well that it is impossible to tell the writing of the two men apart. At the same time, Chen Boda made his mark as one of the Party's principal theorists and a most skilful propagandist. He was particularly noted for his devastating works on Chiang Kai-shek and the Four Families of the KMT oligarchy. Chen also displayed in his writings a far-reaching flexibility; he was able to provide theoretical justification for practically any change in the Party's political line.

After liberation, Chen Boda's prominence was even more marked; from 1949 on he was senior deputy director of the Central Committee's Propaganda Department and simultaneously, from 1952 on, vice president of the Academy of Sciences. The scholars in the academy complained that they found Chen's Fujian accent quite incomprehensible, but they studied his speeches with care nonetheless, for his interpretation of Party policy was considered authoritative. Chen was actively engaged in the implementation of Mao's agricultural policies; in 1956 he was rewarded for his work and loyalty to Mao by being appointed an alternate member of the Political Bureau. Two years later he became editor-in-chief of *Hongqi*, the Party's main theoretical organ. During the first two decades of the PRC, no one can be said to surpass Chen Boda in his concerted effort to propagandize Mao Zedong's views and present them as a meaningful and significant contribution to the further development of Marxism–Leninism.

Among Mao Zedong's closest entourage, a third individual should be noted, whose importance and influence was probably equal to that of Lin Biao and Chen Boda. This was Kang Sheng (1898–1975). Of gentry origin, Kang was a native of Shandong, born in the same province as Mao's wife, Jiang Qing (a fact which was to assume significance later on). He joined the CCP during the 1925–7 revolution. After its disastrous collapse, he worked in the Shanghai underground, concerned primarily with security and intelligence activities. During his stay in the Soviet Union from 1933 to 1937 Kang received further training in this field from the Soviet security organizations, then headed by Yagoda and Yezhov. Kang spent the years of the war against Japan in Yan'an as a member of the Political Bureau and head of the Social Affairs Department, the Party's security and intelligence service. His notoriety was first perceived during the Rectification Campaign of 1942–4, when he was responsible for the witch hunt of suspected Guomindang agents within the Party, which led to a serious distortion of the campaign's aims. In 1949, after a number of years as a leading Party member in his native province, Kang Sheng was transferred to Beijing to become once again responsible for security work. Kang was reputed to be a skilful seal-carver and an enthusiastic admirer of traditional Chinese painting. It is believed that his private art collection grew in size remarkably during the 'cultural revolution'. In passing, it may be worthwhile to note that the author of a hagiographic two-volume biography of Mao Zedong, who claims to have excellent connections with some top PRC personalities, eulogized the 'prestigious' Kang Sheng as a 'very good revolutionary' noted for his 'integrity and ideological correctness'. Such a statement can be considered as tantamount to praising Beria for 'humaneness'. *Caveat emptor*.

It is clear that the grave problems produced by the Great Crisis were of deep concern to the CCP leadership and continued to be discussed extensively at all the top-level meetings in 1961 and 1962. At the Ninth Plenum on 14–18 January 1961 the new economic policy stressing the primacy of agriculture and advocating readjustment and consolidation – i.e. retrenchment of the entire economy – which had been put forward in August 1960 was now officially confirmed. The six regional bureaus were reintroduced to strengthen control over the provincial and lower levels of the Party apparatus. The Party itself had grown by this time to 17 million members, 80 per cent of whom had joined the movement after 1949.

A particularly significant and unusual top-level meeting was the enlarged Work Conference of the Central Committee, which took place from 11 January to 7 February 1962 and was attended by 7000 cadres from all levels throughout the country. Judging from the fragmentary material available on the debates, the divergence of views within the top CCP leadership rose to the surface. Liu Shaoqi voiced his critical opinion of the Great Leap, while Deng Xiaoping challenged Mao's optimistic conclusion that the general situation was very good by stating that if the political situation was favourable, then economic conditions were highly unfavourable as a result of the Party's errors, the Great Leap Forward in particular.

Mao Zedong made use of the occasion for a partial self-criticism, assuming responsibility for the faults of the Great Leap. But he qualified his self-criticism by maintaining that the main source of the errors rested in the 'extremely inadequate knowledge of socialist construction' of the Party as a whole. The main point Mao wanted to stress, which was to assume vital importance within the next five years, related to the purported danger from class enemies; this was connected with the thesis that 'during the entire socialist stage there still exist classes and class struggle, and this class struggle is a protracted, complex, sometimes even a violent affair'.

The close similarity between this assertion and the views expressed by Stalin in the late 1920s and early 1930s should be noted, since it helps to explain, at least partially, the position adopted by Mao from 1956 on regarding the crucial question of the correct assessment of Stalin's place in history and, above all, of the suitability of applying Stalinist policies in China.

In his rather remarkable speech (which was finally published in July 1978) Mao revealed his extensive knowledge of ancient Chinese history; he was obviously well acquainted with the marvellous *Historical Records* of China's first and perhaps greatest historian, Sima Qian. Although at this time, and increasingly so later on, Mao is known to have made a number of remarks deprecating the value of school education, including the flat statement that 'the more books one reads the more stupid one gets', it would seem from his knowledge of China's history that his years in secondary school in Hunan had not been entirely wasted.

It is maintained that a certain relaxation of tension in the intellectual atmosphere took place in 1961–2 in parallel with the new socio-economic policies pursued in the wake of the Great Leap. This tendency is said to be exemplified by the speech made by Zhou Enlai in June 1961 (but published only in February 1979) which is taken to denote a revival of the 'Double Hundred' policy. In fact, there was considerable resentment among intellectuals towards some of the top CCP leaders for the irresponsible introduction of ultimately disastrous policies. These views were to be expressed above all by three individuals, themselves paradoxically connected with the Beijing Party establishment – the historian Wu Han, the journalist Deng Tuo, and the writer Liao Mosha.

Wu Han (1909–69) was already a specialist on Ming history in the 1930s, and by the 1950s was recognized as an eminent authority on the subject. Among his many works was a biography of Zhu Yuanzhang, the peasant founder of the Ming dynasty, considered to be the best biography written by a modern Chinese. It was also thought highly of by Mao Zedong, always attracted by the personality of Zhu. Having formerly been a member of the Democratic League, Wu Han joined the CCP in 1954, and since 1952 had held the post of deputy mayor of Beijing.

Already in 1959 Wu Han had dealt in an article with the activities of Hai Rui (1515–87), an upright, model official of the late Ming period, known as a defender of the peasants against feudal exploitation. In February 1961, Wu Han returned to this subject in a play entitled *The Dismissal of Hai Rui*. It dealt with another episode in this hero's life when, demonstrating his famous integrity, Hai Rui remonstrated with the emperor for his numerous shortcomings which were causing the common people much suffering. For his courageous act Hai Rui was imprisoned and tortured, his life being saved only by the emperor's timely death. It is quite likely that the play was interpreted by many of its audience, well versed in the use of historical analogy in the Chinese literary tradition, as referring to the fall of Peng Dehuai. If this was the intention, it came close to being a case of *lèse majesté*, and three years later, on the eve of the 'cultural revolution', such a view of Wu Han's work was indeed enunciated.

Deng Tuo (1911–66) had been engaged in journalism in one of the Liberated Areas during the war against Japan and continued to work in this field after liberation. In 1952–7 he held the responsible position of editor-in-chief of the *People's Daily*, the CCP's principal newspaper. A highly talented writer, possessed of considerable erudition and knowledge of Chinese history and literature, Deng began in March 1961 to write a special column in a Beijing newspaper. His sarcastic, barbed essays, while clothed in an appropriately esoteric and Aesopian form, were soon recognized by the Beijing cognoscenti as subtle attacks on some of Mao Zedong's characteristics, including his long-windedness. For example, Deng's essay entitled 'Great Empty Talk' pithily described a long speech as something in which really nothing is said and confusion is made worse by explanations which do not explain. Deng's advice for those fond of indulging in empty talk was simple: 'Read more, think more and talk less.'

In October of the same year Wu Han and Deng Tuo joined forces with Liao Mosha to produce a series of devastating satirical articles entitled 'Notes from the Three-Family Village'. Liao Mosha (b. 1907) had joined the communist movement as a youth and been active in Shanghai in the League of Left-Wing Writers before the War of Resistance; in the 1950s and early 1960s he was an official of the Beijing CCP establishment.

By the autumn of 1962 the three men ceased their literary satire, for they sensed that the political situation was becoming once again unfavourable for expressing such unorthodox thoughts. Deng Tuo ended his series of articles in September with a piece entitled 'The Thirty-six Strategies'; the best of these thirty-six was a retreat. However, the activities of these men had been carefully recorded. In the first years of the 'cultural revolution' all three were arrested under false charges. Wu Han and

Deng Tuo 'died as a result of persecution', to use the official terminology which appears in the documents dealing with the trial held in November 1980 of the 'gang of four' and Lin Biao's associates. In fact, Deng committed suicide and Wu died in prison, while his wife was hounded to death and his daughter was driven to suicide. Liao Mosha was imprisoned for eight years, surviving to testify at the 'gang of four's' trial and give an account of his sufferings. How strange that a Western author writing in 1981 saw fit to apply the term 'notorious' to the activities of these brave men.

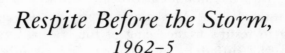

CHAPTER FIVE

Respite Before the Storm,
1962–5

A slow, steady though difficult recovery from the consequences of the Great Leap Forward continued from the beginning of 1963 until the outbreak of the 'cultural revolution' in the summer of 1966. The progress made was primarily due to the ever present and infinite capacity of the Chinese for hard work; it was also due to the relatively moderate and realistic domestic policy which had been established in 1961–2.

According to statistics reconstructed after 1978, grain production rose to around 185 million tons in 1963; by 1965 it had increased to 194.5 million tons. This was still half a million tons less than in 1957, and taking into account the population growth, the per capita rate of production was lower than that achieved before the Great Leap. Cotton output grew moderately: in 1952 it was 1.3 million tons; in 1957, 1.6 million; and in 1965, 2 million. The increase in agricultural production was aided in part by a marked increase in the production of chemical fertilizers: in 1952 the output was 295,000 tons; in 1963, 2.8 million; in 1965, 7.2 million. This spectacular growth was the result also of the import of equipment and entire factories.

Steel production probably amounted to around 9 million tons in 1963. It increased to 12.2 million in 1965. Coal output was about 210 million tons in 1963, rising to 232 million in 1965. The production of cement also showed considerable growth: 1952 – 2.8 million tons; 1957 – 6.8 million; 1965 – 16.3 million. The development of the oil industry was of particular significance, especially if one recalls the prediction of some foreign experts that China would never be an oil-producing country since its resources were inadequate. Output rose from the minuscule figure of 440,000 tons in 1952 to 1.4 million in 1957, between 6 and 7 million tons in 1963, reaching 11.3 million tons in 1965. Electricity generation went up from 7.36 billion kwh in 1952 to 19.3 billion in 1957; by 1963 it had reached 32 billion kwh and more than doubled this figure in 1965 at 67.6 billion kwh.

Against this background a moderate improvement in living conditions took place, especially in the urban areas, and a somewhat more relaxed atmosphere prevailed generally. In some ways the situation resembled that of the early 1950s – a land full of promise, a China with no opium, no beggars, no flies and little crime, a China which seemed capable of lifting herself, almost exclusively by her own bootstraps, out of the terrible morass of inherited poverty and backwardness.

Significant progress continued to be made in the two vital fields of education and health. Much had been done to overcome mass illiteracy, through both adult education and the expansion of the school system. Enrolment in primary schools, which had doubled from 24.4 million in 1949–50 to 51.1 million in 1951–2, reached 64 million in 1957–8 and continued to rise to 80 million in 1964–5. Secondary school attendance, which was 3.1 million in 1952–3, reached a fluctuating level of between 12 and 13 million in the years 1960 to 1965. The number of students in university-level schools rose from 117,000 in 1949–50 to 440,000 in 1957–8. By 1964–5 it had increased to around 700,000.

The advance in health, sanitation and hygiene, aided by mass propaganda campaigns, was equally impressive. The number of doctors trained in modern medicine increased from 41,000 in 1955 to 150,000 by 1965, while the number of graduates in medicine rose from 1300 in 1949 to 6200 in 1957 and 25,000 in 1963. The number of hospital beds mounted from 180,000 in 1952 to 364,000 in 1957 and 660,000 in 1962.

However, there was one very fundamental drawback to these remarkable achievements: the urban areas benefited to a greater degree than the rural ones. The countryside continued to bear

the heavy burden of being the prime source of capital accumulation for the further development of the economy. Moreover,
there was almost no possibility of the peasants' escaping from
the much inferior conditions of the rural areas since they did not
possess the legal right to migrate to the cities or to other rural
areas. Thus, the disturbing and growing gap in the development
of the towns and countryside was becoming more and more
accentuated. The querulous, carping remarks attributed to Mao
Zedong, including the suggestion that the Ministry of Public
Health be renamed the Ministry of Urban Gentlemen's Health,
since 'the broad masses of the peasants do not get any medical
treatment', were not devoid of substance.

During the years 1963–6 a facade of outward unity continued
to be successfully preserved. In reality, serious divergences
within the top CCP leadership concerning both current and
future domestic policies grew in intensity. They must have been
apparent already to the leading CCP members during the Tenth
Plenum (24–27 September 1962). It was here that Mao Zedong
developed still further his concept regarding the existence of a
growing class struggle, a point which he had made at the beginning of the year at the Work Conference of 7000 cadres. Mao
was seeking to reverse the fundamental position adopted by the
Party at the Eighth Congress in 1956. Then, it was stated that the
principal contradiction within the country was between the
demand of the people for rapid economic and cultural development and the capacity for meeting the demand. Now, Mao
maintained that the basic contradiction remained instead the
struggle between the proletariat and the bourgeoisie. But Mao's
use of the term 'bourgeoisie' was imprecise, to say the least, for
already in 1962, and still more in the coming four years, he
tended to employ it to denote not capitalist owners of enterprises, who did not exist any more, but a significant part of the
upper level members of the Party and state apparatus, especially
those whom he suspected of opposing his own policies. According to Mao, these individuals, who supposedly represented an
emerging new bourgeoisie within the Party itself, were prone to
adopt revisionist policies which were purportedly a form of

bourgeois ideology. Hence, the struggle against revisionism was now a pressing task; failure to engage in it could mean the end of China as a socialist country and its emergence as a bourgeois one, as had been the case, according to Mao, with Yugoslavia. It should be stressed, however, that the development of Mao's views on this topic, and in particular on the struggle against so-called revisionism, were inseparable from, and intimately bound up with, the continuing polemic between the CCP and the CPSU.

While Mao Zedong's views enjoyed the support of a part of the CCP leadership, one can safely deduce from the political history of these years that they did not command a majority. Hence, no formal consensus on the policies he advocated could be gained, and this might well explain why no Central Committee plenum was held during the subsequent four years.

In the aftermath of the Great Leap catastrophe, the need to revitalize the Party's rural organization became urgent. It was primarily for this purpose that the CCP leadership agreed to launch a new political campaign, known as the Socialist Education Movement. The programme was formulated by Mao Zedong and his followers and was contained in a draft resolution on rural work published in May 1963, referred to later on as 'The Early Ten Points'. In it Mao gave an optimistic assessment of the economic and political situation in the countryside, defended the correctness of his own policies in launching the commune movement and the Great Leap Forward, and called for a renewal of the class struggle in the rural areas. This was necessary for future socialist construction and for counteracting the supposed growth of capitalist tendencies and the renewed activities of former landlords and rich peasants. It was also to serve to overcome the reputed increasing demoralization and corruption of the rural cadres. In all this the Party was to rely on the poor and lower middle peasants, whose work would be coordinated through the re-creation of associations, which had been in abeyance since the period of the land reform. Raising the political and moral level of the rural cadres was to be achieved in part by their compulsory participation in produc-

93

tive labour. The associations would supervise the Four Clean-up Campaign, as it was called, whose purpose was to examine and reform the activities of the rural cadres.

The Socialist Education Movement, as envisaged by the provisions of 'The Early Ten Points', was meant to bring about a further round of political strife in the countryside; whether this would be conducive to the continued development of agricultural production was open to question. It is more than likely that such senior communist leaders as Liu Shaoqi and Deng Xiaoping, in charge of day-to-day operations aimed at further restoration of the economy, took a dim view of the prospect of renewed domestic turmoil. Certainly, the more specific instructions relating to the Socialist Education Movement, published in September 1963 and known as 'The Later Ten Points', sought to minimize the possible negative consequences by placing the movement under the close control and supervision of the Party establishment on all levels. This was to be achieved through work teams, usually composed of Party functionaries, and dispatched always from a higher level. The teams were to lead and supervise the entire implementation of the Socialist Education Movement. It can be assumed that during its first stage, up to the autumn of 1964, the Party establishment did succeed, at least partially, in keeping the movement within bounds.

The intricate inner-Party struggle over the direction of the Socialist Education Movement was to continue right up to the eve of the 'cultural revolution'. In fact, Mao Zedong's growing dissatisfaction with the way in which the Party apparatus, led by Liu, Deng and their associates, implemented the Socialist Education Movement was one of the more important factors which inclined him to embark upon that ill-fated venture. A large part of the motivation for the 'cultural revolution' can be found in the last important document pertaining to the Socialist Education Movement, the 'Twenty-three Articles', which is said to represent the views of Mao and his entourage.

The difficulties which Mao Zedong encountered in getting his views on the movement accepted and acted upon by the majority of the senior leaders in the Party establishment caused him to think increasingly in terms of waging a decisive political struggle against them. The goal was to restore his undisputed control over the Party; if accomplishing this aim entailed removing his opponents and striking a blow at the Party apparatus under their sway, then so be it. However, as a realistic and superior strategist – a quality he had certainly demonstrated from 1937 to 1949 – Mao took full account of the forces at his disposal. There are sufficient grounds to maintain that by 1963 he had come to regard the highly politicized PLA as the only truly reliable component of the CCP. It should be recalled that Mao had retained direct authority over the PLA through his chairmanship of the Party's vital Military Affairs Commission (MAC), the real decision- and policy-making body in all military matters.

It is logical to assume that Mao Zedong had every reason to be satisfied with his earlier decision to place Lin Biao at the head of the PLA and in charge of the day-to-day operations of MAC. In the years 1963–6 Lin Biao continued the work he had begun in 1960 of transforming the PLA into Mao's principal political base and glorifying the Party chairman and his ideology. A series of intensive campaigns were launched to propagate the ideal behaviour of the PLA. Such, for instance, was the 'Good Eighth Company of Nanjing Road', an army unit stationed in Shanghai which had proved capable of resisting all the dubious attractions of big city life and keeping its virtue unsullied. In early 1963 all the Chinese media carried in great length the story of the ideal soldier – Lei Feng, a paragon of selflessness and devotion.

The really significant campaign which revealed the political aims pursued by Lin Biao commenced in February 1964 with an editorial in the *People's Daily* under the title 'Learn from the People's Liberation Army'. It stressed the political reliability of the PLA which had become a 'great school of Mao Zedong Thought' and had successfully implemented the principle of 'politics in command'. This signalled that its political role was to be increased still further, and from 1963 on, when new political departments were established in a large number of central ministries, they were staffed by PLA personnel.

A number of Western authors maintain that one of Lin Biao's tasks, on Mao Zedong's instructions, was to counteract a trend towards professionalism, which had supposedly become widespread among the senior officers of the PLA in the years after the Korean War. Although it is clear that differences of opinion must have existed about the proper balance that should obtain between political indoctrination and military training itself, there is insufficient evidence to sustain the thesis that this presented a serious problem. Moreover, whatever reservations PLA officers might have had regarding some of Lin Biao's policies – for example they might well have been unenthusiastic about the abolition in February 1965 of the system of ranks which had been introduced a decade earlier – the loyalty of the senior PLA commanders, practically all Long March veterans, to Mao Zedong personally was unquestioned. Most of them continued to regard him as the omniscient and infallible leader who had led them to victory.

The truly important problem rested elsewhere. It had been axiomatic in the history of the CCP that, as Mao himself had stated in 1938, 'The Party commands the gun, and the gun must never be allowed to command the Party.' The increased politicization of the PLA in the early 1960s created a situation in which the future observance of this salutary provision was by no means assured. Matters were further complicated by the simple fact that a large part of the PLA, practically all its officer corps and certainly its entire commanding staff, was composed of men who considered themselves loyal Party members. Thus if the PLA were ever to be used as an instrument of struggle in a political campaign and attack against the majority of the CCP leadership, very thorough preparation and much ingenious and devious manoeuvring would be necessary, in which the fullest use would have to be made of Mao Zedong's prestige and authority. In fact, plans to utilize the PLA precisely for such a purpose had been basically completed in the spring of 1966, and it was the full assurance that he would be able to rely on this formidable and crucial force that did much to embolden Mao Zedong to embark on the 'cultural revolution'.

In 1965 and early 1966 the PLA markedly contributed, in line with Lin Biao's orders, to further expansion of the cult of Mao Zedong. By now it had reached gigantic proportions, certainly enough to make Stalin turn over with envy in his grave. Statues, busts and portraits of the Great Helmsman were scattered and plastered over the length and breadth of China, while all the media poured out an unceasing paean of praise and worship.

It was also at this time that the curious compendium of *Quotations from Chairman Mao Zedong* was put together on the orders of Lin Biao. His injunction to 'study Chairman Mao's writing, follow his teachings and act according to his instructions' was reproduced in his own calligraphy on the page following Mao's photograph. It would be interesting to know what the millions of Chinese who possessed a copy of the booklet did with this page after 1971. At any rate, the *Quotations* were proclaimed as the quintessential and indispensable epitome of Mao Zedong Thought. As the source of all wisdom, the 'Little Red Book' quickly became a talisman to be carried and displayed on all possible occasions as a proof of faithful adherence to the cause of the Great Teacher.

It is indisputable that the propagation of this cult, to which Lin Biao, Chen Boda, Kang Sheng and others of Mao's own coterie were devoting so much effort, met with Mao Zedong's wholehearted approval and support. After the fall of Khrushchev, Mao remarked ironically to his American Boswell, Edgar Snow, that the Soviet leader could have avoided such a fate had he created an appropriate cult for himself.

However, the question inevitably arises as to what motives, other than obvious political advantage, led Mao Zedong to give his blessing to these endeavours of his closest associates. The 1981 Resolution on CCP History admits that 'the personality cult grew graver and graver', that Mao Zedong 'began to get arrogant . . . gradually divorced himself from practice and from the masses, acted more and more arbitrarily and subjectively'. This is all too true, but it is a fragmentary answer at best, for it deliberately omits other developments in Mao Zedong's personality. Not only did his arrogance increase, his vanity did as well. It was this which led him to break the Party rules, instigated at his own suggestion, against any glorification of its leaders. It was vanity which caused him to approve the transformation of his native village into a Chinese Mecca. Both Zhou Enlai and Liu Shaoqi had strictly forbidden any similar attempt being made in their own birthplaces. One might well ponder whether, already at this stage, Mao Zedong did not share the belief of some of his faithful followers that he was indeed omniscient and infallible, whether he did not consider his concepts and vision of the future as the only valid ones, and therefore sacrosanct and unchallengeable. For surely only this state of mind explains how Mao came to perpetrate some of the grievous errors – such as the Great Leap Forward with its ghastly consequences in terms of human suffering – which were committed in the decade 1956–66. However, the present CCP leadership, while holding Mao 'chiefly responsible', maintains that 'the blame for all these errors cannot be laid on him alone'. A justified assertion, but it is left hanging in mid-air. None of the senior CCP leaders, with the honourable exception of Peng Dehuai, appear to have attempted to counteract effectively Mao Zedong's increasingly arbitrary behaviour which ultimately succumbed to the overwhelming power of imperial tradition and assumed a completely autocratic character. There is also no evidence to show that they took any steps against the cult of Mao, which grew rapidly like a monstrous excrescence. Nor did they either seriously oppose or try to alter the increasingly ultra-leftist tendency which, since 1957, Mao Zedong had been systematically imposing on the Party's general policies. They might not have danced the Hopak, but the question as to what they did do during this period to prevent the ensuing disaster is still a valid one. The partial answer given by the surviving leaders in 1981 – that they share, more by omission than commission, the responsibility for the errors – corresponds to the truth as the facts show it, and is encouragingly honest.

During the years when, in the wake of the Great Leap Forward, China was plunged into a devastating economic crisis, the controversy between the CCP and CPSU deepened appreciably, with every neuralgic point becoming more inflamed. The divergences between the two parties were still being expressed primarily in an ideological form, on the assumption – rapidly and increasingly less valid – that they shared an identical world outlook which could and should facilitate a reconciliation of the differences between them. The issues involved remained basically the same as those which had emerged clearly after the 20th Congress of the CPSU in 1956. The question of how to assess the current world political situation and hence determine the strategy and principal tasks of the international communist movement remained in the forefront. But the problem of who was to do the determining was always of utmost importance; the Chinese communist leaders intensified their demand for equal rights with the CPSU in this crucial sphere, and the Soviet leaders adamantly and consistently refused to acknowledge the demand.

It would be quite erroneous to dismiss the ideological nature of the CCP–CPSU dispute as so much idle verbiage, although in view of the suffocatingly scholastic forms it assumed the temptation to do just that is well-nigh irresistible. The leaders of both parties viewed the world primarily in ideological terms, or at least felt obliged to express their opinions in this fashion. They attached the utmost importance to seeking to prove that only they, and not their opponents, were the true purveyors and representatives of orthodox Marxism–Leninism. Hence, the growing clash of national interests between the PRC and the Soviet Union, intimately bound up with the evaluation of the current international situation and therefore the formulation of foreign policy, was also dressed up in ideological apparel. However, the question of whether these national interests were estimated correctly by each side and, even more important, whether a real, irreconcilable, 'antagonistic' contradiction existed between the two countries is quite a different matter. There is a good case for the thesis that there were no fundamental objective reasons for a conflict of national interests between the PRC and the Soviet Union, both of which considered themselves to be socialist. Leaving aside a fatalistic interpretation of history in which all

99

events are foreordained, the conclusion has to be that subjective factors, including above all the activities, behaviour and even idiosyncrasies of the leaders of both parties, played a major, if not dominant, role in bringing about the crisis in relations between the two countries. It is here that any attempt to present even a tentative Marxist analysis of this vital problem becomes insuperably difficult, for the rational categories of Marxist thought do not lend themselves to a full elucidation of subjective, often irrational factors. And irrationality did become an ever more prominent feature of the CCP–CPSU polemic, with pique, resentment, contempt and ultimately hatred coming more and more to the surface.

In 1960 and 1961, national congresses of ruling communist parties, always attended by numerous delegations from other fraternal parties and usually an occasion for innocuous congratulatory speech-making, became now a forum for the Sino-Soviet dispute. During the Congress of the Rumanian Communist Party in Bucharest on 24–26 June 1960, the customary festive atmosphere was rudely shattered by an acrimonious exchange between the heads of the Soviet and Chinese delegations – Khrushchev and Peng Zhen. A few months earlier in a prominent editorial entitled 'Long Live Leninism' (16 April), the CCP had sharply criticized Soviet policies, especially in foreign affairs, as revisionist. Khrushchev rebutted these views at the Bucharest congress. Having beforehand distributed to those present the text of a secret letter from the CPSU to the CCP, he launched a bitter attack on the Chinese communist leadership, and Mao Zedong personally, accusing them of nationalism, adventurism and other deviationist sins. Peng Zhen replied in kind, criticizing Khrushchev for seeking crudely to impose his views and will on other parties and for his 'patriarchal, arbitrary and tyrannical' behaviour. It should be noted that the withdrawal of the Soviet experts from China, mentioned earlier, took place within a month of the Bucharest meeting.

In spite of the level of animosity, both parties still sought to avoid an open break, while also exerting all possible efforts to ensure that the other side would bear full responsibility for it if it were to occur. Thus the CCP continued its dialogue with the CPSU and agreed to participate in the world conference of eighty-one communist parties to be held in Moscow on 11–25 November 1960. The Chinese delegation was headed by Liu Shaoqi, Deng Xiaoping and Peng Zhen. It is ironical that within less than six years these three men were to become the principal victims of the 'cultural revolution', for they were stalwart supporters of the general line pursued by the CCP in its conflict with the Soviet party. The divergences within the Chinese leadership pertained primarily, if not exclusively, to domestic policies.

Deng Xiaoping delivered the principal two Chinese speeches at the Moscow conference, taking the CPSU to task for opportunism, revisionism and numerous other faults, as well as criticizing its foreign policy and relations within the international communist movement. The Chinese found themselves in a small minority during the prolonged and embittered debates. All the ruling parties of Eastern Europe, with the exception of Albania, and the majority of the non-ruling parties as well, supported in varying degrees the Soviet position on most issues. A compromise was ultimately arrived at in the form of a declaration, accepted by all the parties present, which dealt with all the basic issues raised in the debates but did not solve any of the problems dividing the CCP and the CPSU; it served only to preserve a frail, temporary and quite superficial facade of unity in the international communist movement.

The disagreements between the CCP and CPSU grew in strength throughout 1961, though their attacks on each other were somewhat muffled by the use of surrogates – which fooled nobody. Beijing multiplied its virulent diatribes against the 'revisionist' sins of Yugoslavia, with whom the Soviet party was still seeking a rapprochement, while Moscow was no less vehement in its denunciations of Albania. At the 22nd Congress of the CPSU (17–31 October 1961) Khrushchev violently attacked the Albanians, and the head of the Chinese delegation, Zhou Enlai, spoke in their defence. Then to emphasize his disapproval of Khrushchev's policies in general, he ostentatiously placed a wreath on Stalin's grave and left Moscow before the end of the congress, to be publicly welcomed at Beijing airport by Mao Zedong himself. In December the Soviet Union broke off diplomatic relations with Albania.

In the autumn of 1962 two important events in the international arena contributed significantly to the further deterioration of Sino-Soviet relations. During the Cuban missile crisis the Chinese castigated Khrushchev relentlessly, first for adventurism in sending the missiles to Cuba, and then for capitulationism when he agreed to withdraw them. However, it was the border dispute between China and India, culminating in the brief war between the two countries from 20 October to 12 November 1962 that really raised the dispute between Beijing and Moscow to a new pitch of animosity and hostility. The Chinese claimed that not only had the Soviet Union not sided with them, as the solidarity of the socialist camp and proletarian internationalism required, it had actively supported the Indian stand since Soviet neutrality was actually biased in India's favour. The success of China's military operations and the political advantage the country gained from the speedy withdrawal of the PLA forces from the occupied territory did nothing to alleviate the CCP leadership's raucous anger with the Soviet Union.

By the summer of 1963 the crescendo of CCP–CPSU polemics had reached an ear-piercing level. On 14 June, the Chinese sent and published a letter to the CPSU, entitled 'The CCP's Proposal Concerning the General Line of the International Communist Movement'. In about 20,000 words they outlined their position on practically every key issue under debate. The CPSU lost no time in giving its side of the case and replied on 14 July in an even lengthier epistle – around 25,000 words – called the 'Open Letter of the CPSU to Its Members'. These two weighty documents formed the briefs for what to date has been the last direct, formal confrontation between the two parties. It took place in Moscow on 15–20 July; the USSR's delegation was headed by M. Suslov, principal Soviet ideologist, and China's by Deng Xiaoping. Deng's speeches on this occasion, like those delivered by him to the conference of eighty-one communist parties, also in Moscow, have unfortunately not been published.

If one of the purposes of the Moscow meeting was to find ways of repairing relations between the CCP and CPSU, then it was a total failure. The encounter marked the formal end of relations between the two parties, which were infinitely more significant than state relations between the PRC and the Soviet Union.

But the fiasco of the Moscow meeting did not put an end to the polemic between the two parties; on the contrary it flourished more than ever before. The CCP answered the Soviet letter of 14 July in a series of nine lengthy, ponderous open letters, the first appearing on 1 September 1963, the last on 14 July 1964, in which it sought to rebut the Soviet views point by point. The Chinese presentation reflected, of course, the development of Mao Zedong's assessment of the CPSU and the Soviet Union. In January 1962, Mao had already expressed the view that the Party and state leadership of the Soviet Union had been usurped by revisionists. By May 1964 he had reached the conclusion that a dictatorship of the bourgeoisie had been established in what had been the first socialist state in the world.

The Soviet media did not rest idle, and a deluge of propaganda directed against the CCP flooded the world. In it the Chinese communists were represented as irresponsible, nationalistically minded, dogmatic and sectarian adventurers. They were accused of a multitude of sins, although their cardinal one – being incorrigibly insubordinate – was never actually spelled out. The Soviet propagandists also intensified their public attacks on Mao Zedong personally, applying practically every pejorative political adjective in their quite extensive vocabulary. In private, their attitude to the Chinese leader was less elaborate; they simply referred to him as a 'treacherous muzhik'.

This pot and kettle recrimination became the established mode of dialogue between the CCP and the CPSU for nearly the next two decades, its intensity fluctuating according to the international situation and domestic considerations but on the whole undiminished until the early 1980s.

One of the charges raised against Khrushchev which led to his removal from power in October 1964 was his faulty handling of the Chinese issue, and within less than a month of his fall Zhou Enlai appeared once again in the Soviet capital – for what was to be the last time – to hold talks with the new CPSU leadership. But any hope of a rapprochement between Moscow and Beijing – assuming that real intentions to achieve reconciliation existed on each side, which is by no means certain – soon proved misplaced. The Chinese came very quickly to the conclusion that nothing had fundamentally changed in the Soviet Union and expressed this within two weeks of Zhou Enlai's return from Moscow in an editorial containing the telling phrase 'Khrushchevism without Khrushchev'.

It would be quite futile to try to summarize the hundreds of thousands of words poured out by both sides in their polemical dispute during these years. The CCP's senior leaders, and Mao Zedong in particular, devoted an inordinate amount of time to these endeavours, which might have been used more advantageously for dealing with the immense domestic problems arising from the Great Leap Forward.

There was a curious feature of the Sino-Soviet dispute, which has seldom been noticed. In their exertions to prove themselves the sole correct interpreters of Marxism–Leninism, the Chinese communists began to employ – whether consciously or not is hard to determine – the conceptual framework and terminology used by the Communist International in the years 1928–34. This was without question the most sterile, dogmatic and sectarian period in the annals of the international communist movement and the history of Marxist thought. During this time Stalin had sought to turn the independent non-Soviet communist parties from independent representatives of their own working class into obedient servants of the national interests of the Soviet Union. In the process he inflicted severe damage on many of them, including the German, Polish and, not least, Chinese parties. It is therefore supremely ironical that the Chinese communists, and especially Mao Zedong who had successfully led the struggle to assert the CCP's independence from Stalin's dictates, should have reverted to the moth-eaten phraseology and erroneous guidelines of a bygone era, which had brought their own movement to the brink of total disaster. Perhaps the explanation for this lies in the intensity of the hostility towards Soviet policies vis-à-vis China; it seems to have seriously stultified the customary capacity of the Chinese leaders for lucid and consistent thought.

The consequences of the confrontation between the CCP and the CPSU were manifold, but two have to be taken note of here. The efforts exerted by both parties in this conflict inflicted incalculable damage on the international communist movement. The leader of a non-ruling communist party put the matter succinctly at the time: 'Between the two of them they will finish us off completely.' The CCP and the CPSU leaders had split the 'socialist camp' – to the great delight of the world's anti-communist forces – thereby striking a truly grievous blow to the Marxist ideology which both sides professed to cherish and uphold. In October 1951, Mao Zedong had proclaimed proudly that 'the firm unity between the two great countries of China and the Soviet Union . . . has ended for good the era in which imperialism could dominate the world'. By 1966 – only fifteen years later – little remained of this bold assertion and optimistic vision of the future.

CHAPTER SIX

Preparing the 'Cultural Revolution',
January 1965–May 1966

Against the background of the inconclusive results of the Socialist Education Movement, Mao Zedong had reached, by the
beginning of 1965, the conclusion that the power to formulate
fundamental Party decisions no longer rested fully in his hands.
This seemed to be true of the major part of the Party apparatus,
of the media which were run by it, and also of considerable seg-
ments of the state administration, with the very important
exception of the People's Liberation Army.

The task of regaining this power became one of the prime
motives, although by no means the only one, which induced
Mao Zedong to take the first steps on the road leading to the
'cultural revolution', for which he, and he alone, was responsible. He 'initiated and led it'; no Mao Zedong, no 'cultural
revolution' – a simplistic statement, but in this case true.

Mao's fundamental premise, which had been evolving for at
least five years, was that the class struggle must necessarily
become sharper as the process of building socialism unfolded;
class struggle thus constituted the key link in the formulation of
the Party's general line. This idea, which was in many ways similar to the tenets put forth by Stalin in the late 1920s and early
1930s, was also closely bound up with Mao's perception of the
revolution as a permanent phenomenon. In this instance the
revolution was now to be waged against the purported representatives of the bourgeoisie and counter-revolutionary revisionists who had seemingly acquired control of much of the
Party and state apparatus, i.e. those whom Mao suspected of
opposing his views and policies. The prime target was soon to

become Liu Shaoqi, the number two man in the Party and state establishment. At a later date, Mao revealed to Edgar Snow that already in January 1965 he had made up his mind that Liu must be removed from his posts. There is no evidence to show that Mao attached the slightest importance to the fact that most of the men he considered his opponents had been, in reality, his faithful followers and comrades for as long as three to four decades.

These 'enemy' elements, defined as 'persons in power taking the capitalist road', had allegedly formed 'a bourgeois head-quarters inside the Central Committee which pursued a revisionist political and organization line and had agents in all provinces, municipalities and autonomous regions, as well as in all central departments'. The power which had purportedly been usurped by these elements could be recaptured only by 'carrying out a great cultural and political revolution, in which one class would overthrow another'. These ideas were to become, in the course of the 'cultural revolution', the components of the 'theory of continued revolution under the dictatorship of the proletariat'. They formed as well the basic content of the interpretation presented by Mao and his propagandists of the entire history of the CCP and the PRC. This, according to them, was nothing else but an unceasing struggle between two political lines – a correct, 'proletarian' one, represented by Mao Zedong and his followers, and a 'bourgeois' line upheld by the 'capitalist roaders'. It is hardly necessary to add that this bears no relation to the true picture of CCP history.

The present CCP leadership, in its 1981 Resolution on Party History, convincingly demonstrated the spuriousness of Mao's theses and maintains that they 'conformed neither to Marxism–Leninism nor to Chinese reality'. In that case, where did they originate, and how were they able to find credence – for they did – among millions of Chinese? Mao's theories did, after all, serve to set in motion a movement which was to convulse the entire country and bring upon it an unmitigated catastrophe, or, in the moderate language of the Resolution, 'the most serious setback and heaviest losses suffered by the Party, the state and the people since the founding of the People's Republic'.

A tentative answer to the first question should be sought primarily in the mode and manner in which a ruling communist party exercises power. Having struggled for and achieved the victory of the revolution, the Party becomes singularly vulnerable to the danger of deformation through its monopolistic position, which lends itself only too easily, if necessary countermeasures are not undertaken, to the abuse of power. The Party can turn itself into a new ruling caste, interested primarily in enjoying the perquisites of its position. As time in the saddle lengthens, a tendency towards overweening arrogance and a belief in personal indispensability and omniscience is liable to manifest itself in Party leaders. This applies particularly to a supreme leader, in whose hands a vast decision- and policy-making authority has become concentrated. No matter how talented and how significant his contribution was in the past, the supreme leader of a ruling communist party is exposed to various perils; the most common of these is isolation and a growing divorce from reality. His inspection trips 'to maintain contact with the masses' will be turned by his subordinates into a viewing of Potemkin's villages; the reliability of information received from his underlings will become progressively more dubious, for it will be doctored to fit what is known of his preconceptions. All this is not peculiar to China; the history of other socialist countries is replete with such examples, but in the case of the Middle Kingdom, with its almost 4000 years of imperial and bureaucratic tradition, these problems emerged with singular force. They affected Mao Zedong to a marked degree and go some way towards explaining his 'entirely erroneous appraisal of the prevailing class relations and political situation in the Party and State'.

There were at least two main reasons for the initial mass support of the 'cultural revolution'. Although it ultimately shattered the Party establishment, it was launched by Mao Zedong in the name of the Party. The credibility of the CCP was still largely intact and untarnished, in spite of the disaster of the Great Leap Forward. The Party's position had been, after all, well earned; it had come to power as the result of an authentic revolution, not as the by-product of geographical factors, and it had to its credit a number of outstanding achievements in the first seventeen years of the PRC. The tremendous personal authority of Mao Zedong as the founding father of the PRC and the most outstanding leader of the CCP, which had been systematically built on by the propagation of the cult of his personality, also assured the initial acceptance of the slogans of the 'cultural revolution'.

Two principal forces were at hand for Mao Zedong to use against his alleged opponents in the Party and state establishment. One of these, and ultimately by far the more important, was the PLA, which had been already carefully prepared for this purpose by Lin Biao. This force was kept in reserve, however, and the task of leading the attack was assigned to the youth of China. There were a number of reasons for this. Chinese youth, especially the students, had played a significant role in the past five decades in the Chinese political arena, notably during the May Fourth movement in 1919 and the December Ninth in 1935. It was this tradition of political activism which was now drawn upon, for quite different purposes than had been the case in the past.

Mao Zedong had frequently voiced his concern and disquiet over the condition of Chinese young people, their lack of political experience, awareness and maturity. In January 1965, he repeated these thoughts to Edgar Snow: having 'never fought a war . . . never known capitalism in power' the young 'knew nothing about the old society at first hand . . . and thus could negate the revolution, make peace with imperialism, bring the remnants of the Chiang Kai-shek clique back to the mainland'. This deeply pessimistic view, which threw doubt on all the achievements in education and indoctrination of the seventeen years of the PRC, were expressed again by Mao, even more sharply, during his talks with Malraux in August of the same year. Mao felt that Chinese youth demonstrated 'strong dangerous tendencies', by which it can be understood that he considered their political commitment particularly unsatisfactory. The young people must be put to a test; Mao did not spell out what form this would take, but clearly he wanted to train the coming generation to be 'revolutionary successors', a phrase frequently employed by Mao and his followers. There was one other important factor involved in the desire to mobilize China's youth for the ensuing political campaign. Without mass participation, the attack on Mao's nominal opponents would appear a purely factional struggle within the upper stratum of the CCP. The involvement of the young, in their hundreds of thousands, would give the implementation of Mao's aims the appearance of an authentic mass movement, a spontaneous revolution desired by the people themselves. This cynical exploitation of the inherent idealism of young people had dire consequences for the moral development of an entire generation.

According to Mao, the upper stratum of the Party and state bureaucracy in the Soviet Union had become a privileged bourgeois caste whose revisionist policies had allegedly resulted in the restoration of capitalism. He maintained that the same danger faced China unless the campaign against revisionism was waged. In addition to expressing frustration at being unable to implement his policies, Mao's pronouncements at this time indicated a lack of faith in the CCP which began to sound ever more loudly.

It was primarily in the field of art and literature that Mao Zedong chose to press on with his campaign against revisionism in China. Already in January 1964 he had maintained that the overall situation in these two domains was highly undesirable and disturbing, that the activities of writers and artists showed that they were perilously close to the brink of revisionism, and that if proper measures were not taken they could become the nucleus of a future Petöfi Club – a highly debatable reference to the role of the Hungarian intellectuals in 1956. In these comments Mao revealed, not for the first time, the curious anti-intellectual tendency which increasingly became a dominant feature in his thought. It is difficult to explain this phenomenon, since he was no mean intellectual himself, but it might well have derived in part from his own experiences with higher intellectuals in his early youth in Beijing.

For the purpose of revolutionizing art and literature, the

Political Bureau decided in January 1965 to establish a special five-man group to draw up a proper programme of action and then to supervise the developments. It was to be headed by Peng Zhen, the number five man in the hierarchy of the Political Bureau. Born in 1902 into a poor peasant family in Shanxi, Peng had been a Party member since 1923 and was involved in the underground CCP movement in north China. After six years' imprisonment for these activities, he became one of the leaders of the Party's north China bureau. Peng spent the years 1941–5 in Yan'an, becoming a Political Bureau member in 1945. From 1951 he was first secretary of the Beijing Party Committee and the capital's mayor. The choice of Peng was in some respects curious, since he had not demonstrated any particular enthusiasm for the Socialist Education Movement. Moreover, it was his subordinates, Wu Han and Deng Tuo, who had been so outspoken in the early 1960s.

There is no evidence to show that Peng's group was particularly active in its appointed tasks and the issues involved were raised again at a lengthy meeting of the enlarged Standing Committee of the Political Bureau in September and October of the same year. Mao Zedong reiterated his demand that bourgeois reactionary thinking be properly criticized, referring specifically to the problem of Wu Han and his famous play. No satisfactory results, from Mao's point of view, emerged from this meeting and he now proceeded, with the aid of his wife Jiang Qing, to take the matter into his own hands. Jiang Qing was born in 1914 in Shandong into an impoverished family. Her given name was Li Yunhe and she had been a bit-part cinema actress in Shanghai where she had mixed with the heavily communist-influenced art and literature circles of the city. Known then under the name of Lan Ping, she made her way in 1939 to Yan'an. Shortly thereafter, Mao who was separated from the wife who had accompanied him on the Long March, married the Shanghai actress, giving her the name of Jiang Qing. It is maintained that many of the senior communist leaders objected to this marriage, with the exception of Jiang Qing's fellow provincial Kang Sheng, who vouched for her. Jiang Qing played no visible political role in Beijing until the early 1960s when she associated herself with Lin Biao and began to assert her views, particularly in the field of the arts.

According to Mao, Beijing was a watertight kingdom ruled by Peng Zhen, which could not be penetrated even by a needle. He therefore concentrated his campaign on Shanghai, where Jiang Qing turned for assistance to two individuals whose careers were to be inseparably intertwined with those of her and her husband for the next eleven years – Yao Wenyuan and Zhang Chunqiao. Yao (b. 1931) was a literary critic and hatchetman known for his ultra-leftist views and his skilful but brutal poison pen. Zhang (b. 1917), whose political past is open to question, had been engaged in propaganda work for three decades and was at this time head of the propaganda department of the Shanghai Party Committee. This trio now prepared, no doubt with the active assistance of Mao Zedong himself, an article dealing with Wu Han and his play, which was published under the nominal authorship of Yao in a Shanghai newspaper on 10 November. This piece of supposed literary criticism was primarily a political attack not so much on Wu Han himself as on people holding much higher positions in the Party establishment; many authors consider it the first salvo of the 'cultural revolution'. Wu Han's work was characterized as a 'poisonous weed' and the manifestation of bourgeois opposition to the dictatorship of the proletariat. The article was quickly reprinted by the PLA *Liberation Daily*, but only after much pressure was exerted did it finally appear in the *People's Daily* on 30 November.

Peng Zhen and his colleagues in Beijing sought to defend Wu Han, saying that the whole matter should be treated as an academic and not a political discussion. However in December, Mao Zedong, residing in Hangzhou in what was probably the favourite of his numerous provincial residences, let it be known that the assault on Wu Han must be regarded as a political issue, and that the allusion in his play was transparent; Peng Dehuai was indeed Hai Rui. During this time, and up to May 1966, Mao was spending most of his time touring the provinces and the lack of any reference to him in the central press gave rise to much speculation about his whereabouts and the state of his health.

In December a blow was struck, primarily by Lin Biao, against a senior official in the PLA, the chief of the general staff, Luo Ruiqing (1906–78). He was deprived of his post and, in February, arrested in spite of his distinguished record of forty years' service to the Party and the PLA. It is difficult to disentangle the motives for this particular move, although Western authors have devoted much space to speculating about it. Attention is devoted by them to contrasting two undoubtedly significant articles published by Luo Ruiqing in May 1965 and by Lin Biao in September of the same year, in which the general problems of the world situation and of China's strategy were raised. In particular, it is thought that the two men represented a different approach to the problems raised by the Vietnam War and the deterioration of Sino-Soviet relations. It should be recalled that during this period the Chinese communists continued to regard the United States as their prime enemy, and the increased involvement of the Washington administration in its forlorn adventure in Vietnam would certainly have caused the Chinese apprehension. The Tonkin Gulf incident, engineered by the Americans in August 1964, in which two American destroyers were allegedly attacked by North Vietnamese craft, was followed in February 1965 by the start of the Americans' systematic bombing of North Vietnam. At the same time, the number of American troops in Vietnam was increasing sharply; the figure rose from 15,000 in April 1965 to over 200,000 a year later. While it is possible to note differences of approach in Luo's and Lin's views, it seems clear that, while the Chinese were determined to continue their aid to the Vietnamese, they were not planning to involve themselves directly in the conflict, unless faced with a direct attack on their own country. It seems more likely that Luo Ruiqing's fall was connected primarily with domestic issues, i.e. the question of control over the PLA.

In his endeavours to defend both his subordinates and himself, Peng Zhen ordered the preparation of a special report on the ideological situation, nominally issued by the five-man group of which he was the head. This document quickly gave

113

rise to much Party in-fighting, which was ultimately used to bring about Peng's own downfall. During the same period, Lin Biao and Jiang Qing organized a PLA forum on art and literature in Shanghai. They gave much publicity to their ultra-leftist views and castigated most of the literary and artistic achievements of the past seventeen years as a 'black and sinister line' of the bourgeoisie.

The pressure against Peng Zhen and the Beijing propaganda establishment intensified towards the end of March 1966 when Mao Zedong called for Peng's removal. In the second half of April at a meeting of the Political Bureau Mao was able to force through a resolution to remove Peng from his posts. Within a few months he was portrayed as one of the four members of an anti-Party clique which was to be attacked with particular venom during the first years of the 'cultural revolution'. The other members were Luo Ruiqing, Lu Dingyi, the former head of the Central Committee Propaganda Department and minister of culture, and Yang Shangkun. Yang was born in 1907 and had been a CCP member since 1926. He had studied in the Soviet Union in 1927–30, then spent three years in a Shanghai underground movement. Later he was active in the Kiangxi Soviet, participated in the Long March and held important posts in the Party apparatus up to 1966. During the decade of the 'cultural revolution' he was one of the most severely persecuted senior communists. Rehabilitated in 1978, Yang has been a member of the Political Bureau since 1982.

In the spring of 1966 Lin Biao was also devoting much time and effort to strengthening further the position of the PLA. In April the *Liberation Daily* stressed that 'the PLA was the most loyal instrument of the CCP . . . and the mainstay of the dictatorship of the proletariat'. In the same month the PLA took an active part in reorganizing, after the removal of Lu Dingyi, the Central Committee's Propaganda Department.

PART TWO

The 'Cultural Revolution'
1966–76

CHAPTER SEVEN

The First Stage,
May 1966–April 1969

The successes obtained in the first months of 1966 in their struggle against those deemed to be political opponents made it possible for Mao Zedong and his adherents to effect a transition to a new, decisive stage – the launching of the 'cultural revolution'.

An enlarged meeting of the Political Bureau which took place in Hangzhou on 4–16 May was of crucial significance in the unfolding of events. After what must have been a tense and dramatic debate, the meeting approved the 16 May Circular, an inner-Party document which was to be published only one year later. There are of course no records available of what precisely occurred at the Hangzhou meeting and what positions were taken by the participants. Nor is it known whether formal voting ever took place on specific issues. It seems likely, judging from the practice of other ruling communist parties, that the principal leader – Mao Zedong in this case – summed up the debate, presenting an agreed-upon consensus which formed the basis for appropriate resolutions. The 16 May Circular has been correctly called the 'programmatic document' of the 'cultural revolution'. It contains, or reflects, all the erroneous theses evolved in the preceding years by Mao Zedong, which formed the theoretical basis for initiating the 'cultural revolution'. They were formulated here in a particularly violent fashion and the ultimate conclusion was to the effect that 'some of the counter-revolutionary revisionists we have already seen through, others we have not. Some are still trusted by us and are being trained as our successors, persons like Khrushchev, for example, who are still nestling beside us.' This was an ominous forewarning of further untrammelled political strife. Who was supposed to be China's Khrushchev? At the time this was far from clear; within six months it became obvious that the intended victim was none other than Liu Shaoqi.

The bulk of the circular, however, was devoted to a severe and extensive criticism of the report which had been submitted by Peng Zhen in February. The report was declared invalid and the five-man group headed by Peng was dissolved. The decision was announced to set up a new Cultural Revolution Group (CRG), directly under the Standing Committee of the Political Bureau. This new group had in fact already been assembled and had been functioning since April; it was now simply given formal sanction for its activities. The CRG was headed by Chen Boda, and the most important of its eighteen members included such intimate collaborators of Mao Zedong as Jiang Qing (deputy head), Kang Sheng (adviser), Yao Wenyuan and Zhang Chunqiao. By August, acting under Mao's direct orders, the CRG became the supreme ruling body of the CCP, leaving the Political Bureau almost powerless.

Since its contents were made known to most of the Party activists, the 16 May Circular served as a stimulus – and this was the main reason for its issue – to unfolding the campaign against Mao Zedong's supposed antagonists. Initially, it was directed primarily towards the universities and middle schools throughout the country, but it spread especially quickly in the capital itself.

It was Beijing University – Beida, the oldest and most famous of all the universities in the country – which witnessed the sharpest manifestations of the new strife. A group of ultra-leftists headed by a certain Nie Yuanzi, a philosophy instructor in her fifties who was acting at the instigation of Kang Sheng's wife, proceeded to attack the university administration. Its president Lu Ping had a fine record as a leader of the student movement in December 1935 and was also the first secretary of the University Party Committee. On 25 May the ultra-leftists put up a big-character poster listing their charges against Lu Ping. It was written in the inflammatory and hysterical language so characteristic of the first stage of the 'cultural revolution': 'Let us unite and hold high the glorious red banner of Mao Zedong Thought . . . resolutely, thoroughly, totally and completely wipe out all monsters and demons and all counter-revolutionary revisionists of the Khrushchev type and carry the socialist revolution through to the end.'

The poster caused much confusion and ferment at Beida, where the PLA was also busy seeking to mobilize supporters for Nie's campaign. At this moment, a decisive intervention in support of Nie's activities was made by Mao Zedong himself. He ordered the poster to be broadcast on the radio and published on 2 June in the *People's Daily*, thus turning a local university affair into a national issue.

The publicity given to the Beida poster was preceded by an even more inflammatory editorial entitled 'Sweep out all monsters and ghosts', which had far-reaching, ill-fated consequences. The editorial appeared on 1 June, the day the *People's Daily* was taken over by the PLA. Its attack embraced not only leading, unspecified senior CCP officials but also, implicitly, the intelligentsia as a whole. In 1980, Chen Boda was charged with responsibility for the editorial, which had in effect been a declaration of war on the intellectuals. Nonetheless, the views he expressed corresponded completely with the general line being promoted by Mao Zedong.

The great chaos had begun. It was now endowed by the PLA *Liberation Daily* with the grandiloquent title of Great Proletarian Cultural Revolution. Great? Yes, if this is understood as a reference to the scope of devastation and ravages inflicted upon the Chinese. Proletarian? It is hardly fair to blame it on the working class, who had nothing to do with its initiation. Cultural? It is difficult to find another decade in modern Chinese history when so much damage was done to Chinese culture and its representatives. Revolution? By no stretch of the imagination could it be called a true revolution; it produced only 'great disorder under heaven', the effects of which were more akin to those of a counter-revolution.

119

In the meantime, Lin Biao, apart from extolling the 'cultural revolution' and Mao Zedong, was concerned with other matters. On 18 May Lin charged by innuendo the 'anti-Party clique' with preparing a *coup d'état*. It is maintained that using this fabrication as the pretext, Lin brought additional PLA units, which he considered especially reliable, into the capital.

The growing convulsion in Beida and other Beijing universities and secondary schools had obviously been greatly stimulated by Mao Zedong's approval of the Nie Yuanzi poster. However, the Central Committee sought to calm the uproar, and in June work teams were dispatched to Beida and other schools to bring the situation under control. The responsibility for this decision was later attributed to Liu Shaoqi and served as an important factor in the campaign which led to his downfall.

Simultaneously, the PLA and the CRG set about mobilizing still further the student youth of Beijing and giving it new organizational forms. The first unit of the Red Guard was established on 29 May in a middle school attached to Qinghua University. Within a few weeks the Red Guards spread to practically all the schools in Beijing; by the end of July the movement had been extended to most of the schools in all the major urban centres. Thus an undoubted mass movement, embracing millions of young Chinese, had been created and set into motion. The process of its formation was, nonetheless, spontaneous only to a limited degree. Its fate turned out ultimately to be a tragic one, and its place in Chinese modern history certainly does not resemble that of the truly stirring and progressive movements, such as the famous May Fourth and December Ninth. Moreover, the Red Guard movement was an extremely complex phenomenon, for its participants represented many varied tendencies which reflected the usually unrecognized and unacknowledged contradictions that had arisen in post-1949 Chinese society. During the first months of its existence it was cunningly manoeuvred by the CRG and the PLA for purposes the true nature of which was quite unknown to the vast majority of its members. The heady slogans of the 'cultural revolution' which called upon the country's youth to undertake the gigantic

120

task of remoulding China once again, of carrying on the revolution and defending its venerated leader, inevitably found an enthusiastic response in the ardent hearts and eager minds of young people.

At the same time, participation in the new movement offered the young a fine chance to escape, at least temporarily, from the rigid discipline and monotony of their humdrum everyday lives, to engage in an attractive and thrilling adventure and, above all, to become a vanguard force in the shaping of their country's future. The appeal was irresistible. But the young of China were the victims of what, in the final analysis, was nothing more than a cynical political manipulation.

One could see, while travelling in north China, a multitude of starry-eyed youngsters, full of the purest idealism, setting off southwards with packs on their backs, red flags in their hands and the Little Red Book safely tucked away in their pockets, heading for Jinggangshan to retrace the route of a glorious revolutionary past. But others, under the influence of the hysteria whipped up by the media and egged on by the rabble-rousing speeches of Lin Biao and the leaders of the CRG, turned their attention even then to tormenting, torturing and beating, often to death, their own teachers. Some of the Red Guard units, such as the notorious one from the Beijing Aeronautical Institute, quickly degenerated into a bunch of vicious thugs; for an eye-witness there was a startling and shocking resemblance between their behaviour and that of Nazi storm-troopers.

It was now time for the principal actor of the 'cultural revolution' to reappear on the scene. The only glimpse of Mao Zedong granted to the public since November of the preceding year was a photograph published in May showing him receiving a foreign delegation. Appropriately enough, it was an Albanian group, led by Prime Minister Shehu who was later liquidated by Hoxha; the sorry tyrant of Tirana was Mao's main, cherished ally. On 17 July, all the Chinese media went into ecstatic rapture recounting how on the preceding day the seventy-three-year-old Mao Zedong had performed an astonishing feat; accompanied by hundreds of his admirers he had in sixty-five minutes swum fifteen kilometres down the Yangtse near Wuhan. The publicity surrounding this event was huge, and the message crystal clear; the Great Leader, Great Commander, Great Teacher and Great Helmsman was trim and fit, ready to do further battle.

By 18 July, Mao was back in Beijing. One of his first initiatives was to let it be known that he disapproved of what the work teams had been doing in the schools; in his view, they were obstructing the 'cultural revolution'. As a result, within a few days the work teams were withdrawn, and on 26 July the decision was announced to close down all the universities and secondary schools for six months so that the students could devote their entire time to the 'cultural revolution'. In the event, the six months dragged on for two to three years. At Beida, where Jiang Qing, accompanied by Kang Sheng and Chen Boda, made her first triumphant public appearance on 22 July with an appropriately flamboyant and demagogic speech, the result of the moves was to place the university under the control of the CRG.

In a letter sent on 1 August to the Red Guard of the Qinghua Secondary School, Mao Zedong gave his blessing to the new organization, especially approving their contention that 'it is right to rebel'. This served as a tremendous fillip to the Red Guard movement which now spread like wildfire through the country. Five days later Mao published his own big-character poster, entitled 'Bombard the headquarters', which was a clear call for the Red Guard to launch an attack against the Party establishment.

A more complicated and difficult task faced Mao Zedong and his coterie; this was to obtain formal ratification for everything they had done thus far from the only body entitled to do so – the Central Committee. Important changes in the composition of the ruling bodies of the Party were envisaged, and thus preparations to hold a Central Committee plenum – the first since September 1962 – were quickly speeded up.

The decisive Eleventh Plenum was held in Beijing on 1–12 August in an atmosphere of vastly increased tension. Once again, its proceedings are shrouded in secrecy; apart from one speech made by Lin Biao and the decisions and communiqué issued at its conclusion, no other material pertaining to the discussions is available. Moreover, it is not even known exactly who attended the plenum, although it is assumed that Mao and his adherents were probably unable to muster a majority. Some of the actual members and alternates of the Central Committee did not attend for various reasons, but the session was packed with Mao's supporters from the provinces.

The Sixteen-Point Decision approved at the Eleventh Plenum reformulated the basic theses of the 'cultural revolution' and aimed to provide a concrete programme of action. It emerges quite clearly from the text that the principal purpose of Mao and his followers was to continue the assault on his purported opponents in the Party leadership, since it was stated that 'The main target of the present movement is those within the Party who are in authority and are taking the capitalist road'. Everything else was subordinated to this aim. The prescriptions as to how the struggle was to be conducted, which were intended to preserve a modicum of sanity and common sense, were not worth the paper they were written on, since they were completely ignored in the ensuing cataclysm. Moreover they were negated by the rabble-rousing speeches of Lin Biao, Jiang Qing and other CRG members, who openly incited the Red Guards to violence.

The reorganization of the supreme Party authorities, contrary to all the stipulated provisions of the Party constitution, was also noteworthy. The principal change was the elevation of Lin Biao to the post of sole vice chairman of the Central Committee; this signified the demotion of Liu Shaoqi, Zhou Enlai, Zhu De and Chen Yun, who had all been vice chairmen up to this moment. Thus Lin Biao was now clearly the number two man in the Party leadership – a position held until then by Liu Shaoqi – and hence Mao's presumed successor. Kang Sheng and Chen Boda were promoted to the Standing Committee of the Political Bureau. This was the time when Mao Zedong's 'personal leadership characterized by "Left" errors took the place of the collective leadership of the Central Committee', while the cult of his personality was 'frenziedly pushed to an extreme'. However, the moderate and balanced language of the 1981 Resolution quoted here cannot – and does not attempt to – convey the extraordinary dimensions of the prevailing frenzy which had all the hallmarks of an artificially induced mass psychosis. Anyone wishing to oppose the cult would have had to possess incredible courage, for to do so meant to take one's life into one's hands. Some, like the Beida student Lin Zhao who believed that ever since the Anti-Rightist Campaign in 1957 Mao's policies had resulted in disaster for China, did so, only to meet a tragic fate. After eighteen years of imprisonment, she was shot in 1975 for the crime of having opposed Mao Zedong.

The victory gained at the Eleventh Plenum was soon celebrated by Mao Zedong with a mammoth rally held in Beijing on 18 August. Close to one million of his young supporters jammed into the immense expanse of Tiananmen Square, greatly enlarged since 1949, to gaze admiringly at the Great Leader standing on the terrace above the archway of the gate leading to the Forbidden City, the spot from which he had proclaimed the establishment of the People's Republic of China. The main speech was given by Lin Biao in his high-pitched voice, who was already being honoured with the appellation of Mao's 'closest comrade in arms'. Later, Mao Zedong, dressed in a PLA tunic, permitted the youngsters to place a Red Guard armband on his sleeve, thus eloquently affirming his support for the new movement. The meeting ended with the huge crowd chanting *'Mao zhuxi wan sui, wan wan sui'* – ten and another ten thousand years to Chairman Mao; the *wan sui* had been used formerly only for emperors.

Mao's meeting with his youthful adherents marked the beginning of an enormous hegira to Beijing of Red Guards from the entire country, during which seven more gigantic parades were held, the last on 26 November. Between 11 and 13 million young Chinese took the opportunity of free travel to stream into the capital for the purpose of 'exchanging revolutionary experiences'. The not inconsiderable logistical problem this caused in terms of transport, housing and feeding was handled quite competently. The huge costs involved were quite another matter.

For the participants the experience was undoubtedly truly exhilarating, since for most of them it was probably the first and last time in their lives that they had the chance of seeing their country's fabulous capital. What they think of this episode now, twenty years later, when they gaze at the faded snapshots of themselves on Tiananmen, grinning and full of confidence, would make a fascinating sociological study.

During the parades the area of Tiananmen itself was off limits to all foreigners. However, it was possible to follow the marchers to within a kilometre of the square and without the slightest difficulty – perhaps due to the innate friendliness of the Chinese – to observe the proceedings. The columns, sixteen abreast, marched in good order, and small wonder for the entire spectacle was skilfully stage-managed by a large number of PLA cadres interspersed among the marchers. It was they who, clutching typed sheets in their hands, periodically shouted out the slogans of the day to be re-echoed by the Red Guards. The only stumbling block was a large contingent from Xinjiang who failed to respond to the cheer-leaders' prompting; the Uighurs' knowledge of Chinese was obviously somewhat weak.

Beijing television, at that time still in its infancy, covered the scenes in the square itself and zoomed in on the reviewing rostrum to present a close-up view of the leaders assembled there. They stood in accordance with the precedence newly established at the Eleventh Plenum. The punctiliousness with which order of rank was, and still is, observed in the PRC is rather a remarkable phenomenon which awaits a serious study and explanation; in the meantime, it has created a thriving field for speculation among Western 'China hands'. In November, although they were already the subject of increasingly severe attacks, both Liu Shaoqi and Deng Xiaoping took their allotted positions on the rostrum. The sight of their facial expressions, a remarkable study in contrasts, was a memorable and unforgettable experience.

Already in July and August many Red Guard units in Beijing and other cities began, under the influence of the incessant deluge of strident propaganda spewed out by all the media, to put

125

into effect the recommended struggle against 'The Four Olds' (ideas, culture, customs and habits), combining it with an assault against the reputed bearers of these evils, the 'revisionists', 'bourgeois authorities' and others designated as the 'counter-revolutionary' enemies of People's China. The Red Guards were soon joined in their endeavours by the equally numerous Revolutionary Rebels recruited from the workers and employees in all branches of the economy and all levels of the Party and government establishments. The result was a veritable rampage of terror and vandalism, conducted with complete impunity, which continued throughout most of the remaining months of this dreadful year.

Incalculable and irreparable damage was inflicted on China's cultural heritage by this 'cultural revolution'. In the homes of the 'enemies' plundered by the Red Guards, priceless old volumes were consumed in countless bonfires. Later on, innumerable private libraries were confiscated or turned in 'voluntarily' by their owners to be pulped. The paper was recycled and used to print additional tens of millions of copies of Mao Zedong's works, practically the only thing available then in the bookshops. Recordings of European classical music were smashed, stamp collections confiscated, art objects destroyed or simply stolen. Even goldfish were condemned as a manifestation of a bourgeois style of life. The mindless destruction swept across the length and breadth of China, from the shrine of Confucius in Qufu to the hundreds of monasteries despoiled in Tibet. In Beijing itself it was possible to see a superb life-size statue of Buddha dumped on a refuse heap before being carted away to be melted down. Unfortunately, only in some instances was the devastation pre-empted, as in the case of the Summer Palace where the paintings on the wooden balustrades were covered with whitewash to prevent their defacement. Vast sums have been spent since 1978 on repairing the ravages of 1966–76. And much publicity has been given to new splendid archaeological discoveries, partly to distract attention from the senseless nihilistic deeds of the 'cultural revolution'. But the wanton destruction might well be considered of minor importance, for the human factor is the only truly significant one, and the human costs were infinitely more shocking.

Hundreds of thousands of Chinese died as a direct result of the 'cultural revolution'; many had perished already during the terror of 1966. As Mao Zedong observed in 1956, 'Once a head is chopped off, history shows it can't be restored, nor can it grow again as chives do, after being cut.' The information revealed in November 1980 during the trial of Mao Zedong's and Lin Biao's closest surviving associates – an account which should be obligatory reading for all Western admirers of the 'cultural revolution' – portray only a fragment of the horrors and atrocities inflicted upon the Chinese people during this decade. A total of 729,000 people were 'framed and persecuted', of whom 34,900 were 'persecuted to death'.

As could be expected, the intellectuals, including many veteran, authentic communist revolutionaries, were in the forefront of those victimized, and suicides – the time-honoured Chinese form of protest against oppression and intolerable humiliation – soon followed on a vast scale. Among these thousands of victims was the noted sociologist and president of Wuhan University, Li Da (1890–1966). Li had attended the First Congress of the CCP in 1921 along with his fellow delegate from their native province Hunan, Mao Zedong. Li's own Red Guard students tormented him and brought about his death by refusing to permit him medical treatment. The famous Manchu novelist and playwright Lao She (1899–1966) was found drowned in a Beijing pond, after two days of being beaten to a pulp by the Red Guards. The eminent Marxist historian Jian Bozan (1898–1968) finally refused to tolerate any further humiliation and committed suicide with his wife. The same step was taken by the noted translator of Romain Rolland, Fu Lei and his wife, the parents of the pianist Fu Tsong. According to an impeccable source, sixty members of the teaching staff of a famous Shanghai university committed suicide that summer and autumn, while forty professors at one of the Beijing colleges also took their lives. All this in the name of ideological purity.

To prolong the list of atrocities committed during the 'cultural revolution' – it is truly a long one and could fill a book this size – is pointless. There is a man in China who needs no reminder of them, for all he has to do is look at his eldest son, Pufang, once a brilliant physics student, now condemned to a wheelchair for the rest of his life. The Red Guards either pushed him out, or forced him to jump, from a third-storey window; he was left lying unattended on the pavement below with a broken back. The man in question is trying to see to it that a 'cultural revolution' will never happen again. His name is Deng Xiaoping.

From the very outset the Red Guard movement was characterized by an unusual degree of confusion, both in its organization and in its activities. A great multitude of separate Red Guard units, bearing a large variety of fanciful and picturesque names, were set up in the universities and secondary schools, differing in size and influence. In spite of the attempts made, it proved impossible to establish organizational unity on a national scale, although some of the principal Red Guard groups in Beijing did seek to liaise with similar organizations in other cities. The rival groups, all proclaiming their undying allegiance to Mao Zedong and his Thought, soon engaged in an increasingly sharp internecine tug of war for control of their area of activity. This struggle also reflected to a considerable degree the social contradictions among the Red Guards themselves. The students coming from families which constituted the dominant stratum of the Party and government establishment quickly came into conflict with those of worker and peasant background, whose position was in many ways much more disadvantageous. The strife among the Red Guards grew in intensity after their return home from the pilgrimage to Beijing, and it was aggravated by the dispatch of large numbers of the capital's most active 'revolutionaries' to other important urban centres for the purpose of stimulating the further development of the 'cultural revolution'.

By their actions in July and August, Mao Zedong and his coterie had succeeded in gaining partial sway in Beijing and complete control of the central media. The Sixteen-Point Decision made it abundantly clear that these achievements were only the first step in the unfolding of the 'cultural revolution'. The main aim pursued in the next stage, from the Eleventh Plenum to the end of 1966, was to mount a decisive attack on the 'capitalist roaders', still managing to hold on to their positions in the Party and government apparatus, both in the capital and the provinces. The Red Guard and the Revolutionary Rebels were the vanguard of this assault, while the PLA was still kept as a reserve force to be utilized, if necessary, at a later stage.

The evaluation of the current situation and the elaboration of policies to be followed in the future were the subject of lengthy secret debates during a Central Committee Work Conference on 8–25 October. In his speeches Mao Zedong is said to have stated that he had not expected that 'all the provinces and cities would be thrown into confusion' by the Red Guard movement. He called, nevertheless, for a continuation of the 'cultural revolution', since it had been in existence for only five months. At the end of the conference both Liu Shaoqi and Deng Xiaoping are reported to have made lengthy self-criticisms, in which they recounted the political errors they had purportedly committed since 1949. Liu's speech, as well as Mao's, were quickly leaked by some members of the CRG to Red Guard units under their patronage, and found their way to the public through big-character posters. However, the reliability of the texts is open to question. Their purpose was clearly to identify the number one and number two 'capitalist roaders in authority', to undermine their personal prestige and to facilitate further attacks on Liu and Deng, and all the very many senior Party government officials considered to be their close associates.

In December, acting on the orders of and inspired by Lin Biao and the CRG, the Red Guards became still bolder in their activities, passing from propaganda to direct physical attacks on the most prominent 'enemies' of the PRC. A picked Red Guard unit from the notorious Beijing Aeronautical Institute flew off to Chengdu to arrest Peng Dehuai, thus inaugurating the nine years of torment already described. On 12 December, the four members of the 'anti-Party clique' – Peng Zhen, Lu Dingyi, Luo Ruiqing and Yang Shangkun – all already under arrest, in some cases at the instigation of Jiang Qing, were dragged off by the Red Guards to the Workers Stadium in Beijing for a six-hour-long public kangaroo trial. Each man carried a large placard on his chest bearing his name, and was subjected to the milder version of the 'jet plane' treatment (keeping the head bowed low while stretching the arms straight back). Speaker after speaker railed at them for their heinous crimes, the cardinal one being, of course, opposing Mao Zedong. The crowd of 10,000 Red Guards gloated with glee, roaring its approval of the humiliation of these veteran revolutionaries.

At the same time, attacks by Revolutionary Rebels on 'capitalist roaders' holding prominent positions in the central government departments also intensified. The case of the minister for the coal industry, Zhang Linzhi, is a particularly drastic example, although by no means isolated, of the methods used in this struggle. Zhang was a veteran Party member who had been active in the CCP underground in the early 1930s, probably under Liu Shaoqi and Peng Zhen. He was set upon in mid-December by Revolutionary Rebels of the Institute of Mining. 'He was interrogated 52 times in 33 days and tortured to wring confessions out of him . . . besides being beaten and kicked, he was forced to wear cast-iron headgear weighing 30 kilos . . . on 21 January Zhang was paraded at the Institute campus and tortured until he died that night.'

Why the gratuitous cruelty? How much of it can be attributed to the baneful influence of a still recent feudal past? A part of the answer might rest in the blind, fanatic faith of many of the Red Guards in the Great Helmsman and the slogans of the 'cultural revolution'. Nonetheless, other elements seem to be of no less importance, in particular the widespread tendency to conformism in what was undoubtedly an unusually tense and dangerous situation. To be suspected, and therefore probably denounced, by one's schoolmates or fellow workers for failure to demonstrate sufficient zeal in 'carrying forward the glorious red banner of Mao Zedong Thought' was fraught with truly serious consequences. Furthermore, a cultural trait appeared to be reflected in the antics of the Red Guards. There was no art form as popular, genuinely beloved and influential among the Chinese as the traditional opera. Imitating its characteristically stylized poses came naturally to those participating in Red Guard spectacles, endowing them with a peculiarly theatrical air. Thus a girl clerk at Beijing airport would be demure, quiet and courteous one day, and the next day, during a demonstration against 'foreign revisionists', she would become a venom-filled and hate-spewing vixen, thereby earning high marks for a correct revolutionary stand.

In mobilizing the youth of China, Lin Biao and the CRG made conscious, although never explicit, use of the widespread resentment among the population of the many privileges enjoyed by the members of the upper ruling stratum to which, of course, they themselves belonged. Such sentiments had become apparent during the short period in the spring of 1957 when some freedom of expression had been allowed. There is no reason to assume that these feelings had either disappeared or been alleviated to any great extent in the intervening decade. The point at issue was not the still relatively tolerable ten to one differential between the highest and lowest salaries of government officials; in the PRC, as in other countries with a similar system, the multitude of perquisites was always of much greater importance. And the higher the position on the hierarchical ladder, the greater the number of perks; they covered an extensive field from superior housing, medical care, holiday facilities, and official cars, to special airplanes and a luxurious excursion steamer on the Yangtse. In this fashion the rulers were tangibly distinguished from those they ruled. This was true from the earliest years, when the top PRC dignitaries drove along the avenues of the capital, then almost devoid of cars, in their huge imported Soviet limousines to which a Chinese touch had been added – silk curtains to provide discreet privacy for the passengers. This is not to imply that the inhabitants of Zhongnanhai – the western part of the Imperial City, converted into a residential area for the most senior leaders of the CCP and also housing the offices of the Central Committee and State Council, which is still guarded by a special PLA unit, No. 8341 – had succumbed en masse to the temptations of a new luxurious mode of existence. The majority – Liu Shaoqi and Zhou Enlai especially – continued to lead modest, frugal lives, as they had before the victory of the revolution. However, the gulf was there and the resentment of the unprivileged was skilfully inflamed and easily manipulated. As the leader of a ruling European communist party remarked privately at the time, 'There is nothing easier than mobilizing people, especially the young, against the "yellow curtains" [the special stores open only to high Party and government officials]. I could organize such a mass movement myself in twenty-four hours.'

Many demagogic arguments were being advanced by the propaganda media at this time. The claim was made that participation in the 'cultural revolution' would stimulate mass creativity, and the institution of 'extensive democracy' would lead to the further 'education and emancipation' of the masses. These views were clearly reflected in, or perhaps rather based on, Lin Biao's speech of 3 November, and assiduously disseminated during the next months. Although they had very little in common with Chinese reality they were, oddly enough, eagerly picked up in all good faith by some Western observers sympathetic to the 'cultural revolution'. Even more curiously, these concepts still reverberate, as if valid, in some recent works of Western authors.

In spite of the intensity of attack by Red Guards and Revolutionary Rebels, relatively little progress had been achieved by the end of 1966 in bringing about the overthrow of powerful provincial Party officials considered to be 'capitalist roaders'. The principal reason for this rested in the skill with which these very experienced politicians defended their positions. One of their favourite gambits was to rally their own Red Guard units against those attacking them, who were usually outsiders, often from Beijing itself. At the same time, the efficiently functioning Party machines which the provincial leaders had been heading, in most cases for a long period, were able to muster considerable support from the workers to oppose the disruptive, anarchic activities of the student Red Guards.

However, the successes gained in this period by the local leaders proved to be only temporary, for in 1967 most of them fell victim to the 'cultural revolution' forces. This was probably largely due to the fact that in most cases there was no co-ordination between their defensive actions, and thus they were toppled one by one. This can be taken to prove that there was no organized Liu–Deng faction in the CCP leadership – a charge raised by the CRG and Lin Biao – for had it existed the defence put up by the provincial Party apparatus would certainly have been more effective. One other factor weakened provincial leaders. The vast majority were veteran Party members, who had been faithful followers of Mao Zedong. The offensive waged against them was inspired and headed by the man they had admired as their own leader for two to four decades. This placed them in a dreadful quandary as to the course of action that they should pursue, for perhaps the man who had been proved correct so many times in the years 1935 to 1949 was right once again.

The struggle between the conflicting forces became particularly tense and dramatic in China's largest metropolis – Shanghai. With a city population of 6 million and a metropolitan total of over 10 million, Shanghai was not only the largest city in the country but also its greatest industrial centre. Hence, Mao Zedong and his closest followers attached the utmost importance to gaining control of the ugly city sprawling at the mouth of the Yangtse. The task was entrusted to two of Mao's and Jiang Qing's most intimate collaborators – Zhang Chunqiao and Yao Wenyuan. Although both these men spent most of their time in the capital as key members of the CRG, they were instrumental in organizing the Red Guard units and Revolutionary Rebel forces that were ultimately to form the Shanghai Workers' Revolutionary Rebel Headquarters. The main purpose of this new organization was to launch a strident campaign against the Shanghai Municipal Party Committee. A very prominent role in the establishment of the Workers' Headquarters and in the further unfolding of events in Shanghai was played by a certain Wang Hongwen (b. 1935), a lowly public security functionary in one of Shanghai's many textile mills. During the next decade Wang, as a member with Zhang and Yao of what has often been referred to as the 'Shanghai clique', made a spectacular career, 'rising like a helicopter' to the very summit of the CCP hierarchy.

From mid-November on, Zhang, Yao and Wang were aided in their assault on the city's Party establishment by the influx into Shanghai of tens of thousands of Red Guards, primarily from Beijing. The formidable Nie Yuanzi claimed to be their main leader, and at a mass rally on 25 November she announced that her mission and intended goal was the overthrow of the city's 'capitalist roaders'. But the Shanghai Municipal Party Committee was headed by two very capable and experienced veteran communists, its first secretary, Chen Pixian, and the city's mayor, Cao Diqiu. Chen was born in 1917 and was persecuted throughout the decade of the 'cultural revolution'. He is now a secretary of the Central Committee. Cao Diqiu died as a result of persecution. These men were largely successful in keeping the situation in Shanghai under control until the middle of December. The Party Committee they led also enjoyed much deserved support among the city's skilled workers; Chen and Cao had no difficulty in organizing their own, sizeable Scarlet Guards to counteract the Workers' Headquarters. It is maintained that the latter, in turn, was able to rally to its side the numerous contract workers, usually peasants from the nearby countryside, whose resentment at their much inferior economic and social position made them sympathetic to the radical slogans of the 'cultural revolutionaries'. The confused conflict between these two principal groups, each in fact a loose federation, led to a series of strikes, mainly of railway workers and dockers, which totally paralysed Shanghai's transport. The economic situation was further complicated by the attempts of the Party leaders to maintain and enlarge their support among the workers by meeting some of their demands for financial compensation and other benefits. For these actions they were to be denounced later for having committed the crime of 'economism'.

Against this background of mounting confusion – and the pandemonium in Shanghai during these weeks was indescribable – the Workers' Headquarters, following directives from Beijing and assured of support from Shanghai's PLA garrison, took over on 4 January 1967 all the city's main newspapers. In a final assault culminating in a mass rally attended by a million people they brought about the overthrow of the leaders of the Municipal Party Committee. Victory was celebrated by placing two of the leaders, dunce caps on their heads, on the top platform of a lorry's aerial ladder and driving them triumphantly for hours around the city.

The coup was approved with enthusiasm by the CRG in Beijing, while the central media presented it as an example to be emulated throughout the country – which it was. However, the problem of establishing a new governing body for the city remained. The three members of the 'Shanghai clique' for a short while sought to organize the new authority on the lines of the Paris Commune. Both Mao Zedong and Lin Biao had been toying with this idea, and the latter had made in his speech on 3 November an approving reference to the principles of the Paris Commune, which he regarded as a fine example of the 'extended democracy' that he was advocating. Thus, Zhang and Yao considered that they could proceed in this direction with the full blessings of Beijing, and on 5 February the Shanghai People's Commune was established with a great blaze of publicity. Not surprisingly, Zhang and Yao were elected its director and deputy director. But, in the meantime, Mao Zedong had second thoughts regarding the advisability of adopting the Paris Commune model – for its principles were authentically democratic. Mao now concluded that such a move smacked of anarchism; in other words, that local authorities established in this fashion could not be easily controlled by the central government. Hence, no approval was forthcoming from the capital. Instead, on 23 February, the Shanghai People's Commune was quietly buried without any ceremony, to be replaced by the

Shanghai Revolutionary Committee, composed of representatives of the PLA, the 'revolutionary masses' and the 'revolutionary cadres'. This 'three-way alliance' was now the form of government to be achieved throughout the country. Zhang and Yao remained at the head of Shanghai's new governing body, although they spent most of their time in the capital. For the remaining nine years of the 'cultural revolution' Shanghai continued to be for them, and Wang Hongwen, an extremely important political base.

During the last months of 1966, there was intricate conflict at the very top of the pyramid of power in Beijing, illustrated by the strange case of Tao Zhu (1906–69). A Hunanese participant in the famous and ill-fated Canton Commune of 1927, Tao had an impressive record in the ensuing two decades of revolutionary struggle. Posted after liberation to south China, he served as the first secretary of Guangdong from 1956 to 1965. In the first months of the 'cultural revolution', Tao Zhu was transferred to Beijing, where he became head of the Central Committee's Propaganda Department after the removal of Lu Dingyi and was promoted to the Standing Committee of the Political Bureau. In January 1967, his career came to an abrupt end. Charged by Lin Biao and some members of the CRG with assorted political crimes, primarily opposition to the 'cultural revolution', he was first put under house arrest and then exiled to Anhui where, deprived of proper medical attention, he died of cancer two years later. In 1978, Tao Zhu was fully rehabilitated as a victim of Lin Biao and the 'gang of four'. He is also described as having been, like so many other prominent CCP members, 'persecuted to death'.

The course of events in the winter of 1966–7 had shown that, in spite of their violent actions and the chaos they created, the student Red Guards by themselves were incapable of bringing about the desired overthrow of Mao Zedong's reputed opponents in the Party and government apparatus. On 26 December 1966 and 1 January 1967, it was proclaimed that the working class must be encouraged to participate directly in the 'cultural revolution'. Such a policy had already been partly applied in

Shanghai; it was now to be extended to the entire country. The results, as far as the economy was concerned, were far-reaching; as might have been expected, production in many fields fell even further in 1967 than it had in 1966. And the hope expressed in the Sixteen-Point Decision that it would be 'possible to carry on both the Cultural Revolution and production without one hampering the other' soon proved to be quite forlorn. The Revolutionary Rebel groups in the factories proved almost as prone to factional conflict as the student Red Guards. Thus strife among the working class became practically a permanent feature in the urban centres during the coming decade, most strongly manifested in the period up to 1969.

The situation was complicated still further by the fact that the one movement which had embraced a majority of workers – the trade unions – was also being assaulted by the 'cultural revolutionary' forces. In January 1967, the leaders of the All-China Federation of Trade Unions, suspected of being supporters of Liu Shaoqi, came under sharp attack. Shortly thereafter the Federation, as well as its component unions, ceased all its activities. The same was true of practically all other mass organizations, such as the Women's Federation.

The most important mass organization to fall victim to the 'cultural revolution' was the Communist Youth League (CYL). Intended to be the training and recruiting ground for the future generation of the Party, and the rallying point of the most politically active youth, the CYL had been built up over the years with much care and attention by the CCP. By 1964 its membership had reached around 35 million. In the summer of 1966, when the development of the Red Guard movement was being energetically encouraged by the CRG, the CYL was quickly relegated to the sidelines, to be disbanded at the time of the Eleventh Plenum in August. The principal reason for this course of action rested in the close connection of the organization, especially of its leading cadres, with the central Party apparatus. Since the aim of weakening the leaders of the CCP establishment was foremost in the minds of Mao Zedong and his collaborators, the youth organization, supposedly under the control and influence of the CCP, could be dispensed with. Its disappearance from the political arena facilitated the untrammelled growth of the Red Guards, who were much more amenable to assaulting the Party establishment than the CYL ever would have been. A considerable number of the CYL's leaders, including its first secretary Hu Yaobang, were removed from the political stage and underwent persecution very similar to that of so many high Party officials.

Born in 1915 into a poor peasant family in Hunan, Hu Yaobang ran off at the age of fourteen to Jinggangshan to become one of the Red Army's famous 'little red devils', described so well by Snow in his pioneering *Red Star Over China*. A member of the Young Communist League (YCL) from 1930, Hu joined the Party in 1933, becoming at the same time, at the age of eighteen, the general secretary of the YCL. After completing the Long March he remained one of the top YCL leaders. During the war with Japan he studied at the famous Anti-Japanese Military and Political Academy in Yan'an, before becoming a political officer in the Eighth Route Army. He continued to serve in this capacity during the final struggle against the Guomindang when he held high political posts in what became the Second Field Army, thus working directly under its political commissar, Deng Xiaoping.

After liberation, Hu Yaobang spent three years as a Party official in Sichuan and was then transferred to Beijing. In 1953 he became the top leader of the New Democratic Youth League (renamed the Communist Youth League in 1957), a position he retained until 1966. As a member of the Party Central Committee from 1956, Hu was again a close associate, for ten years, of Deng Xiaoping, then the Party's general secretary.

In January 1967, the strife in the provinces, between the Red Guards and their opponents as well as between Red Guard factions, became increasingly vehement. In Nanchang, the capital of Jiangxi – the site of the famous uprising in 1927 led by Zhou Enlai and Zhu De, still commemorated as PLA Day – the conflict between the workers and students ended with hundreds of serious casualties, especially among the students. In Nanjing the clashes between these two groups in the same month were even greater, with dozens of people killed. According to Red Guard posters and the press, even more sanguinary incidents, with still greater casualties, took place in Xinjiang, where a PLA-sponsored unit suppressed the activities of the local Red Guard group. The situation was no better in Yunnan and Guangxi; in the latter the groundwork was being laid for what became in effect a local civil war of almost two years' duration.

The Guangdong capital, Guangzhou, also became the setting for violent conflict which was to last for many months. Its location accounted for the fact that relatively more news regarding events in the city reached the outside world – avidly noted down by the Hong Kong-based American China watchers – than was the case with inland provincial capitals. January saw the prelude to a long period of increasing factional strife in the metropolis of the south, which ultimately resulted in very heavy loss of life. The Guangzhou Red Guards, already much divided among themselves, attacked the Guangdong Party Committee and its first secretary Zhao Ziyang, quickly accomplishing their overthrow. Zhao was born in 1919 of a landlord gentry family in Henan. He was a veteran cadre, having joined the Young Communist League in 1932 and the Party in 1938, working thereafter as a Party functionary. Four years after his overthrow in Guangdong he returned to work in the Party apparatus. He joined the Political Bureau as an alternate member in 1977, and a full member in 1979. In 1980 Zhao became a member of the Political Bureau Standing Committee and premier.

The growing turbulence and violence of the 'cultural revolution', over which the leadership in Beijing had largely lost control, led Mao Zedong to take the fateful decision to order the PLA into direct action. The students had not fulfilled his hopes; they had not succeeded in accomplishing the task of overthrowing successfully his alleged 'capitalist roader' adversaries, nor did they show many signs of emerging as the worthy 'revolutionary successors' he had wanted them to become. But a year and a half had yet to pass before Mao discarded his 'little red generals' once and for all. Now, in order to continue the general attack and deepen the 'cultural revolution' – and this intention was clearly stated in his New Year message – Mao turned to his reserve force, the PLA, which he had considered all along to be the most politically reliable component of the state apparatus and of the Party itself. But it was precisely this dual nature of the PLA that made its deployment an exceedingly complex and hazardous venture. The degree of risk involved became evident as early as July 1967 during the astounding Wuhan incident.

The principal and most urgent task assigned to the PLA – formulated by Lin Biao in his directives of 23 and 28 January – was to support the 'left' in the attempt to overthrow the provincial 'capitalist roaders' who were still successfully holding on to their positions. To this end new provincial Revolutionary Committees were to replace both the Party committees and the former provincial government authorities. However, the PLA commanders in the field were given little assistance in sorting out who among the contending factions – all of them loudly proclaiming their undying allegiance to Mao Zedong and his Thought – really represented the 'left'.

In Heilongjiang and Shanxi, where the PLA was instrumental in setting up Revolutionary Committees early on in the campaign, it was clear that by far the strongest element in these new 'three-way alliances' was the PLA itself. This pattern was to be followed later throughout the entire country. However, due to the utter chaos brought into being by the 'cultural revolution', the process of establishing the Revolutionary Committees proved much more arduous than the Beijing leadership had expected. By August 1967 the new ruling bodies had been set up in only Beijing, Shanghai and four provinces. Matters were complicated still further in some provinces when the incumbent high Party officials, with the aid of local PLA officers, organized the 'taking of power' themselves and created their own Revolutionary Committees. The legitimacy of this procedure would then be challenged by Beijing and the whole process would have to start again from the beginning.

The immediate effect of Mao's New Year message was to stimulate on an immense scale the activities of the Red Guards and Revolutionary Rebels in the capital itself. Thus, in almost every ministry an attempt to overthrow the leading officials was being made and, in many cases, carried out successfully. Practically every building in Beijing housing a central institution was plastered from top to bottom with big-character posters, which consumed a tremendous amount of paper. Luckily, due perhaps to the innate frugality of a poverty-stricken people, most of it was scrupulously collected later on and recycled.

To a sympathetic admirer of the Chinese Revolution for three decades, the country seemed to be tearing itself to bits. In February a group of vice premiers and top military officials, all Political Bureau members and distinguished veteran revolutionaries, took a critical stand against the distortions of the 'cultural revolution' in an effort to assist Zhou Enlai in his Herculean attempts to preserve a modicum of viability and sanity in the face of the threatened collapse of the entire state administration.

The men in question were Chen Yi, Li Fuchun, Li Xiannian, Nie Rongzhen, Tan Zhenlin, Xu Xiangqian and Ye Jianying; there were of course many more senior Party members, in particular Zhu De and Chen Yun, who shared their views. Their action was labelled by Lin Biao and the CRG as the 'February adverse current' and all of them 'were attacked and repressed', albeit in different degrees.

Zhou Enlai's significant career has been dealt with by many authors, although a definitive and satisfactory biography has still to see the light of day. His role during the 'cultural revolution' will be dealt with later. Zhu De – the co-founder of the Red Army – had the good fortune to have his life story up to 1946 narrated splendidly by Agnes Smedley. But the contribution of the seven men mentioned above, each of whom deserves a full-length biography, is perhaps not as well known to the non-specialist reader.

Chen Yi (1901–72), minister of foreign affairs, is undoubtedly the best known to the outside world of this group. Coming from a Sichuanese scholar gentry family, Chen took part in 1919 in the Work and Study Programme in France where, like many other students, he quickly became politically active, only to be expelled from France in 1921 for his activities. A number of the most prominent Chinese communist leaders were to emerge from this student group, which ultimately became the French branch of the CCP, led by Zhou Enlai. A Party member since 1923, Chen joined the National Revolutionary Army during the 1925–7 revolution. After the Nanchang Uprising, Chen hastened to catch up with the troops who had retreated from the city, and he was one of the officers who, under Zhu De's command, brought the survivors of this ill-fated venture to join Mao Zedong in Jinggangshan in 1928. This marked the beginning of over twenty years' distinguished service in the Chinese Red Army by Chen, who emerged as one of its most brilliant top commanders.

When the decision to undertake the Long March was made, Chen Yi, seriously wounded, was deputed to remain in Jiangxi to conduct a forlorn desperate rearguard action. With the remnants of his troops he waged guerrilla warfare for three years. After the outbreak of the war against Japan, his force became part of the New Fourth Army; in January 1941, after Chiang Kai-shek's treacherous attack on this unit, he became its acting commander. In the last three years of the War of Resistance Chen, together with Liu Shaoqi, his political commissar, greatly expanded it from the original 10,000 men to over 300,000. During the Seventh Party Congress in 1945 he was elected a full member of the Central Committee.

In the final struggle against the Guomindang, Chen became the principal communist military commander in east China and his forces, known from 1948 as the Third Field Army, played a decisive role in the final stage of the war, taking part in the huge and crucial Huai-Hai campaign. As the liberator of Shanghai, Chen became its mayor, spending most of his time there until 1954 when he became vice premier. In 1955, he was nominated one of the ten marshals of the PLA. At the Eighth Party Congress in 1956 he was elevated to the Political Bureau and in February 1958 he replaced Zhou Enlai as foreign minister, remaining throughout the entire PRC period Zhou's close friend and invaluable right-hand man.

A person of wide intellectual interests and attainments, Chen Yi was particularly noted as a prolific author of poetry in the classical vein. His comrade for forty years, Tan Zhenlin, quoted one of Chen's poems to describe his character 'like the evergreen pine which stands straight and unbending in high wind and heavy snow' – the classic simile for an upright scholar.

Li Fuchun (1900–75), a Hunanese from a bankrupt scholar-gentry family, had become already in 1916, as a member of the New People's Study Society, an early associate of Mao Zedong. In 1922, during a five-year stay in France (1919–24), he joined the French branch of the CCP, and then returned to China. In 1925 Li became a political instructor under Zhou Enlai in the famous Whampoa Academy and later took part in the Northern Expedition. Following the Guomindang's betrayal of the 1925–7 revolution, Li Fuchun worked in the Party's underground organization in Shanghai until 1931, when he moved to the Central Soviet Area in Jiangxi. Already a Central Committee member, Li participated in the Long March. During the War of Resistance he worked as a high-level Party official, beginning to deal with financial and economic problems. He spent the years of the War of Liberation as one of the top Party leaders in the north-east.

Li was to hold key posts in the economic field. In 1954 he became vice premier and concurrently chairman of the State Planning Commission. Promoted to the Political Bureau in 1956, he became in 1958 a member of the Secretariat also. By 1959 Li Fuchun was considered to be the PRC's top economic official, having replaced Chen Yun in this capacity. At the Eleventh Plenum in August 1966 Li became a member of the Standing Committee of the Political Bureau. His support of Zhou Enlai in February 1967 caused Lin Biao and the CRG to view him with suspicion; thereafter, he was gradually removed from the basic policy- and decision-making process. In 1969 he ceased being a Political Bureau member.

Li Xiannian was born in 1909 into a poor peasant family in Hubei. An apprentice carpenter, he joined the 1927 Hubei uprising against the brutal suppression by the Guomindang of

143

the peasant movement. The Red Army was gradually built up in this area which became part of the famous Eyuwan (Hubei-Henan-Anhui) Soviet; Li, a CCP member since 1927, rose to be one of its leading commanders. In 1932 the army was forced by heavy KMT pressure to retreat to Sichuan where, two years later, they were joined by the communist forces from Jiangxi engaged in the Long March. In the winter of 1936–7 Li Xiannian took part in the disastrous expedition of some Red Army units to Xinjiang, in which his forces were practically annihilated.

During the War of Resistance Li was sent to his native province with the task of organizing the anti-Japanese resistance movement. He quickly gained fame as one of the ablest guerrilla commanders and his forces ultimately became part of the New Fourth Army. In the final struggle against the Guomindang, he served as a deputy to Liu Bocheng in what was to become the Second Field Army. After 1949, Li spent most of his time in Wuhan as a key Party and government official in central-south China. In 1954 he was transferred to Beijing to become vice premier and minister of finance. A Central Committee member since 1945, he was promoted to the Political Bureau at the Eighth Party Congress in 1956 – a position he has held without interruption to the present. Since 1983 Li Xiannian has been president of the PRC.

Nie Rongzhen was born in 1899 in Sichuan into a landlord gentry family. A participant in the Work and Study Programme, Nie went to France in 1919 and was expelled for political activities in 1922. After a year in Belgium, he went to study in Moscow for two years. A CCP member since 1923, Nie returned to China in 1925, to become a political instructor in Whampoa under Zhou Enlai. He took part in the Northern Expedition and played an important role in the Nanchang Uprising. Nie ultimately made his way to Guangdong to participate in December 1927 in the Canton Commune. The years 1929–31 were spent by him in underground Party activity in north China, after which he was assigned to the Central Soviet in Jiangxi. Here Nie served primarily as a high-level political commissar in the Red Army, with which he made the Long March. During the war

144

against Japan he was instrumental in organizing one of the principal Liberated Areas in north China, gaining a reputation for being one of the Eighth Route Army's most skilful guerrilla commanders. His forces grew from an original 2000 to around 150,000 men.

In 1945 Nie was elected to the Central Committee at the Seventh Party Congress. North China remained the scene of his activities during the War of Liberation; towards the end of the war he was in command of the North China Field Army, and his troops took part in the peaceful liberation of Beijing. Up to 1954 Nie held important military posts as acting chief of staff and, like all the other communist leaders, high Party positions as well. In 1955 he was granted the rank of marshal. A vice premier since 1956, Nie assumed in 1957 what was probably the most significant post of his career: the chairmanship of what was ultimately to be called the Scientific and Technological Commission. In this capacity Nie was responsible for overseeing, among other things, the development of China's atomic energy programme and especially its military aspects. In August 1966 he was made a member of the Political Bureau, but was dropped from it in 1969. He was re-elected in 1977 and served on it until his resignation in September 1985.

Tan Zhenlin (1902–83), born in Hunan into a landless peasant family, was a printer and bookshop clerk by trade. Having joined the CCP in 1926, Tan took part in September 1927 in the Autumn Harvest Uprising in his native province, led by Mao Zedong. After its defeat he was one of a small group of survivors who followed Mao's retreat to Jinggangshan. In the years of the Jiangxi Soviet, Tan became one of Mao's closest associates, working primarily as a political commissar in various Red Army units. When the principal Red Army forces left Jiangxi to embark on the Long March, he was assigned the task of conducting guerrilla operations against the Guomindang in Fujian.

At the outset of the war with Japan, Tan's forces, like other CCP guerrilla groups in the south, were assembled to form the New Fourth Army. By 1941 he had become the commander of one of its seven divisions. In 1945 at the Seventh Congress Tan was elected a member of the Central Committee. During the War of Liberation his troops continued to fight in east China under the overall command of Chen Yi and became part of the Third Field Army. Tan was one of the principal commanders in the crucial Huai-Hai campaign.

After 1949 Tan Zhenlin held top Party and administrative posts in east China until his transfer to Beijing in 1954. Here his principal position was that of deputy secretary general of the Central Committee. From 1956 onwards he became increasingly involved in problems of agriculture, coming forth as a strong advocate of Mao Zedong's policies, including the Great Leap Forward. He was promoted to the Political Bureau in 1958 and became a vice premier the following year. Of those in the group who supported Zhou Enlai's efforts to moderate the 'cultural revolution' Tan was undoubtedly the most vigorous, not only in words but in action, organizing his own Red Guard units to defend the institutions under him. He was also one of the most repressed by the leaders of the 'cultural revolution', undergoing a total political eclipse from 1967 to 1973, when he was once again elected to the Central Committee. From then until his death he continued to hold prominent Party and state posts.

Xu Xiangqian, the son of a poor scholar gentry family, was born in Shanxi in 1901. In 1924 he enrolled in the Whampoa Academy and graduated from its first class to follow a lifelong military career, albeit quite different from that of his Guomindang classmates. Having joined the CCP in 1927, Xu became one of the leaders of the Canton Commune. After its bloody suppression by the Guomindang, he led a unit of survivors, 1500 strong, to join the struggle of the historic first Chinese Soviet, the Hai-lu-feng. Only sixty of his men survived the destruction of that revolutionary base. In 1929 Xu was sent to the Eyuwan Soviet, to become its principal military commander. His record in defending this area against overwhelming odds was outstanding. However, he was forced in 1932 to retreat with his troops to Sichuan. During the last part of the Long March, Xu participated, like Li Xiannian, in the disastrous expedition to Xinjiang.

During the War of Resistance Xu Xiangqian became one of the principal commanders of the rapidly expanding Eighth Route Army. A Central Committee member since 1945, Xu fought with Peng Dehuai in north China during the last struggle against the Guomindang, earning a well-deserved reputation as one of the PLA's most skilful leaders. After 1949, Xu held important posts in Beijing and in 1955 was granted the rank of marshal. In August 1966 he became a member of the Political Bureau, but was dropped from it, probably by 1968. His importance increased markedly after Mao Zedong's death in 1976; in 1977 he once again became a member of the Political Bureau where he remained until his retirement in 1985, serving also as a vice premier and minister of defence from 1978 to 1981.

Ye Jianying (1897–1986) was the son of a Hakka merchant family from Guangdong. He graduated in 1919 from Yunnan Military Academy, and after serving in various military units he became a deputy director of the Instruction Department in the Whampoa Academy, subsequently taking part in the Northern Expedition. In 1927, the year in which he joined the CCP, he became as commander of an officer training regiment one of the principal leaders of the Canton Commune. After its downfall, Ye took refuge in Moscow where he studied for two to three years, probably in a military academy. Returning to China in 1931 he made his way shortly to Jiangxi, where by 1933 he was chief of staff of the main Red Army forces in the Central Soviet Area. It was as chief of staff that he participated in the Long March. In 1936 Ye assisted Zhou Enlai in the intricate resolving of the Xi'an Incident, and after the outbreak of the war with Japan he also took part in negotiations and liaison work with the Guomindang. From 1941 until the end of the war Ye served as chief of staff of the Eighth Route Army. His skill as a negotiator was to be demonstrated once again in the period preceding the outbreak of the War of Liberation. In the course of this struggle Ye, a Central Committee member since 1945, served as a top-level staff officer in north China, having gained the reputation of a first-rate strategist.

After 1949, Ye Jianying remained until 1954 in his native

Guangdong as probably the most important Party official. Transferred in 1954 to Beijing, and given the rank of marshal in 1955, he continued to hold top military posts. In August 1966 he became a member of the Political Bureau, retaining that position until his resignation in September 1985. His key role in the period immediately following Mao Zedong's death will be dealt with in its proper place.

The efforts of these men to halt or at least slow down the momentum of destruction in February 1967 produced very few results; the 'cultural revolution' continued on its harmful path for a further nine years. Its consequences were even more far-reaching than those of the Great Leap Forward, although perhaps not quite as high in human costs. Nonetheless, as with the question of responsibility for the tragedies which afflicted China in connection with the Great Leap Forward, the present CCP leadership maintains that responsibility for the disaster of the 'cultural revolution', while clearly being principally that of Mao Zedong, cannot rest with him alone. This point seems to be borne out by the inability of men with such distinguished records as the seven individuals mentioned above to face up to and deal effectively with the situation. Of course, it is also clear from the careers of these leaders that their active opposition to the calamitous course of events differed quite considerably. It also should be kept in mind that, under Chinese circumstances, there was one option which they could not exercise. They were not in a position to retire to a country estate or cottage and peacefully write their memoirs, paint pictures, practise their calligraphy, write classical poetry or cultivate their gardens à la Candide.

It has been stated by no less an authority than Deng Xiaoping that 'it is no exaggeration to say that were it not for Chairman Mao there would be no New China'. This is a highly debatable thesis. But it is not an exaggeration to say that without these seven men and such leaders of the first generation of the Chinese communist movement as Zhu De, Liu Shaoqi, Zhou Enlai, Deng Xiaoping, Chen Yun, Peng Dehuai and many others, the victory of the Chinese Revolution would not have been attained. No one man, no matter how brilliant and wise in his time, could have led the CCP to its triumph without them.

In the meantime, the campaign waged by the leaders of the 'cultural revolution' against those designated by them as their main enemies – Liu Shaoqi and Deng Xiaoping, the number one and number two 'capitalist roaders' – was rapidly gaining momentum. The self-criticism which these two men were supposed to have made in October 1966 was not considered sufficient to discredit them, and hence open attacks on them by name were soon set in motion. The first large-scale demonstration in which their names were publicly pronounced – preceded by those two ominous words '*da dao*' (strike down), always screamed in a hysterical high-pitched tone – was held in Beijing on 25 December 1966. It was organized by Kuai Dafu, a malevolently demagogic leader of the Red Guard of Qinghua University, at the instigation of Zhang Chunqiao, whose instructions ran, 'make their names stink'. (Kuai's political career was terminated in 1971 when he was found to be dispensable; in 1980 he was in prison.) The demonstrators carried for the first time large caricatures of Liu and Deng, which in 1967 became a common sight. The two senior communist leaders were portrayed with hate-filled viciousness, their distorted heads presented as pierced by the pens of their virtuous critics.

In the first months of 1967, the assault on the 'bourgeois headquarters' of Liu and Deng continued to mount in fury and frenzy – all of it carefully prepared and orchestrated by the Cultural Revolution Group, which continued to enjoy Mao Zedong's full support. It was soon extended to the two men's families, especially Liu's wife Wang Guangmei. A strikingly handsome, well-educated and distinguished woman, Wang Guangmei was subjected in 1967 to countless humiliations at the hands of the Red Guards, notably during two separate all-night kangaroo trials held in public. She behaved with great dignity and courage during her ordeals, remaining utterly loyal to her husband. From 1968 on she was to spend more than eight years in prison. The direct instigator of Wang Guangmei's torment was none other than Jiang Qing who in her rabble-rousing speeches to Red Guard audiences spewed out, in what was purportedly a political campaign, her boundless spite, jealousy and hatred of the PRC's First Lady.

It is high time to devote a few paragraphs to the life stories of the two men who were being portrayed as the greatest enemies of People's China, and whose destruction was proclaimed as imperative for the sake of preserving and continuing the Chinese Revolution.

Liu Shaoqi, born in Hunan in 1898, came from a rich peasant family, as did Mao Zedong. His first association with Mao took place in 1917, when he joined the New People's Study Society in Changsha. Liu joined the Socialist Youth League in 1920 in Shanghai. A CCP member from 1921 – the year of its foundation – Liu spent six months studying in Moscow and, after returning to China in 1922, devoted himself to organizing the labour movement; he was to become one of its principal communist leaders in the period up to 1927, when he was secretary general of the then powerful All-China Federation of Labour. After the defeat of the 1925–7 revolution, Liu Shaoqi worked as a leader of the communist underground in Guomindang-ruled areas until 1932, when he moved to the Central Soviet Area in Jiangxi. A Central Committee member since 1927, he joined the Political Bureau either in 1932 or 1934, being already regarded as one of the Party's top leaders.

Leaving Jiangxi in 1934 along with most of the other communist leaders, Liu Shaoqi completed the Long March and then made his way to north China, where for the next two years he led the underground Party organization, playing a crucial role in stimulating the growing national salvation campaign of the students, as revealed in the December Ninth movement. During the War of Resistance, Liu alternated between activities at Party headquarters in Yan'an and work in the Liberated Areas. By the time of the Rectification Campaign (1942–4), Liu's stature as a major Party leader and theoretician was universally recognized. Of his many works probably the most interesting, and certainly the most influential, was *How to Be a Good Communist*, written in 1939. Liu's position was confirmed at the Seventh Party Congress in 1945, when he delivered one of the three principal reports. From 1945 on, Liu was considered to be the second-ranking leader of the CCP, and his personal history henceforth became even more inseparably intertwined with the final victory of the Chinese Revolution and the building of People's China.

Deng Xiaoping was born in 1904 and came from a Sichuanese gentry family. In 1920 he joined the Work and Study Programme in France where, like his fellow provincials Chen Yi and Nie Rongzhen, he soon became engaged in political activities, joining the SYL in 1922 and the French branch of the CCP, led by Zhou Enlai, in 1924. After a short period in Moscow, Deng returned to China to become a political officer in Feng Yuxiang's army. After the downfall of the 1925–7 revolution he spent two years in the Shanghai Party underground; subsequently, he was sent to Guangxi, where he became one of the leaders of the little-known revolutionary movement in that province. After the destruction of the Guangxi Soviet in 1932, Deng moved with its survivors to the Central Soviet Area in Jiangxi where he became a political commissar in the Red Army.

Having taken part in the Long March, Deng Xiaoping continued to work as a high-ranking political officer in the armed forces. During the war against Japan he was attached in this capacity to Liu Bocheng, the Red Army's most renowned strategist, forming a close association which lasted throughout the ensuing military campaigns up to 1949. Deng was elected to the Central Committee at the Seventh Party Congress in 1945. Continuing to work with Liu Bocheng as his political commissar, in what became the Second Field Army, Deng was nominated secretary of the Special Party Committee which co-ordinated the action of all the PLA troops engaged in the historic Huai-Hai campaign.

The first three years of the PRC were spent by Deng in the south-west. From 1952 on he was in the capital, assuming ever higher positions in the Party and government hierarchy. A vice premier since 1954, Deng became a Political Bureau member in

1955, and the Eighth Party Congress in 1956 marked his further elevation to the post of general secretary. Henceforth, as the sixth-ranking member of the Party leadership, he was given the accolade in the media of being one of Mao Zedong's 'closest comrades in arms'. His role in the aftermath of the Great Leap Forward and his active participation in the Sino-Soviet dispute have already been noted.

It follows from the careers of Liu Shaoqi and Deng Xiaoping that to tear to shreds their prestige and political standing and negate their significant contribution to the victory of the Chinese Revolution was no easy task. A virulent flood of lies and slander had to be unloosed – as it was – and even then it is difficult to ascertain to what degree the defamation was given credence by, especially, the numerous veteran Party and PLA cadres whose own lives had been intimately bound up with those of Liu and Deng. It is clear from what did happen that many of their closest associates who held key positions in the Party and state apparatus, as well as in the PLA, adamantly refused to believe any of the vile charges heaped upon the two men. However, they must have, of necessity, undergone immense inner torment, for it was the Party and its supreme leader who were conducting the campaign against Liu and Deng. Party discipline compelled them to be obedient to the Party's orders and political line, even if, in their hearts, they knew full well that a monstrous injustice was being committed. But were they really completely powerless to prevent the injustice? Given the increasingly undemocratic nature of policy- and decision-making at the apex of the CCP hierarchy, and Mao Zedong's overweening and autocratic leadership, by 1967 the answer rests, more than likely, in the affirmative. The two men who were, of course, in the most helpless position of all were Liu and Deng themselves. Although still living in Zhongnanhai, they were soon placed under house arrest. It is obvious that both men had more than just serious reservations about the 'cultural revolution'; they had strong objections which arose out of the concern they felt for the future of the country and the revolution. Their removal from their posts put an end, once and for all, to the legend of monolithic unity of the leadership of the CCP. In reality, it had never been that monolithic, but a consensus had been attainable in the years up to 1966. Why did this prove impossible thereafter? Largely because of the sharpness of the political struggle brought about by the 'cultural revolution'. This was constantly rendered more acute by Mao Zedong and his coterie, who were now pressing for the achievement of a total, crushing victory over their purported antagonists.

Two factors, in particular, greatly aided Lin Biao, the CRG and their patron in pushing on with their assault and obtaining considerable support at various levels of society, without which the accomplishment of their aims would perhaps have been impossible. The first of these has been alluded to briefly earlier: the propensity of a ruling communist party to attract highly dubious elements into its fold. This is a phenomenon which has to be experienced and witnessed to be fully appreciated. Once Party membership becomes a *sine qua non* for advancement, particularly in the political field, it is inevitable that opportunists and careerists swarm to the Party. Although they excel in mouthing the current political line and slogans, their political reliability is nil, since in reality most of them deep down despise the ideology they profess to cherish. Their moral worth is on a similar level, for they are willing to commit any base acts they deem necessary for clawing their way up the ladder of a successful career. They are eager to demonstrate their zeal, especially by attacking fiercely the enemy of the day. All this was by no means specific to China. But the 'cultural revolution' created an excellent situation for scum of this type to rise to the surface and jump on the bandwagon. While some of the activists of the 'cultural revolution', especially among the very young, may have been fanatic, misguided 'true believers', probably the majority were guided primarily by pure opportunism and the desire for power. If it was otherwise, then it is almost impossible to find a satisfactory explanation for the factionalism which characterized both the Red Guards and the Revolutionary Rebels and grew into a straight power struggle.

The second factor was the incredibly tense atmosphere

aroused by the 'cultural revolution', especially during its first two years. The constant stress by all the media on the 'life and death' nature of the struggle against the 'bourgeois headquarters' of Liu Shaoqi and Deng Xiaoping created a situation in which any attempt to oppose what was going on became even more perilous than had been the case earlier. If the experienced and prestigious senior communist leaders could not manage to prevent the further unfolding of the 'cultural revolution', or even mitigate to any appreciable extent the damage it was inflicting on the country, it is idle to expect that this would be done by those in the middle and low levels of the Party and state establishment. And this was precisely why the 'cultural revolutionaries' created an atmosphere akin to terror; it helped them immeasurably to achieve their aims.

In March 1967, a new element, perfidious even by the standards of the 'cultural revolution', was introduced into the campaign to defame Liu Shaoqi. It was claimed that a large, obviously dangerous, clique of 'renegades and traitors', headed by Liu, had been in existence for almost two decades, the members of which occupied top positions in the Party and government apparatus. Dozens of arrests followed; the list of these new victims of the 'cultural revolution' was headed by Bo Yibo. Born in Shanxi in 1908, a CCP member since 1925, Bo had been an important Party leader in his native province during the war with Japan. A Central Committee member since 1945, in 1956 he became an alternate member of the Political Bureau and a vice premier concerned with economic affairs.

The allegations against Bo Yibo and the others were based on the fact that shortly before the outbreak of the war against Japan, he and sixty other CCP members were sitting in a Guomindang prison in Beijing, held on suspicion of communist activity. On the instructions of the Central Committee, Liu Shaoqi, then head of the CCP underground in north China, negotiated for the release of these men. The KMT authorities stipulated, as a face-saving manoeuvre, that the men sign a pledge to refrain from future political activity. On the Party's orders they did so, and of course all of them, after their release, promptly went back to work for the Party, becoming in most cases, like Bo Yibo, important leaders of the communist-led resistance movement. The completely justifiable action of these men was now denounced as treason to the Party, and Liu was charged with prime responsibility for the entire incident. As far as is known none of those arrested appeared in public again until 1978. In that year the survivors, including Bo Yibo, were all fully rehabilitated and once again took up high Party and government positions.

It has been maintained that at the end of March a dramatic meeting of the Political Bureau's Standing Committee, attended by all eleven members, took place at which the decision to deprive Liu Shaoqi of all his Party and government posts was passed by a majority of one. However, the story is open to question, since it is derived from information leaked by a member of the CRG and then revealed in the Red Guard press and big-character posters. It was later reported by Japanese journalists, the most assiduous and successful collectors of news from these sources; most of them read Chinese fluently and, if dressed in Chinese-style clothes, could circulate in the capital with relative ease.

What is quite certain is that in May 1967 a special group was established to inquire into the past 'misdeeds' of Liu Shaoqi and Wang Guangmei. It was headed by Jiang Qing, Kang Sheng and Xie Fuzhi, the minister of public security. The composition of the group assured that no effort would be spared to concoct as watertight a frame-up as possible. The records of the November 1980 trial throw a light, although assuredly only partial, on the methods employed to obtain the desired 'evidence'. Xie Fuzhi (1898–1972), born in Hubei, participated in the same peasant uprising in 1927 as Li Xiannian. Subsequently he rose to high posts as a commander and political commissar in the communist-led armed forces. Xie became a Central Committee member in 1956, a vice premier in 1965 and an alternate member of the Political Bureau in August 1966. At the outset of the 'cultural revolution', Xie threw in his lot unreservedly with Kang Sheng and Jiang Qing. For his actions during the course of the 'cultural revolution' Xie Fuzhi was expelled posthumously from the CCP in October 1980.

It should be noted that while the Ministry of Public Security was, of course, one of the principal instruments employed by the leaders of the CRG to persecute their selected victims, it was itself an object of repression. Some of its functionaries, and more than half of its vice ministers, found themselves in jail, and at least one of them was 'persecuted to death'. The public security organs in the PRC never possessed the degree of independent power that their equivalents in the Soviet Union had, especially in the years up to Beria's death.

The case of Xie Fuzhi, like that of Kang Sheng, Chen Boda and, above all, of Lin Biao, necessarily gives rise to further reflection on the question of how the holding of powerful positions affected the behaviour of these men. Their record during lengthy service in the cause of the Chinese Revolution seems well-nigh impeccable, and their contribution to its victory, especially Lin Biao's, outstanding. Clearly, the phenomenon of careerism and opportunism was by no means restricted to those who joined the Party after 1949; it applied also to a number of those belonging to the CCP's first, heroic generation.

Once again, the influence of a still recent and prodigiously lengthy autocratic past, and of an even more recent period of warlord rule, provides a partial answer. But this is still insufficient to explain satisfactorily the process by which men with a fine revolutionary record stretching over three decades were transformed into nothing more than avid, ruthless and unprincipled seekers of power. That power corrupts and absolute power corrupts absolutely is, of course, a bromide, but nonetheless apt when applied to the PRC from 1959 on, for after the fateful Lushan meeting power was exercised by those at the highest level in an increasingly absolutist, authoritarian fashion.

The 'cultural revolution' hastened the process of degeneration of a number of erstwhile revolutionaries by stimulating the struggle for power at all levels, especially the highest. Moreover, the CCP leaders, especially the highest, were completely immune from any form of restraint on the part of public opinion, or even of the membership of the Party, for by this time very little, if anything, remained of the democratic features of the Yan'an period, and all talk about the 'mass line' and 'mass participation' had been reduced to hypocritical cant. This created a situation in which the formulation of policies and decisions increasingly took on the shape of imperial palace intrigues, which further stimulated the process of degeneration.

In the years preceding the outbreak of the 'cultural revolution' much effort had been devoted to the expansion of contacts with the outside world, primarily for the purpose of strengthening the PRC's position in the world arena and extending its influence. Particular attention had been paid to the developing countries of the Third World, and especially to the newly independent states of Africa. This was illustrated by the highly publicized, and on the whole successful, visit paid by Zhou Enlai and Chen Yi to ten African countries from 14 December 1963 to 4 February 1964. At the same time, China had embarked on a relatively ambitious, considering her own poverty and needs, aid programme for the Third World, contributing for this purpose around US $300 million in the decade ending in 1964. The largest and best known of the projects undertaken by the Chinese was the building of the vital Tanzania–Zambia Railroad.

The results gained from these endeavours were largely negated by the 'cultural revolution'. There were almost fifty foreign missions in Beijing and the growing and incomprehensible chaos in China was of course reported by all of them. But it was the representatives of the Asian and African states, some of whom had looked on the achievements of the PRC with much sympathy and interest, who were among the most shocked by the excesses of the 'cultural revolution'. In their eyes, the prestige of the PRC was receiving a grievous self-inflicted blow. The leaders of the 'cultural revolution', totally wrapped up in their assorted campaigns, could not have cared less, since gaining a victory for themselves was, in their view, infinitely more important than maintaining China's status in the world.

One of the first manifestations of the senseless self-destructive policies of the 'cultural revolution' was the recall of all the heads, with one exception, of Chinese missions abroad, supposedly so that they could participate directly in the 'cultural revolution'. These experienced diplomats had acquired a well-deserved reputation for the skill with which they sought to represent their country's interests. Needless to say all of them were veteran Party members. But after their return home, a number of them fell victim to the machinations of the CRG; the charges trumped up against them included that of carrying out 'revisionist' foreign policy, and they ended up in prison or labour camps. This repression reflected the systematic campaign against the foreign minister, Chen Yi, set into motion at this time by Lin Biao, Jiang Qing and Kang Sheng. There were at least three reasons for the assault: Chen's closeness to Zhou Enlai, who in reality was the principal intended target of the 'cultural revolutionaries'; his outspoken, blunt contempt for the antics of the Red Guards; and his obviously serious reservations about the entire programme of the 'cultural revolution'. A particularly strong attack against Chen Yi was launched in January 1967 by the newly established Revolutionary Rebel organization within the Foreign Ministry, whose actions were stage-managed by a member of the CRG. On 24 January, Chen was compelled to attend a mass rally of ten thousand people and engage in self-criticism; he made use of the occasion to issue a prophetic warning to the effect that the 'cultural revolution' was setting off a chain reaction of resentment and anger which would continue for the entire lifetimes of its participants.

The action against Chen increased in April, by which time the buildings of the Foreign Ministry were plastered with big-character posters carrying the edifying legend 'Smash Chen Yi's dog's head'. Most of his assailants had been still in slit pants at the time the valiant marshal was leading his guerrillas in south China. The final escalation came in August, when the Revolutionary Rebels took complete control of the Foreign Ministry for two weeks.

Although Chen Yi defended himself throughout with brilliant panache, the struggle took its toll. By the autumn of 1967, wearing rumpled PLA fatigues instead of his superbly tailored Sun Yat-sen jacket of the 1950s, he had visibly aged ten years during the preceding twelve months. He never recovered his health, ceased to function in his post in 1968, and died of cancer on 6 January 1972. Four days later, Mao Zedong appeared at Chen's funeral – the only time during the last decade of his own life that he attended such a ceremony – to pay his respects to a fellow poet and comrade for forty-four years. A belated, regretful apology perhaps?

In the two years that had passed since the fall of Khrushchev in October 1964, Sino-Soviet relations had sunk even lower, if this was possible. One of the main points at issue was the attitude towards the war in Vietnam, in view of the constantly increasing level of American intervention. In February 1965 a bitter debate was begun on the question of trans-shipment of Soviet aid to Vietnam. Although Moscow implied that the Chinese were creating difficulties in this respect, in reality they permitted the transport of Soviet materiel through Chinese territory on railway lines, but rejected other Soviet proposals, including those for the use of air bases. The Chinese distrust of Moscow's intentions was expressed bluntly in a Central Committee letter to the CPSU dated 14 July 1965. The Soviet media quickly replied, charging the Chinese with sabotaging all efforts aimed at co-ordinating joint assistance for the Vietnamese.

By February 1966, Chinese attacks on Soviet policy had risen to a new pitch. The Soviet 'social imperialists' – for they had graduated to that distinction already – were now accused of collusion with the United States in an attempt to encircle and contain China, and thus were 'accomplices of US imperialism in its opposition to the revolutionary people of Asia, Africa and Latin America and to the revolutionary people all over the world'. By the outbreak of the 'cultural revolution', the Soviet Union was viewed by Mao Zedong as an out and out enemy. It would seem that his assessment of the United States was as yet unchanged, since the official PRC position was that 'for 16 years US imperialism had consistently followed a policy of hostility towards

China, and throughout these years it has never stopped its aggression and threats against this country'. However, it is very difficult to ascertain whether in 1966 and 1967 these two countries were considered to be equally hostile and potentially dangerous to the PRC, or whether one of them was regarded as the greater enemy.

It was against this background of mutual enmity and an unceasing barrage of hostile propaganda that a series of incidents almost brought about a break in Sino-Soviet diplomatic relations. The critical stage came in January 1967, after a group of Chinese students holding a demonstration at the Lenin Mausoleum was unceremoniously removed from the scene by the Moscow police. The response in Beijing was to hold an eighteen-day-long siege of the Soviet Embassy. For most of the period tens of thousands of demonstrators noisily milled around the extensive area of the Embassy. The demonstrations, in which a considerable number of PLA units participated, were organized quite efficiently; the military arrived in their own transport, while factory crews and other civilians were brought in on PLA lorries. So much for spontaneity. Loudspeakers roared out a raucous paean of hatred – taped, of course – twenty-four hours a day. The pandemonium was so severe that all the Soviet women and children had to be evacuated home. Their departure from the airport gave the heroic Red Guards another occasion to display their revolutionary zeal and courage. Their attempts to harass the women and children were forestalled, on the whole successfully, by the intervention of diplomats from both Eastern and Western Europe, who displayed in this emergency an unusual and rare esprit de corps.

A number of other foreign missions in Beijing underwent similar treatment, although on a smaller scale, during the next few months, in an artificially instigated atmosphere of xenophobia. Some of the incidents, like the night-long tormenting in a police station of the French Counsellor's wife to force her to confess that she had struck a Chinese, were hushed up by the authorities at home. One European ambassador managed to prevent a scheduled assault and siege of his own mission by relaying a message to Zhou Enlai, in which he stressed the futility and disruptive consequences of such actions.

This curious mode of conducting foreign relations reached its apogee in August, when events in Hong Kong, connected with the spill-over of the 'cultural revolution' into that city, were used as a pretext for the sacking of the office of the British Chargé d'Affaires. In the event, both the chancery and the residence were demolished almost totally, including some fine objects of Chinese art. This was carried out by the Red Guards under the direction of a member of the CRG. The staff were brutally manhandled, but special treatment was reserved for the Chargé himself. Donald Hopson, who had earned a DSO and MC in the Second World War during the Normandy landings, was beaten until blood streamed over his face. At an opportune moment, a public security man escorted him away from the mêlée.

None of the governments involved, Soviet, French and British, broke off diplomatic relations with Beijing; all decided to wait for the tide to turn. As far as their representatives were concerned, they were expected to take what had happened in their stride, as something that was all in a day's work – which they did.

Although the PLA had been ordered into action earlier in the year with the task of facilitating the organization of further Revolutionary Committees and helping to stabilize the situation, there was little sign in the spring of 1967 that it had achieved much success in fulfilling its mission. On the contrary, the reports from the provinces spoke of the mounting resentment of many Red Guard and Revolutionary Rebel groups against the PLA for having suppressed their activities and sided instead with the Party apparatus. In a number of cases this antagonism was soon to lead to direct clashes between the Red Guards and PLA units, with the latter becoming increasingly confused by the contradictory nature of the directives received from Beijing.

It is worth noting that the 1981 Resolution on Party History considers that 'The chaos was such that it was necessary to send in the PLA' which 'played a positive role in stabilizing the situation'. It is quite true that the chaos had reached such proportions that only the employment of the armed forces – a measure usually grasped as a last resort – could possibly save the country from total disintegration. However, this in itself was proof of the political bankruptcy of those who initiated the 'cultural revolution', a point which the Resolution does not make. Moreover, it took the PLA over a year and a half to stabilize the situation since, as will be seen, the difficulties encountered were much greater than expected. There is no mention of this aspect in the Resolution; perhaps it is too obvious and too painful a subject for the Chinese who lived through this dreadful period of domestic strife. This seems to be supported by the fact that the authors of the Resolution simply skipped over the period from February 1967 to April 1969. This leaves many questions unraised and unanswered, but the reluctance to deal with them is partly understandable. These months were probably the most reprehensible and unedifying, even worse in some respects, than the initial period of the 'cultural revolution', and a greater blow to the prestige and credibility of the Party than any other event in the history of the PRC.

The deployment of the PLA 'also produced some negative consequences', but this evaluation is given no elaboration. It can be assumed that one of the most negative results was the enhancement of the PLA's political status which led to a distortion of the appropriate relationship between the CCP and its armed forces; to put it more strongly, it constituted a direct challenge to the hallowed principle of the Party controlling the gun.

By May, the situation in some areas became critical. In Zhengzhou, the important industrial centre and railway junction of Henan, the supporters of a student Red Guard group, banned by the PLA, came into conflict with the army and a Revolutionary Rebel workers' unit backed by it. Bloody riots raged through the city for many days, and casualties were numbered in the hundreds. Similar incidents took place in the large city of Luoyang, to the west of Zhengzhou, where severe clashes again took place between students and workers.

The rich, beautiful, vast and populous province of Sichuan –

the size of France with a good bit of Germany thrown in, and with over 90 million inhabitants – became the scene of still greater strife. In May, its capital, Chengdu – one of the most attractive cities in all of China – witnessed armed struggles of unparalleled brutality and ferocity between rival Red Guard and Revolutionary Rebel groups, escalating a situation which was already akin to a local civil war. Incidents of the same nature took place simultaneously in other Sichuanese cities, including the former Guomindang wartime capital on the Yangtse – Chongqing.

It has been maintained by a number of authors – including the present writer – that the 'cultural revolution' remained throughout most of its existence, especially during its first and most turbulent stage, primarily an urban phenomenon. It undoubtedly overflowed, probably to a quite considerable extent, to the suburban rural areas, but the force of its impact on the countryside as a whole is still difficult to ascertain on the basis of the data available. It seems, however, that in view of the scale of fighting in some areas, such as Guangxi or Yunnan, it would be wrong to underestimate the disruption caused in non-urban areas. The only provisional conclusion that can be made at present is that, fortunately for China, the effects of the 'cultural revolution' were less in the villages than in the cities. Had it been otherwise, the consequences of this calamity would have been even more severe.

What does seem certain is that by the spring of 1967 the turmoil and strife initiated by the 'cultural revolution', which far exceeded the expectations of its authors, had brought about the collapse of the Party apparatus on a national, provincial and district level. In the course of the struggle during the preceding twelve months, the Party committees on these levels – the real ruling bodies of the country – had simply ceased to function in the great majority of cases since, according to the 1981 Resolution, they 'became partially or wholly paralysed'. Consequently, the effectiveness of the central authorities in Beijing was also severely and extensively undermined. Gone were the days when instructions, relayed simultaneously by telephone to all the first secretaries of the provincial Party committees, could ensure a more or less uniform implementation of general policy. Thus, one of the greatest achievements of the PRC – the country's real unification – was seriously jeopardized.

Outwardly, the Beijing leadership showed no signs of being perturbed by the chaos into which their country had been plunged. Holidays were celebrated as if everything was in perfect order. And thus, in the muggy, humid evening hours of May Day 1967, Mao Zedong stood once again on the terrace of the Gate of Heavenly Peace, gazing down blandly and impassively on the surging crowds of over half a million of his fellow citizens who had spent long hours on their feet waiting for his arrival. Next to him on one side stood the 'standard-bearer of the Great Proletarian Cultural Revolution' Jiang Qing, her face wreathed in delighted smiles, as a sycophantic courtier paid her respectful homage. On his other side stood his 'closest comrade in arms' – at least for another four years – Lin Biao. For all three it appeared to be a moment of great triumph, and the innumerable banners held up and waved enthusiastically by the densely packed ranks of people proclaimed all the accolades then being accorded to the 'reddest sun in our hearts'. The cult had by now reached its pinnacle, and the dazzling display of fireworks seemed to symbolize it.

In the same merry month of May, the Red Guards dragged from his prison cell to a mass rally and the customary public kangaroo trial another of the men whose contribution to the victory of the Chinese Revolution had been crucial – the legendary He Long (1896–1968).

He Long's early life could have come straight out of the famous Chinese picaresque epic *All Men Are Brothers* (*The Water Margin*), a work which Mao Zedong greatly admired. A Hunanese peasant, He Long had been in his youth both a secret society member (belonging to the Ko-lao-hui, Elder Brother Society) and an outlaw. By 1918 he joined a provincial army unit, rising to the rank of regimental commander. Under the influence of the revolutionary movement of 1925–7, He became a communist and his troops were a major component of the forces participating in the Nanchang Uprising. Henceforth,

He's career was that of a top Red Army leader, in command of his own revolutionary base in south China. His wife, two sisters and one brother were all executed by the Guomindang. In 1935 he successfully led his army on its own Long March to meet the other Red Army contingents in Shaanxi. During the War of Resistance, He Long, the most colourful of the communist military leaders, was entrusted with the command of one of the three original divisions of the Eighth Route Army. In the final phase of military struggle in 1946–9, He led the PLA troops in the north-west, the future First Field Army. A Central Committee member since 1945, he was elevated to the Political Bureau in 1956, having become a vice premier in 1954. A soldier's soldier, renowned for his personal bravery, he received the rank of marshal in 1955.

Even before the 'cultural revolution' He Long had not disguised his disapproval of the policies pursued by Lin Biao in the PLA. His reservations about the 'cultural revolution' were also not concealed. Hence he was attacked in the autumn of 1966 and a particularly vituperative campaign of vilification was launched against him in January 1967, the probable time of his arrest. Lin Biao also charged him with taking part in planning the mythical *coup d'état* of February 1966. Reduced to chewing the straw in his mattress for food, He Long was 'persecuted to death' and perished in prison in 1968. A few years after Lin Biao's disappearance from the political arena he was fully rehabilitated.

In the summer of 1967, the huge triple city of Wuhan (Wuchang to the south of the Yangtse, Hankou and Hanyang to the north), a key industrial centre and the site of some of China's most important factories such as the Wuhan Iron and Steel Works, became engulfed in a prolonged and bitter conflict. The main contestants were the One Million Workers, composed mostly of Revolutionary Rebel groups from the factories, and the Workers' Headquarters which incorporated various student Red Guard units and some workers. The conflict between these two coalitions was fundamentally over the control of Wuhan. The clashes began in the spring and involved, as they intensified, the PLA, itself divided in its sympathies. By June, the rivalry had degenerated into bloody armed conflict with hundreds of fatalities, which the local PLA commander, Chen Zaidao, was unable to suppress or control. Production in Wuhan's numerous factories was inevitably seriously affected.

The situation in Wuhan became so grave that the Beijing authorities decided to intervene and dispatched a special mission to the city, headed by Xie Fuzhi and Wang Li, a member of the CRG. Chen Zaidao had tended to side with the less extreme and stronger of the two contending coalitions, the One Million Workers; he was ordered by Xie and Wang to reverse his stand, which he refused to do. In the ensuing contretemps the two emissaries were arrested by one of Chen's units and Beijing was faced with what had all the hallmarks of a local military rebellion. An airborne division, ground units and gunboats were quickly dispatched to Wuhan, prepared to attack Chen's large garrison. Nonetheless, mostly due to the successful mediation carried out by Zhou Enlai, the crisis was resolved relatively peacefully. Xie and Wang were rescued from captivity, and Chen Zaidao and his colleagues departed for Beijing to face the consequences of their actions. Within a few weeks the situation in Wuhan became relatively stable. However, the incident itself gave rise to a series of new attacks on the PLA by a number of the most extreme Red Guard organizations, launched under the slogan of 'dragging the capitalist roaders out of the PLA'.

One of the most active of the extremist groups in this period was the mysterious May Sixteenth outfit, probably acting at the instigation of certain CRG members. After the dissolution of this group and the arrest of many of its participants, it was held to be responsible for most of the excesses and atrocities committed in 1967, including the taking over of the Foreign Ministry and the destruction of the British Mission. However, in view of the highly conspiratorial nature of Beijing politics during these months and the intricate in-fighting between and within at least two factions of Mao Zedong's closest collaborators – those led respectively by Lin Biao and Jiang Qing – it is very difficult to establish who, in reality, were the instigators and patrons of the

May Sixteenth organization. By September, six of the secondary members of the CRG had been removed from the scene, most of them winding up in prison. All were charged with being 'ultra-leftist' and some with responsibility for the activities of the May Sixteenth movement. However, the truly important ultra-leftists – Lin Biao, Kang Sheng, Xie Fuzhi, Chen Boda, Jiang Qing, Zhang Chunqiao and Yao Wenyuan – remained in dominant positions in the CCP leadership and, hiding behind the authority and prestige of Mao Zedong, continued their struggle for power and the assaults on all their alleged enemies. Probably one of the very few elements that this disparate crew had in common was their hostility to the one individual who was capable of occasionally frustrating, if not blocking their schemes – Zhou Enlai.

The role of Zhou Enlai during the 'cultural revolution', particularly in its first and most turbulent stage, is assuredly one of the most vexing of the many problems of this troubled decade. There is so far no evidence that Zhou at any crucial moment, especially in July and August 1966, ever sought to oppose in a determined fashion Mao Zedong's resolve to launch the 'cultural revolution'. Publicly, he continued to avow his support for Mao's leadership and all the policies that the latter had now set into motion. It is difficult – practically impossible – to assume that a man of such intelligence and capability as Zhou Enlai would not have had serious reservations about the incoherent concepts and reckless measures characterizing the 'cultural revolution'. It seems inconceivable that his objections did not mount during the first year as the disastrous consequences became ever more apparent and the state administration which he headed crumbled day by day. Yet he did not change his course and, proclaiming his allegiance to the 'cultural revolution' and, more importantly, to its leader, he concentrated his efforts on the almost insuperably difficult task of seeking to prevent the total disruption of the state apparatus and to lessen the damage which was being inflicted upon the country.

Involved in practically every one of the successive crises, always mediating between conflicting groups and seeking to find a moderate course – usually unattainable – Zhou Enlai's indefatigability in these months was stupendous; at the age of sixty-eight it was not unusual for him to work up to sixteen hours a day for weeks on end. His diplomatic skill was used to the utmost in his relations with the connivers in Mao Zedong's closest entourage, especially Jiang Qing and Lin Biao. While Zhou also had access to Mao, it would seem that his influence on the man he had worked with so closely for three decades was limited, less than that of the two main contenders for power. And power was the one thing that Zhou was not striving for; this, to a large degree, accounts for his survival. In public, Zhou's composure remained unshaken, as one could observe in his contacts with some of the most loutish of the Red Guard leaders.

However, Zhou was constantly faced with the problem of preserving his own integrity. It is only the Chinese who have the right to judge whether and to what degree he was successful in this respect. What is indisputable is that the compromises he entered into did make it possible for him to retain his position and utilize it, not for himself, but to save as much from the wreckage as he could. His greatest action was to save people – no mean achievement under the conditions of the 'cultural revolution'. Not all the ones who should have been saved – Liu Shaoqi and He Long for example – but nonetheless a great number. Not always when they were the object of direct attack by Lin Biao or Jiang Qing, but often later, at a more propitious moment. More than one veteran revolutionary was rescued from rotting to death in prison or labour camp by Zhou's efforts. To accomplish this 'he said and did many things which were against his conscience'. The words are those of Deng Xiaoping, as are the following: 'But the people forgave him, because, had he not done and said those things, he himself would not have been able to survive and play the neutralizing role he did, which reduced losses.' The behaviour of the people of Beijing in January 1976, when the cortège carrying Zhou's body passed through the streets, confirms the truth of Deng's evaluation.

Although the Wuhan incident had been resolved, the intensity of strife in the provinces subsided only to a limited degree in the autumn and winter of 1967. The struggle for power between rival groups had been embittered by earlier conflicts, and a general tendency to settle accounts and take revenge became prevalent. The depth of the political crisis was also revealed by the lack of progress in the efforts of the central authorities in Beijing to achieve such compromises between contending provincial factions as would make possible the creation of the three-in-one alliances and the establishment of further Revolutionary Committees. In this respect practically nothing had been achieved, in spite of much pressure, for by the end of 1967 Revolutionary Committees existed in only nine of the twenty-seven provinces and municipalities of equal status. The situation began to change only in the first five months of 1968, when finally a further nineteen committees were set up. In this the role of the PLA proved to be crucial. The political weight of the armed forces grew correspondingly since, in practically all cases, the provincial PLA commanders and political commissars dominated the leadership of the new Revolutionary Committees.

Since February 1967, when the PLA was first sent in to participate directly in the 'cultural revolution', its increased involvement in the political struggle nationally and locally gave rise to additional problems. Some of these resulted from the fashion in which this mighty 'pillar of the dictatorship of the proletariat' – the words are Lin Biao's – carried out its newly assigned functions, since its attempts to restore order inevitably brought it into conflict with numerous Red Guard groups. Moreover, the complex factional in-fighting within the ruling circles in Beijing itself, which reached new heights during this stage of the 'cultural revolution', affected the PLA high command considerably. This was evident in the kaleidoscopic shifts of those holding such key positions as that of chief of staff, head of the General Political Department or head of the PLA Cultural Revolution Group. These changes no doubt also reflected the strivings of Lin Biao to place his closest followers, primarily his former subordinates in the Fourth Field Army, in as many decisive posts as possible, at the expense of course of those high-ranking officers who had served in the field armies commanded by Chen Yi, Liu Bocheng, Peng Dehuai and He Long. In some cases the transfer of prominent military personnel was carried out relatively quietly; in others, such as the abrupt removal and arrest in March 1968 of the acting chief of staff, it was accompanied by the customary barrage of defamatory political accusations.

The cardinal problem, however, was that by the autumn of 1967 the PLA was still far from having succeeded in stabilizing the situation. It was almost surely this factor which caused Mao Zedong to renew in September his directives to the PLA, commanding it to restore order nationally. Mao had spent the preceding two months on a lengthy trip to five provinces – Henan, Hubei, Hunan, Jiangxi and Zhejiang. The conditions in the first two were especially chaotic and disturbing, and it is maintained that Mao concluded that civil war had actually broken out. He is also supposed to have expressed his growing disenchantment with the Red Guards – the putative revolutionary successors to whom he had attached such high hopes.

It is doubtful, however, whether the turmoil and chaos of the first year of the 'cultural revolution' caused Mao Zedong either to question the correctness of his own policies – or to alter his view of his own role as the country's supreme leader. On the contrary, the cult of his person, propagated ever more assiduously by Lin Biao, Chen Boda, and all the Chinese media, reached still greater heights. Almost a thousand million copies of the Little Red Book had been distributed to serve perhaps as a revolutionary substitute for the sayings of Confucius – *The Analects*. Moreover, when the fiftieth anniversary of the Russian Revolution came to be celebrated all over China, everyone in the country, whether literate or not, could see how the chairman viewed his place in world history. By November gigantic posters were to be seen everywhere; the content of the message was clear and unmistakable, for under the dates 1917–1967, five large overlapping portraits in profile were superimposed. Thus Mao Zedong was proclaimed – not only to the Chinese but to the entire world as well – as the one and only legitimate successor to Marx, Engels, Lenin and Stalin, with all the ideological and political consequences that this implied. It was somewhat ironical that such a claim was being championed precisely at a time when he was leading the country into immense and tragic upheaval.

Although the PLA had succeeded in establishing the provincial Revolutionary Committees by the end of May – eight months later than scheduled – this did not signify that its prime mission, the restoration of order, had been accomplished as well. In the spring and summer of 1968 violence erupted once again in many parts of the country. The situation became particularly dangerous in Guangxi, where large-scale pitched battles were fought between the contending parties, primarily between Red Guard and Revolutionary Rebel groups and the PLA. Full use was made of modern weapons by both sides, for the Red Guards employed both arms filched from PLA depots – a countrywide practice in 1967 and 1968 – and also a large quantity of military equipment pilfered from Chinese and Soviet shipments destined for the Vietnamese. The number of deaths ran into thousands, possibly tens of thousands.

The severe conflict in Guangzhou between the two main rival Red Guard coalitions – the Red Flag and the East Wind – which had raged so fiercely in 1967 before being put down by the PLA, flared up again in the spring of 1968. The armed forces were compelled to intervene once more and by June armoured cars of the PLA were patrolling the city's main streets. The restoration of order resulted in additional heavy casualties.

In July, two rival Red Guard units at Beijing's Qinghua University, both laying claim to being the only true revolutionary upholders of Mao Zedong Thought and comprising only a small minority of the student body, continued their murderous feud on the thoroughly devastated campus, whose buildings had been converted into fortresses. Their methods of 'revolutionary struggle' included the pulling of their captives' teeth to extort confessions of counter-revolutionary activities. A non-violent end was finally put to these excesses when a large number of unarmed workers from the Beijing factories were sent in under PLA guidance to take over the campus.

It is maintained that by this time Mao Zedong had had enough of the 'little red generals' he had released genie-like two years earlier to accomplish his aims. At a meeting on 27 July with five prominent Red Guard leaders, including Nie Yuanzi and Kuai Dafu, Mao berated them bitterly for their actions and for letting him down. His repudiation of the Red Guards was followed very quickly by concrete measures; within six months close to 20 million of the erstwhile Red Guards found themselves sent down to the countryside, to live and work alongside the peasants, where the possibilities for continuing their 'revolutionary struggle' were non-existent. It would be extremely interesting and worthwhile to ascertain how the experiences of these two years, in which they were first encouraged, fêted and glorified as the nation's wave of the future and then cast aside as unreliable and expendable, affected the thinking of this generation, now in their thirties and forties. It should be borne in mind that the suspension of studies during this period and the ensuing rustication deprived almost all of this age group of the possibility of acquiring the knowledge and skills the country needed so desperately. It can be regarded partially as a lost generation – a high price for achieving the political aims of the leaders of the 'cultural revolution', but only one of many.

At the end of August 1968, the PLA was ordered once again to restore order throughout the country. This time it finished the task. By the end of the year strife on a major scale had been eliminated, although the casualties involved were high. The decision to stabilize the situation was based primarily on domestic needs, but it was also a reaction to two significant and related external factors.

The first of these was the Czechoslovak crisis. While the optimistic vision of the Dubcek leadership to build socialism with a human face was anathema to Mao Zedong and his collaborators and castigated by them as 'revisionism', the entry of Soviet troops on 20 August was immediately denounced by the leaders in Beijing with all the invective customarily applied to the Soviet Union at that time.

The second factor was the marked build-up during 1968 of

Soviet armed forces on the Sino-Soviet borders, and the growing number of incidents there, especially in Xinjiang where
some of the nationalities lived on both sides of the frontier. The
implications of both these situations loomed significantly in the
thinking of the Beijing leadership and influenced to a very considerable degree their determination to stabilize the domestic
situation immediately. Both these factors led to still further
deterioration of Sino-Soviet relations which found its climax in
March 1969 with armed clashes on the Ussuri River.

It was in these domestic and international circumstances that
Mao Zedong ordered the holding in Beijing of the enlarged
Twelfth Plenum of the Central Committee on 12–31 October.
Apart from the final communiqué, practically no material relating to the plenum was released. No list of those attending was
published, but it can be assumed that around two-thirds of the
members and alternates of the Central Committee elected at the
Eighth Congress in 1956 were not present. Like its predecessor
in August 1966, the plenum was packed with Mao's adherents,
primarily from the provinces.

One of the topics discussed was the next Party Congress. It
had been due to be held in 1967, then in 1968; it was now scheduled for 1969. A draft of a proposed new Party constitution was
distributed to those attending the meeting. Mao Zedong and his
associates were preparing to rebuild, in a mould they thought
appropriate, the Party which they had spent two years shattering.

A major item on the agenda of the Twelfth Plenum was the
acceptance of the report on the examination of the 'crimes' of
the number one capitalist roader, Liu Shaoqi. As noted earlier, it
had been prepared by a commission of inquiry headed by Jiang
Qing, Kang Sheng and Xie Fuzhi. The commission had done its
job very thoroughly. In what turned out to be the greatest
frame-up in the history of the PRC, Liu was declared to be a 'renegade, traitor and scab'. The plenum resolved 'to expel Liu
Shaoqi from the Party once and for all, to dismiss him from all
posts both inside and outside the Party'. Already under house
arrest in Zhongnanhai, he was now placed in a prison in Beijing.

Within a year of the Twelfth Plenum he was transferred, a diabetic and suffering from pneumonia, on a stretcher to solitary confinement in a building serving as a prison in Kaifeng. On 13 November 1969, Liu died in his cell, with only his jailer present. It was years before his wife and children were informed of his fate.

Fate was to be kinder to the number two capitalist roader – Deng Xiaoping. After a period of house arrest in Zhongnanhai, Deng and his wife were exiled in October 1969 – the same month as Liu's transfer to Kaifeng – to Nanchang in Jiangxi. Kept under strict police surveillance and in complete isolation, Deng and his wife eked out an existence by working half-days in a tractor factory. Their conditions improved somewhat after Lin Biao's disappearance from the political arena in September 1971, but it was not until February 1973, after three and a half years of enforced vegetation, that Deng and his family were permitted, quite likely due to Zhou Enlai's efforts, to return to Beijing.

In public Mao Zedong professed an admiration for Stalin and his policies, but his attitude towards him was in fact much more ambivalent and complex than his own formal utterances or the CCP's official evaluation of Stalin sponsored by him. Mao's methods of struggle against those he considered to be enemies of the Chinese Revolution differed substantially from Stalin's. The purge of veteran revolutionaries during the 'cultural revolution' gave rise to innumerable cases of persecution, repression and rank injustice, but it never assumed the proportions of the great Soviet purges of the 1930s, which resulted in the extermination of practically the entire revolutionary and civil war generation, and almost all of the old Bolsheviks. Had the Soviet model been followed in this instance, the great majority of the post-1976 CCP leadership would not have been still alive.

By the spring of 1969 the preparations for holding a meeting of the CCP's supreme and theoretically governing body were complete. The Ninth Party Congress, one of the two most questionable in the history of the Chinese communist movement, met in Beijing on 1–24 April, attended by over 1500 delegates.

Since the Party committees on the provincial and district levels had ceased to exist, no pretence was made of electing the delegates at local Party conferences. Instead, they were carefully selected by the central authorities in Beijing. In contrast with the Eighth Congress in 1956, very little of the proceedings was made public.

The principal document available is the political report delivered by Lin Biao. An elucubration of this kind is not usually written by the speaker but by a team of ghost writers. Later developments made the question of authorship in this case controversial, but one thing is certain – the report faithfully represented the views of Mao Zedong.

In the speech, Lin Biao's adulation of Mao, whom he referred to 148 times, reached new heights. He devoted much time to praising the tremendous achievements of the 'cultural revolution' and the bright prospects for the future, ascribing all of this to Mao Zedong's wise leadership. Much attention was also paid to a systematic distortion of the CCP's history, in line with the thesis that there existed a constant two-line struggle. A long section on the international situation and the PRC's foreign policy reaffirmed the Soviet Union and the United States as China's two principal enemies.

Apart from discussing – what was said is not known – and approving Lin Biao's report, the delegates also passed the new Party constitution, the draft of which had been prepared by Zhang Chunqiao and Yao Wenyuan. Predictably, the reference to Mao Zedong Thought, which had been dropped in the 1956 constitution, was restored in an appropriately expanded and exalted form. A special paragraph was devoted to Lin Biao, which deserves to be quoted to illustrate the political atmosphere of the PRC during this period.

'Comrade Lin Biao has consistently held high the great red banner of Mao Zedong Thought and has most loyally and resolutely carried out and defended Comrade Mao Zedong's proletarian revolutionary line. Comrade Lin Biao is Comrade Mao Zedong's close comrade in arms and successor.'

Thus the question of succession was presumably considered

to be resolved, in a manner corresponding quite closely to China's 3000-year-long tradition of monarchic rule.

At the conclusion of what Mao Zedong reportedly had hoped would be a congress of unity and victory, the delegates elected from a full slate of candidates prepared beforehand a new Central Committee. This new body comprised 170 members and 109 alternates, much larger than its predecessor's 97 members and 73 alternates. The dominant position was clearly held by the PLA; 45 per cent of the new Central Committee's members came from its ranks. This was a logical and direct consequence of the role assigned to the PLA during the 'cultural revolution'. It also followed partly from the fact that while the civilian sector of the Party had been decimated and its organizational structure largely destroyed, the Party organization within the PLA had not suffered comparable damage; in fact, by 1969, it was probably the only component of the CCP which was still functioning more or less normally. The problem of observing the principle that the Party should control the gun and not vice versa became more acute as a result of the Ninth Congress and was a significant element in the ensuing political struggle within the top leadership of the CCP during the next two and a half years.

The composition of the new Central Committee also revealed the degree to which the veteran cadres, particularly those previously engaged in the work of the Party and state apparatus, had been pushed to the side of the political arena. Only 30 per cent of the original members of the Central Committee chosen in 1956 were represented in the new body. If one bears in mind the nature of the mechanism of political power, in which Central Committee membership automatically entailed in almost all cases the holding of prominent and decisive positions in the Party or state apparatus, then the true extent of the purge of the highest CCP echelon can be understood more fully.

The policy- and decision-making powers did not, in reality, rest with the new Central Committee, but with the Political Bureau it elected. This had been the case throughout the twenty years of the PRC; the difference now was that the autocratic tendencies, displayed above all by the supreme leader himself, became much more apparent.

At the First Plenum of the new Central Committee on 28 April a Political Bureau of twenty-one full and four alternate members was chosen. Five of them – Mao Zedong, Lin Biao, Zhou Enlai, Chen Boda and Kang Sheng – composed the Bureau's Standing Committee which in practice constituted the real ruling group of the Party, in charge of running it and the entire country on a day-to-day basis.

A valuable insight into the essential nature of the history of the Chinese communist movement in these years can be gained by examining the future fate of the twenty-one full members of the 1969 Political Bureau. By the end of 1976, eight of them were dead. The causes were natural in the case of Mao Zedong, Zhou Enlai, Zhu De, Dong Biwu and Kang Sheng; not so in the case of Lin Biao, Ye Qun (his wife), and Xie Fuzhi. A further eight were in prison – Chen Boda, Jiang Qing, Zhang Chunqiao, Yao Wenyuan, and four of Lin Biao's associates. The surviving five remained as Political Bureau members.

In 1981 the present CCP leadership gave its assessment of the Ninth Congress. According to the Resolution on Party History, it had 'legitimatized' the erroneous theories and practices of the 'cultural revolution', and 'the guidelines of the Ninth Congress were wrong, ideologically, politically and organizationally'. An accurate judgement based on facts. However, there is one particularly significant question – among a number of others – which the Resolution does not deal with fully. What was the real nature of the Party in the period after the Ninth Congress, when it was compelled to act in accordance with these erroneous theories and practices? After the bitter experiences of the first stage of the 'cultural revolution', did an increasing number of Party members 'adopt a sceptical or a wait-and-see attitude towards the "cultural revolution" or even resist and oppose it'? If so, then it is certain that the CCP became an increasingly dispirited, demoralized, and disunited organization, with its highest echelon especially riddled with factionalism, and many of its members paying only lip service to the current programme for the sake of personal survival. Under these circumstances it could hardly have been the 'great, glorious and correct Party . . . the core of leadership of the Chinese people' that it was claimed to be by the 1969 constitution. Once again, however, only the Chinese can truly judge the issue.

In the 1970s many Western authors took the view that the Ninth Party Congress marked, in reality, the end of the 'cultural revolution'. A number of them still adhere to this opinion. However, the view of the present CCP leadership that the 'cultural revolution' was terminated only after the death of its initiator and the downfall of his remaining closest collaborators seems to be more plausible. This viewpoint is justified by the fact that the basic policies of the 'cultural revolution' – incoherent and contradictory as they may have been – continued to be upheld throughout these years, as was the hyperpoliticized atmosphere generated during the first stage of the 'cultural revolution'.

CHAPTER EIGHT

The Intermediate Period,
April 1969–August 1973

Mao Zedong proclaimed the Ninth Congress a 'congress of unity and victory', but the political developments during the following two and a half years showed that the unity was barely skin deep. In reality, the Congress inaugurated a period marked by some of the most intense factional strife in the entire history of the Chinese communist movement, culminating in September 1971 in a political crisis of the first magnitude. It was a conflict waged within the highest leadership of the Party itself, and while its participants differed in their approach to a number of fundamental issues, it was basically a struggle for power.

Since the outset of the 'cultural revolution', two main factions had taken shape at the very pinnacle of the CCP hierarchy – one led by Lin Biao, the other by Jiang Qing. Both have been consistently referred to in the official CCP documents issued since October 1976 as counter-revolutionary cliques; both have been charged with the same crime – 'plotting to capture supreme power'. As has been seen, both factions played a dominant role in the first stage of the 'cultural revolution', simultaneously cooperating with and rivalling each other.

Within a year of the Ninth Congress the activities of the Lin Biao faction, which held seven seats in the Political Bureau, became the major political concern for the remaining members of this ruling body and, above all, for its leader, Mao Zedong. Knowledge of what was going on was restricted largely to this handful; it was not until the Second Plenum in Lushan on 23 August–6 September 1970 that a slightly larger group – the Central Committee – became aware that serious friction had arisen. The rest of the Chinese people remained completely in the dark for well over another year. The style of politics practised at this time by the CCP leadership had an uncanny resemblance to that which prevailed in the imperial palaces of Qin Shihuang, Liu Bang of the Han or Zhu Yuanzhang. Mao Zedong was correct when he observed that 'three thousand years of history weighed heavily on our heads'; autocracy still exerted its baneful influence.

At the Lushan plenum Lin Biao and Chen Boda, who had decided to cast in his lot with Lin, are supposed to have 'launched a surprise attack' when they raised two issues in connection with the revision of the PRC constitution. Lin proposed that the post of PRC chairman be retained, although Mao had repeatedly declared his opposition to the idea. Chen presented an argument, properly buttressed by quotations from Marx and Engels, in favour of inserting a passage relating to Mao Zedong's genius. They were supported by other members of the faction, referred to later by Mao Zedong as Lin Biao's 'big generals'. These were Huang Yongsheng (b. 1908), the chief of staff, Li Zuopeng (b. 1910), the political commissar of the navy, Qiu Huizuo (b. 1915), director of the logistics department, Wu Faxian (b. 1913), head of the air force, and Lin's wife, Ye Qun. The four military officials were, in fact, Lin's closest collaborators; all had been his subordinates in the Fourth Field Army.

The episode ended, for the time being, in the disgrace of Chen Boda who was 'put under investigation' shortly thereafter. His disappearance from public view was of course noted and an attack in the media in March 1971 on a 'sham political swindler' was correctly interpreted by those versed in the esoteric nature of Beijing politics as a reference to him.

It is maintained officially that after the failure in Lushan, Lin Biao began to lay his plans for 'an armed counter-revolutionary *coup d'état*'. His son, Lin Liguo, is said to have organized a small conspiratorial group, the 'Joint Fleet', and to have drawn up in March 1971 a detailed plan for the coup, known as 'Outline of Project 571'. The anointed heir apparent evidently felt unsure of his future; his succession might prove slow in coming, and in the meanwhile he might be removed from his position. In the event, Lin Biao's last public appearance was made on 3 June.

The 'Outline of Project 571' reads like pulp fiction – as, for that matter, does the entire account of the Lin Biao affair. It was quite elaborate, and its principal aim was the assassination of Mao Zedong, to be accomplished as soon as an opportune moment presented itself.

Between 14 August and 10 September Mao Zedong was in south China on an inspection trip which took him to Wuhan, Changsha, Nanchang and Hangzhou. During the trip he is said to have officially briefed the top military and Party officials in these areas on the conflict with Lin Biao. Before leaving Beijing, Mao had taken steps to decrease the influence of Lin Biao on the crucial Military Affairs Committee and had brought in new troops to the Beijing garrison. It is claimed now that the plans of the conspirators to kill Mao during his trip were frustrated by the precautionary measures taken; however, according to Zhou Enlai, the assassination attempt was simply not put into effect. It is somewhat astounding that the most brilliant Chinese tactician of his time proved to be such a fumbling and ineffective conspirator. In the 1981 Resolution the credit for 'ingeniously thwarting the plotted coup' is assigned to Mao Zedong and Zhou Enlai.

On 13 September, Lin Biao, his wife and son are said to have left Beidahe in a Trident No. 256. Two hours later the aircraft crashed in the Mongolian People's Republic, about one hundred kilometres north of the Sino-Mongolian border. All aboard were killed and the bodies badly charred. They were buried on the spot.

The failure to hold the customary festivities on 1 October was taken to indicate that something truly unusual had taken place in Beijing. The disappearance from public view not only of Lin Biao and his 'big generals' (they had all been arrested immediately) but also of many of his closest associates could not remain unnoticed. Thus an account of the Lin Biao affair was transmitted step by step down the hierarchical ladder of the Party and state establishment. The first official public pronouncement was made at the end of July 1972. By that time, of course, the news had percolated through the entire country.

The repercussions of the Lin Biao affair were immense. The attempts to re-create after the end of the first stage of the 'cultural revolution' a modicum of political stability were largely frustrated. Moreover, the credibility of the Party, and especially of its highest leadership, had suffered a severe blow. In particular, the Party chairman's omniscience and infallibility could now be seriously questioned, although to have done so openly would have been foolhardy indeed.

The far-reaching absorption of the top CCP leadership into this factional in-fighting might well have been one of the causes of the slowness in rebuilding the Party, a task which had been assigned high priority by the Ninth Congress and strongly stressed by Mao Zedong himself. It was to be accomplished by re-creating the Party's organizational structure, starting with the provincial committees and then working down to the district and finally to the branch level. The process proved to be much more difficult than had been expected, probably due to the mutual resentment and recriminations which had accumulated since the outset of the 'cultural revolution'. Thus, the first provincial committee – in Hunan – was not established until December 1970, and only a handful of district committees were in existence by then. In 1971, efforts were intensified and by August all the provincial committees were finally reconstituted. It is quite likely that this acceleration was connected with the struggle being waged against the Lin Biao faction. However, another two years were to elapse before the entire Party apparatus was restored to the state existing in early 1966. Nonetheless, the political dominance which the PLA had acquired in the years 1966–9 was still reflected in the composition of the new Party organizations. It was to decrease only gradually, though the Lin Biao affair clearly affected relations between the CCP and its armed forces.

The Sino-Soviet clashes on the Ussuri River in March 1969 did not lead to widespread conflict but they inaugurated a period of unusual tension along the border. In August, a new series of incidents in Xinjiang further exacerbated relations between the two countries and resulted in a build-up of military forces by both sides. Shortly thereafter, Beijing claimed that the Soviet Union had increased the size of its units to over a million men, accompanied by a large though unspecified number of atomic weapons.

Bitter though the conflict had become, the door to negotiations had not been shut completely by either the Chinese or the Soviet governments. On 11 September, the Soviet premier, Kosygin, had a six-hour talk with Zhou Enlai at Beijing airport. The meeting failed to resolve any of the problems, nor did it lessen the hostility which characterized relations between the countries, but it did show a mutual desire to resort to negotiations in the future rather than force. This was reflected in Chinese public pronouncements in October, in which it was stressed that there was no reason why the border question should give rise to war. Sino-Soviet negotiations were initiated on 20 October 1969 and continued for years without ever producing the slightest concrete results, except the crucial one of keeping the issues on the negotiation table and off the battlefield.

The border itself was not where the real problem lay; it was a byproduct of the general deterioration in Sino-Soviet relations from 1956 on. The Chinese side never requested any revision of the frontiers, nor did they claim any specific Soviet territory. What they did demand was that in any future negotiations leading to a final, mutually recognized demarcation of the entire boundary, the Soviet Union should admit that the existing frontier was the result of 'unequal treaties' imposed on China by Tsarist Russia, which of course was the case. From the outset of the negotiations the Soviet side adamantly refused to accept this proposal, thus creating a complete impasse. Moreover, the whole issue, which would never have arisen in the first place had the CCP and the CPSU managed to work out a *modus vivendi* in the late 1950s, quickly became a favourite weapon in the propaganda war conducted by each side against the other and contributed significantly to a further poisoning of relations between the two countries.

More significantly, the view of the Beijing authorities in the late 1960s that the Soviet Union and the United States were equally hostile to the national interests of the PRC had altered by 1970. Some authors deduce from the utterances supposedly made by Mao Zedong in 1969 and 1970 that he now tended to regard China's northern neighbour as the greater enemy of the two, in spite of the war which the United States was conducting in Vietnam. Hence, Mao's resolve to counter the alleged Soviet threat by seeking to establish relations with the United States. In December 1970, he took the initiative and via Edgar Snow invited Nixon to China. The oft-recounted ping-pong diplomacy conducted by Zhou Enlai took place in April 1971, and by July of that year Kissinger was in Beijing for secret talks with Zhou. On 14 July Nixon publicly announced his acceptance of the Chinese invitation.

It was under these circumstances that in October 1971 the PRC finally won the long struggle to take its rightful place in the United Nations. The Washington administration still opposed China's entry but it had ceased to exert as much pressure against the decision as it had earlier.

The Lin Biao affair delayed Nixon's departure for China for a few months. The highly publicized and televised visit finally took place on 21–28 February 1972. The terms agreed upon for the renewal of Sino-American relations, after over two decades of hostile confrontation, were made public in the Shanghai communiqué; they included an ingenious way of bypassing one of the most contentious issues, that of Taiwan, with the US noting the position of the PRC.

Thus the road was cleared to what ultimately became a normalization of PRC–US relations. Liaison offices were set up in 1973, but the establishment of full diplomatic representation was delayed, largely due to problems of American domestic politics, until the end of 1978.

The establishment of direct contact between the PRC and US governments created an entirely new situation in what has often been referred to as the Moscow-Beijing-Washington triangle. Throughout the rest of the 1970s, however, the absence of any meaningful dialogue between the Soviet Union and the PRC – a factor which seems to have resulted more from the multitude of mutual grievances and resentments accumulated during the preceding fifteen years than from any objective clash of national interests – allowed the United States to occupy the most favourable position in this peculiar formation, although it had done precious little to deserve such good fortune.

As the process of rebuilding the CCP unfolded slowly from 1969 on, some of those who had been repressed and removed from their posts in the Party and state apparatus were now rehabilitated and permitted to resume their work. Many of them had spent considerable time in the peculiar institution known as the May Seventh Cadre School. Its name derived from the directive issued on that day in 1966 by Mao Zedong, in which he called for the re-education of the intellectuals by the workers, peasants and soldiers. This was to be accomplished by sending the intellectuals down to the countryside to engage in physical labour similar to that which the peasants pursued throughout their lives.

The May Seventh Cadre Schools, first set up in late 1968, soon became a nationwide phenomenon since every urban institution, whether university or government agency, was obliged to establish such a school for its own staff. In most cases the schools were run by specially delegated PLA members, with stress laid on military discipline and incessant indoctrination. Since the schools, in reality, became independent units, not in any way integrated with adjacent villages, the aim of establishing direct contact with the peasants and their lives was not achieved at all. The time spent in a school was decided by the PLA cadres running it, based on their evaluation of the inmate's 'political level'; in some cases this resulted in incarceration until 1976 when these institutions were finally closed down. Although the May Seventh Schools were the subject of much propaganda in the 1970s and were presented by the media as a splendid solution to the problems of intellectual alienation, one might well conclude from the accounts of those who experienced them that they were little more than glorified labour camps.

The alleviation of the political crisis brought about by the Lin Biao affair called for great efforts to restore once again some semblance of stability and to repair the damage inflicted upon the CCP's image. An intensive propaganda campaign was launched in 1972 for the purpose of exposing the nature of Lin Biao's nefarious conspiracy. According to the present CCP leadership, Zhou Enlai, having 'taken charge of the day-to-day work of the Central Committee', played a crucial role in these endeavours, obtaining 'improvement in all fields'.

However, the situation within the top leadership was certainly not conducive to a quick or easy victory for the forces represented by Zhou Enlai. The Jiang Qing faction within the Political Bureau, which became stronger and more influential after the downfall of its rival, undoubtedly opposed Zhou's efforts. This applied particularly to his proposed analysis of the Lin Biao affair as a manifestation of ultra-leftism – which, in effect, it was. The Jiang Qing clique was quick to understand that such an approach could lead not only to a repudiation of the 'cultural revolution' itself, it could gravely endanger its own position, since its ultra-leftist stand in the years 1966–9 could be demonstrated without the slightest difficulty. Ultimately, Mao Zedong disapproved of the proposals advocated by Zhou Enlai and his colleagues, maintaining that 'the task was still to oppose the "ultra right" '. This view might well have been motivated by Mao's unwillingness at this or any other time to disavow his misbegotten child, the 'cultural revolution'. It seems probable, nonetheless, that the Jiang Qing faction's easy access to him was also an important factor leading to the maintenance of basically ultra-leftist policies.

By the summer of 1973 the political situation was deemed to have been sufficiently stabilized for the Party's theoretically supreme ruling body to meet once again, and the Tenth Party Congress was convened in Beijing on 24–28 August. It was held in complete secrecy, with no information about it being released until after its completion. Once again the delegates were selected and not elected, although the organizational structure of the Party had by now been basically restored and the election of delegates at lower level Party conferences could presumably have been carried out. The delegates were supposed to represent a greatly increased Party membership; it was said to number 28 million, a rise of 11 million since 1962.

The demise of Lin Biao necessitated another revision of the Party constitution, since the bothersome paragraph pertaining to him had to be deleted. But the question of succession remained, and to all appearances the new candidate for this unenviable post was none other than Wang Hongwen, whose career as a member of the Shanghai clique has already been noted. Wang was entrusted with delivering the report on the revision of the Party constitution, while Zhou Enlai gave the principal report on the Party's political line. These two reports and a communiqué are the only documents available pertaining to this Congress.

A considerable part of Zhou Enlai's speech was devoted to the case of the 'renegade and traitor' Lin Biao, and the defeat of his faction was presented as the greatest triumph of the Party since the Ninth Congress in 1969. The political line adopted at that time was presented by Zhou as still fully valid and no other guidelines were mentioned, except for the repetition of generalities and some of Mao Zedong's delphic utterances such as 'dig tunnels deep, store grain everywhere and never seek hegemony'. It is most likely for this reason that the 1981 Resolution takes the Tenth Congress to task for 'perpetuating the "Left" errors of the Ninth Congress'.

The situation within the country, and especially its economic aspect, was dismissed in Zhou's speech in four sentences, and summarized as the 'scoring of new victories in socialist construction'. In this respect Zhou Enlai followed the model of the Ninth Congress where similarly only a few platitudinous phrases were devoted to the issues affecting the welfare of 800 million Chinese.

As a result of the Lin Biao affair new elections to the supreme bodies of the CCP were held during the Congress. The new Central Committee, slightly larger at 195 full members and 124 alternates than the one it replaced, included a majority of those who had held seats in the previous body, but there was one quite significant difference: the representation of the PLA dropped from 45 to 31 per cent. This change reflected not only the consequences of the downfall of Lin Biao, but the determination of the majority of the top leadership to restore the primacy of the Party and to reduce the political dominance which the armed forces had acquired in the course of the 'cultural revolution'. Mao Zedong himself took the lead in formulating this approach; he is said to have expressed this by stating that it was time that the PLA, formerly held up as a model to be emulated, should start learning from the people. In December 1973, a further decisive measure was taken to cut down the political power of the military when there was a reshuffle of eight of the twelve commanders of the key military regions.

Alterations had to be made at the apex of authority too, for Lin Biao had been the Party's sole vice chairman. Five vice chairmen were now nominated – Zhou Enlai, Wang Hongwen, Kang Sheng, Ye Jianying, and Li Desheng who was a Long March veteran and a relatively unknown senior PLA official. His career had advanced rapidly during the 'cultural revolution' and he became an alternate member of the Political Bureau in 1969. The Standing Committee of the Political Bureau, reduced to three members by September 1971, was now enlarged to nine: Mao Zedong, the five vice chairmen, the two octogenarian Party veterans Zhu De and Dong Biwu, and Zhang Chunqiao. The number of full members of the Bureau was kept at twenty-one, and the gaps created by the elimination of the Lin Biao faction were filled either by prominent military leaders such as Xu Shiyu, Chen Xilian and Wei Guoqing or top Party and security officials such as Hua Guofeng, Ji Dengkui, Wu De and Wang Dongxing. One well-publicized peasant, Chen Yonggui, was also included.

Just as in the case of its predecessor, the Tenth Congress was proclaimed as 'a congress of unity, a congress of victory and a congress full of vigour'. How inaccurate these claims were was demonstrated by the political events of the next three years.

CHAPTER NINE

—⚜—

The Last Years,
August 1973–September 1976

The superficial nature of the unity of the CCP heralded triumphantly at the Tenth Congress first became apparent in the
ensuing struggle for succession. The outcome of this contest was
crucial, for it would determine what fundamental policies
would be formulated to guide the country's future.

The numerous ideological campaigns which followed one
another in this period reflected the factional strife within the
highest echelon of the Party, although often the esoteric nature
of the arguments employed served to conceal the true aims of
the contestants. This was particularly true of the movement to
criticize Confucius, inaugurated already in the summer of 1973
but much intensified the following year. A veritable flood of
articles and essays appeared, sponsored primarily by the Jiang
Qing faction which had a special group of writers at its beck and
call in Shanghai and Beijing. The articles sought to depict Confucius as a reactionary who favoured the restoration of the slave
system and opposed the rise of the new feudal order, as represented by the first Qin emperor, Shihuang. It should be noted
that the views expressed in this and subsequent campaigns completely distorted the Marxist analysis of ancient Chinese history.
The purpose was to conduct political warfare by means of historical analogies and allusions, a method often resorted to in
China's past. Thus, for the sake of scoring points against their
opponents, Jiang Qing's polemicists extolled Qin Shihuang –
who had been hated and despised for his tyranny and the sufferings he imposed on the people by the entire first generation of
Chinese communists – as a great progressive leader and unifier

189

of the country. The Legalist School, well known for its almost proto-fascist authoritarianism, was praised in similar terms and its struggle against the Confucianists, allegedly already reactionary at this time, warmly approved. All these distortions of history, which incidentally revealed a thoroughgoing contempt for the country's cultural heritage, could be passed over in silence were it not for the fact that this was one of the basic forms of the current political struggle. The great Confucianist of the present was clearly Zhou Enlai, while the upholders of the progressive Qin emperor were, of course, Jiang Qing's faction. The movement to criticize Confucius became linked with the campaign against Lin Biao, since it was sought now to represent Lin as a Confucianist.

The relative ease with which the Jiang Qing faction was able to conduct its 'cultural' campaigns was explained by the fact that control of the CCP's propaganda and ideological activities rested almost entirely in its hands. It also continued to invoke the authority of Mao Zedong, claiming that he approved of the views it was propagating. However, it is very difficult to ascertain the extent to which Mao – now in his eighties, increasingly debilitated by Parkinson's disease – was able to exercise his dominant influence and participate in crucial policy- and decision-making. By now he had reached a truly tragic stage of becoming – as an acute observer of the Chinese scene has remarked – his own epigone. This transformation may well have occurred as early as 1966.

Zhou Enlai's endless and untiring endeavours had also taken their toll. By 1972 he knew that he was ill with cancer, but he did not cease to labour on. From May 1974 he was almost permanently in hospital. Zhou's illness was surely one of the factors that gave rise to the astounding reappearance in the Chinese political arena of the man castigated in 1966 as 'the number two capitalist roader'. Deng Xiaoping returned from exile in Jiangxi in the spring of 1973, to take up one of his former posts, that of vice premier. At the Tenth Congress he was shown sitting in the back row of the Presidium with Deng Yingzhao, Zhou Enlai's wife and a veteran senior communist leader in her own right.

Deng, now sixty-nine years old, was re-elected to the Central Committee. By January 1974 he had been co-opted to the Political Bureau, and from May he became the acting premier, seeking to implement the policies advocated by the ailing Zhou Enlai, in face of the mounting overt and covert opposition of the ambitious, power-seeking Jiang Qing faction. In January 1975, at the Second Plenum of the Central Committee, Deng was elevated to the Standing Committee of the Political Bureau, becoming simultaneously vice chairman of the Military Affairs Commission and chief of staff of the PLA. A few days later he became first vice premier. This large accumulation of key Party and state functions signified that as well as being acting premier Deng was in fact in charge of the day-to-day activities of the Central Committee.

The re-emergence of Deng Xiaoping signalled the return to political life of thousands of higher and middle echelon experienced veteran CCP members who – in contrast to Liu Shaoqi, Peng Dehuai, Tao Zhu, He Long and many others – had been fortunate enough to survive the horrors of the 'cultural revolution's' first stage. Most of these men resumed the positions that they had held up to 1966, or their equivalent, and almost automatically supported the policies advocated by Zhou Enlai and Deng Xiaoping. Their return to power was no doubt bitterly opposed and resented by the assorted numerous careerists who had jumped on the 'cultural revolution' bandwagon and became its beneficiaries, taking an active part in the downfall of those now returning. Fearful of possible retribution and a 'settling of accounts' for their deeds, these opportunists flocked to support the Jiang Qing clique and upheld its opposition to any further 'reversal of verdicts', i.e. rehabilitation of repressed and persecuted veteran cadres.

The return of the victims of the 'cultural revolution' to their former places of employment created almost insuperable problems. How do you work in the same institution, or the same room, and attend the same Party meetings as the person who slandered and spat upon you – often literally – at denunciation meetings, who held you incarcerated for months on end in a 'cowshed' (a special prison set up by the Red Guards and Revolutionary Rebels in the grounds of their own institutions), who refused you permission to visit your wife dying of cancer, who then stole her watch which you wanted to keep as a memento? For all this, and many more drastic deeds, did take place during the 'cultural revolution'. Chen Yi's warning of its consequences was prophetic indeed; the problem of the persecutors and the persecuted haunts the political life of the PRC to the present day.

In January 1975, the Fourth National People's Congress, nominally the PRC's governing body, assembled for the first time since the end of 1964. Zhou Enlai left his sick-bed to attend it, as he had a few days earlier to preside over the Second Plenum of the Central Committee. In his speech to the NPC – the last he ever gave – Zhou stressed the need for China to embark on a programme of comprehensive modernization in four domains – agriculture, industry, national defence, science and technology. It could be considered his bequest, which the post-1978 CCP leadership is devoting its main efforts to fulfilling.

Zhou Enlai's last public appearance took place in June. The dying man left the hospital to attend a memorial service for He Long. The Chinese media, under the thumb of the Jiang Qing clique, did not devote a single word to either the service or the premier's presence.

From the beginning of 1975, Deng Xiaoping sought to elaborate with the help of a group of his closest associates a new, general approach to the fundamental problems facing the country. The group included Hu Yaobang and Hu Qiaomu. Born in 1914 into a Jiangsu gentry family, Hu Qiaomu had been a CCP member since 1935 and spent the War of Resistance in Yan'an. After liberation he held high posts in the Central Committee, to which he belonged from 1956. He was victimized during the 'cultural revolution'. Hu is known to be the author of a number of key CCP documents and has the reputation of being one of the CCP's ablest theoreticians.

A study was prepared dealing with the problems of acceleration of industrial development, in which stress was placed on the ways and means of bringing about a liberation of productive forces. This constituted, in Deng's view, the fundamental probing test of all future policies. In his speeches during the first half of 1975, Deng maintained that the three instructions recently put forth by Mao Zedong – study the theory of the dictatorship of the proletariat; achieve stability and unity; boost the economy – formed an organic whole and should be regarded as a key link in the work of the Party. Progress in this direction could not be achieved without eliminating the widespread phenomenon of factionalism, obviously one of the main byproducts of the 'cultural revolution', which was being constantly stimulated by the ultra-left policies of the Jiang Qing clique.

In effect, the programme advocated by Deng Xiaoping, who had numerous supporters in the Party and state establishment, especially among the rehabilitated veteran cadres, signified a desire to do away with the principal characteristics of the 'cultural revolution', in particular with two of its central theses – 'politics in command' and 'the class struggle as the key link' with its concomitant emphasis on interminable ideological campaigning and mass mobilization. A second study dealt with the problems concerning work in science and technology, including that of the Academy of Sciences. Finally, a third document was devoted to presenting a general programme of work for the Party and country as a whole.

The policies favoured by Deng Xiaoping and his followers signified the first step in a reversion to the sound and pragmatic course of development pursued in the earlier period of the PRC, as symbolized by the 1956 Eighth Congress. Thus, implicitly, they constituted a rejection and negation of the 'cultural revolution', although in 1975 this could not be and was not – for understandable tactical reasons – spelled out openly. Nonetheless, the Jiang Qing faction quickly understood the danger to its position that a successful implementation of Deng's policies implied, and lost no time in launching its assault on him. It can be assumed that Jiang Qing and her accomplices were also able to influence Mao Zedong, in spite of the critical attitude he is supposed to have displayed towards them at this time, since his approach to Deng's policies and activities – always marked by much ambivalence – became increasingly hostile in the second half of 1975. While he himself had expressed the need for achieving stability after nine years of the 'cultural revolution', he still regarded its results favourably, assessing its achievements in relation to its failures in a ratio of 7 to 3, a formula he applied frequently and widely. In the words of the 1981 Resolution, he 'could not bear to accept systematic correction of the errors of the "cultural revolution" by Deng Xiaoping'. It can be argued that Mao in fact feared such a correction, since it would inevitably lead to an out-and-out repudiation of the 'cultural revolution'. Thus, 'he triggered the movement to "criticize Deng and counter the Right Deviation trend to revise current verdicts", once again plunging the nation into turmoil'. The Jiang Qing faction mounted an increasingly vehement and vicious propaganda campaign against the 'unrepentant capitalist roader'. It followed closely a period in which the ultra-leftist line received, in the course of the discussion on the dictatorship of the proletariat, what was perhaps its fullest exposition.

The vision of the future advanced by Zhang Chunqiao, the 'brain' of the Jiang Qing clique, was one of intensified, long and tortuous class struggle, necessitating the exercise of an 'all-round dictatorship over the bourgeoisie' in all fields. Hence, the ideology and programme of the ultra-leftists became still more akin to fascism: social demagogy on a massive scale; a systematically sustained cult of the Great Leader, whose every utterance must be believed and followed (Mussolini's *credere, obbedire*) even if not understood (this phrase is Lin Biao's, but the Jiang Qing clique adhered to it just as much); contempt for culture, and even greater for the people, treated as malleable clay; glorification of autocratic tyranny (Qin Shihuang); and, still more significantly, the advocacy of ruthless authoritarian methods of suppressing alleged class enemies. Add the arrant nationalism seeping out from the various claims to 'revolutionary superiority', and the ideology resembled fascism in all but name. It probably would not be too difficult to find that an appropriate lumpen and petty bourgeois social basis existed for it as well. Is

194

it necessary to add another pejorative adjective to describe this weird concoction? Perhaps not. But the term 'feudal' does point to the historical sources of many of the ideas advanced and the methods employed by the ultra-left in China, which endowed it with character all its own. The really challenging problem is how and why such a phenomenon could arise in a society in which all the prerequisites theoretically necessary for the construction of socialism had been created earlier. Perhaps something indispensable – democracy, for example – had been omitted.

Paradoxically, Mao Zedong himself had pointed a number of times to the possibility of a ruling communist party changing its colour, transforming itself into a fascist one. This danger was one of the principal arguments he used in support of the struggle against 'revisionism' and the launching of the 'cultural revolution'. But it was precisely in the course of the latter that fascist features clearly emerged, largely as a result of the activities of the two cliques led by his closest collaborators, Lin Biao and Jiang Qing. It will probably never be known whether, in the cloistered existence of his last years, any awareness of these evils arose in Mao's mind.

On 8 January 1976, Zhou Enlai succumbed to his fatal illness. His last words to his doctors and nurses were, 'There is little you can do for me here. Go and look after the others who need you more.' Characteristically, he also specified that no mausoleum should hold his remains, requesting that his ashes be scattered over the rivers and fields of his native land. Three days later, in the bitter and penetrating cold of a Beijing winter, millions of his countrymen stood for hours along the Avenue of Eternal Peace to pay their last respects to a man they revered. The sobbing of the crowd could be heard from a twelfth-storey window.

The memorial service for Zhou Enlai was held on 15 January and attended by the entire Chinese leadership with the exception of Mao Zedong. Deng Xiaoping delivered the eulogy in which he did full justice to Zhou Enlai's outstanding contribution to the victory of the Chinese Revolution and his role in the building of the PRC. It was to be Deng's last public appearance for well over a year. The name of Zhou Enlai also quickly disappeared from the media.

Within less than a month of Zhou Enlai's death it was announced that at Mao Zedong's instigation not Deng Xiaoping, the *de facto* premier since May 1974, but the comparatively unknown Hua Guofeng would become the acting premier and also run the day-to-day work of the Central Committee. Hua was in some respects a representative of the second generation of CCP leaders. Born in 1921 into a peasant family in Shanxi, he joined the communist movement during the War of Resistance, becoming a Party functionary in one of the Liberated Areas. After liberation he continued to work as a Party official in Hunan, advancing steadily from the post of secretary in Mao Zedong's native district to that of the province's first secretary. In 1971 Hua was transferred to Beijing; two years later he became a Political Bureau member and minister of public security. In January 1975 he was made a vice premier.

What lay behind this move was of course Mao Zedong's earlier decision to reject the policies pursued by Deng Xiaoping. The propaganda campaign against Deng broadened considerably in January and February. Deng's proposal to take Mao's Three Instructions as the key link in all work was now interpreted by the Jiang Qing faction as a revisionist attempt to restore capitalism, an attack on Mao himself, a rightist deviation aimed at splitting the Party, and so forth. The barrage of criticism was conveyed not only by the central media but became the subject as well of numerous big-character posters at Beijing's main universities. The identity of the 'unrepentant capitalist roader' and 'China's Khrushchev number two' was not hard to guess.

A new element aimed at discrediting veteran cadres was introduced into this violent dispute. Having fought for decades for the country's liberation, the veteran cadres were now to be considered bourgeois democrats and not Marxist socialists. Moreover, it was claimed that they had become capitalist roaders. Still more significantly, a recent statement attributed to Mao Zedong was produced in March to buttress the political line of the Jiang

Qing clique. It included the following observation: 'You are making the socialist revolution and yet don't know where the bourgeoisie is. It is right in the Communist Party – those in power taking the capitalist road. The capitalist roaders are still on the capitalist road.' If authentic, then the statement reveals Mao's total unwillingness to alter in the slightest his positive assessment of the disastrous policies he had pursued since 1966.

In the spring of 1976, a unique occurrence in the history of People's China took place – the Tiananmen movement, an immense and spontaneous demonstration of protest by a supposedly docile people against injustice and oppression, motivated basically by a sense of pride, dignity and self-respect.

The Tiananmen movement, which in some respects deserves to take its place alongside its famous predecessors, the May Fourth and the December Ninth, was partly a popular reaction to the assaults of the Jiang Qing faction on Zhou Enlai, continued even after his death. Two items carried in a Shanghai newspaper, obviously the work of this clique, referred to Zhou by clear innuendo as a capitalist roader and aroused nationwide indignation. Posters went up in Nanjing attacking the clique and calling for action to prevent its seizing power. The coming of the Qingming Festival – the traditional day of remembrance for the dead – provided the occasion for a further expression of popular sentiment. From late March wreaths and poems eulogizing Zhou Enlai were placed in growing numbers on the Monument to the People's Heroes in the middle of Tiananmen Square. By 4 April, 2 million people from the capital and the provinces had been to the monument to pay their respects to Zhou. The pile of wreaths rose thirty feet high on all its sides. Thousands of poems reflecting the people's feelings were recited and copied by the participants. The workers at a Beijing factory, having heard that the paper wreaths were being removed and burned, brought in an indestructible steel one, 6.5 metres high and weighing over 500 kilos.

On that day a section of the CCP leadership, including Hua Guofeng and the Jiang Qing group, obtained Mao Zedong's agreement that the demonstration was being instigated by counter-revolutionaries and his approval of appropriate measures being taken. Plainclothes policemen were sent to the square to photograph the poems and identify the most active participants; around thirty of them were arrested. During the night of 4/5 April, 200 police lorries were used to remove all the wreaths and poems. In the morning, an angry crowd of over 10,000 people gathered, growing during the day to close to 100,000. They scuffled for hours with the police, demanding the return of the wreaths and poems. In the evening, the police went into action, clubs swinging, against the remaining demonstrators. Over 200 people were arrested. During the following weeks the public security forces scurried through every factory and institution in Beijing, carrying out further arrests, searching for other participants in the demonstration and, above all, the non-existent 'counter-revolutionary' organizers of the Tiananmen movement.

Fear reigned supreme throughout the country, for smaller-scale demonstrations had taken place in a number of other cities as well, including Nanjing, Hangzhou and Zhengzhou. But a crucial step towards ending the 'cultural revolution' had been taken by the people themselves.

The immediate political consequences of the Tiananmen incident became apparent within the next few days. On 7 April it was announced that the Political Bureau had agreed, on the proposal of Mao Zedong, to appoint Hua Guofeng first vice chairman of the Central Committee and premier. In a second resolution, released simultaneously, it was stated that 'The nature of the Deng Xiaoping problem has turned into one of antagonistic contradiction' and, again on the proposal of Mao Zedong, the Political Bureau 'agreed to dismiss Deng Xiaoping from all posts both inside and outside the Party while allowing him to keep his Party membership so as to see how he will behave in the future'.

It appeared, at the time, that Deng's political career had been terminated once and for all. The nationwide propaganda campaign against him took on even more extreme forms. He was portrayed as a counter-revolutionary revisionist, a Chinese Imre Nagy, and also as the principal instigator of the Tiananmen incident. The three basic policy documents prepared in 1975 by Deng and his associates were now referred to as the three poisonous weeds which revealed his aim to restore capitalism. The assault became not only the major topic of all the media, it was the compulsory subject of all meetings, Party and mass organizations alike.

A reception was held in Beijing on 26 April to honour the public security men who had suppressed the Tiananmen demonstration. It was attended by most of the CCP leadership, with the notable, and in retrospect significant, exceptions of Li Xiannian and Ye Jianying. The latter is reported to have arranged the transfer of Deng Xiaoping for his own safety from house arrest in Beijing to Guangzhou.

The inexorable advance of age had been taking its toll of the first generation of Chinese communist leaders. Zhou Enlai's death had been preceded eight months earlier by that of the universally respected Dong Biwu. In July, it was the turn of ninety-year-old Zhu De. The modest, good-natured, unpretentious and unambitious soldier-peasant's contribution to the victory of the Chinese Revolution as the co-founder of the Chinese Red Army, the commander of the Eighth Route Army and the PLA up to 1949, was undeniable; even the falsifiers of CCP history had been unable to efface it successfully during the earlier years of the 'cultural revolution'.

The year 1976 took on a more ominous aspect in this same month when a terrible disaster shook north China. An earthquake of gigantic proportions, 8.2 on the Richter scale, razed the industrial and mining centre of Tangshan; a quarter of a million of its inhabitants lay dead in the ruins. The entire country rushed to the aid of the stricken area, the PLA playing an especially active role in the relief operations. Hua Guofeng promptly visited the Tangshan, but the members of the Jiang Qing group did not bother. Instead, they issued, in the name of the Central Committee, an appeal to the survivors which ended with an exhortation to 'study earnestly Chairman Mao's important directives, to deepen and broaden, with class struggle as the link, the criticism of Deng Xiaoping's counter-revolutionary revisionist line, and the great struggle of the counter-attack against the rightist storm of verdict reversal'.

In the spring of 1976 the custom of having especially prominent foreign guests climax their stay in China by paying a call on Mao Zedong was still being practised. The last to do so on 26 May was Bhutto, the ill-fated prime minister of Pakistan. On 15 June it was announced that Mao would not be receiving foreign guests any more. Thereafter, no further news regarding his activities or the state of his health appeared in the media.

Mao Zedong died on 9 September 1976. With his death a remarkable era in the history of the Chinese Revolution came to an end. It should be abundantly clear from what has been said thus far that the drawing up of an appropriate assessment of his crucial and often decisive role in the first twenty-seven years of People's China, and of his unquestionably outstanding place in modern Chinese history, strictly conforming to and based on known facts, is a formidable task indeed. It is also a subject which has always been, and will no doubt remain, highly controversial. The present writer is still inclined to the view that he expressed some years ago that, ultimately, Mao Zedong's life and deeds might well appear, in the immense span of Chinese history, a moment as brief, in Sima Qian's memorable phrase, as the glimpse through a crack in the wall of a running white colt.

The news of Mao's death was announced with great solemnity. Although it was not unexpected, it undoubtedly came as a shock, not least because there was no way in which the people could know what the future held in store for them. The omniscient and infallible Great Leader had departed. Who would succeed him? For the question of succession seemed to remain open; all that appeared certain was that it would be settled primarily by the top leadership of the CCP. Whether, and to what degree, popular sentiment – as demonstrated in the Tiananmen incident – would be taken into account was as yet unclear, as was the equally crucial issue of what policies a new leader would pursue. Would he or she desire to continue the disastrous course of the 'cultural revolution', or seek a way out of the critical situation it had created?

A nationwide period of mourning was proclaimed for 11–18 September, culminating in a memorial rally at which Hua Guofeng delivered the eulogy. However, even as the sombre ceremonies were being held, the first steps in the denouement were already being taken. There exist at least half a dozen different versions of the dramatic events in Beijing during the three weeks ending on 6 October. Hence, the following reconstruction is only tentative.

The Jiang Qing clique hastened its preparations to take over full power, claiming that Mao Zedong himself had expressed the wish to have Jiang Qing succeed him as chairman of the Central Committee. Control of the central media was the clique's strongest card, and it hoped that if need be it could rely on the People's Militia, much expanded during the preceding years, especially in what was supposed to be the faction's stronghold – Shanghai. Furthermore, help could be expected from some of the military forces in the north-east where Mao Yuanxin, Mao's nephew and a close collaborator of Jiang Qing, was political commissar in the Liaoning military region. Jiang Qing and her accomplices also hoped to obtain the assistance of one of Mao Zedong's closest collaborators who occupied a crucial position in Beijing – Wang Dongxing. Born in 1912 into a poor peasant family in Jiangxi, Wang had served in the Red Army since 1933 and during the last struggle against the Guomindang was Mao's chief bodyguard. After liberation, he remained in the security service of the Central Committee under Kang Sheng, holding from 1955 the post of deputy minister of Public Security. In 1967 he replaced Yang Shangkun in the key position of head of the Central Committee's General Office, becoming also commander of the 8341 special guard unit. Wang was made an alternate member of the Political Bureau in 1969, becoming a full member in 1973.

Plans were also laid for enlisting the aid of the commander of the Beijing garrison, Chen Xilian. Born in 1913 into a poor peasant family in Hubei, Chen joined the Red Army in 1930 to become by 1949 one of its bravest and most outstanding generals. From 1969 Chen also served as a Political Bureau member.

There is no doubt whatsoever that at least three other members of the Political Bureau – Hua Guofeng, the first vice chairman and premier, Ye Jianying, a vice premier and minister of defence, and Li Xiannian, a vice premier and minister of finance – were more than aware of the machinations of the Jiang Qing clique. At the same time, they probably felt able to rely, more or less, on the support of the remaining nine surviving members of the Political Bureau should action have to be taken against the quartet headed by Jiang Qing.

It is reported that in the first days of October a meeting was held by the Jiang Qing group at which the final plan for taking power was to be determined. Chen Xilian and Wang Dongxing had been invited to attend in order to obtain their indispensable assistance. News of the meeting reached Hua and Ye almost immediately. When questioned, Chen admitted his presence at the meeting; Wang went further and disclosed the entire plan of the Jiang Qing faction.

The reaction was swift. On 6 October Jiang Qing, Zhang Chunqiao, Wang Hongwen and Yao Wenyuan were arrested by soldiers of unit 8341, led by Wang Dongxing. Henceforth they were referred to as the 'gang of four', a term attributed to Mao Zedong himself, who is said to have used it in criticizing them to their faces in July 1974 and May 1975. In the 1981 Resolution the passage dealing with this event reads: 'The Political Bureau of the Central Committee, executing the will of the Party and the people, resolutely smashed the clique and brought the catastrophic "cultural revolution" to an end.' The last eight words convey the full significance of the arrests. The leaders of the not inconsiderable stratum of beneficiaries of the 'cultural revolution', who were doing their utmost to prolong and even renew its excesses, had been put out of action. Within days of the arrest of the 'gang of four' their principal supporters in Beijing (including two ministers) and in the provinces, especially Shanghai, had been rounded up. The whole operation was quick, efficient and almost completely bloodless. There was no sign that the 'gang of four' had had any real mass support at all.

The Resolution goes on to state: 'Hua Guofeng, Ye Jianying,

Li Xiannian and other comrades played a vital part in the struggle to crush the clique.' The other comrades were, in this instance, Chen Xilian and Wang Dongxing in the first place. And whom did these five men represent? Assuredly a majority of the Central Committee, the great majority of the senior members of the central and provincial Party apparatus, especially those who had been victimized and then rehabilitated, also a majority of the PLA, the state administration, and public security forces. More than enough to overpower the 'gang of four' and its media.

On 10 October it was announced that, in accordance with a Central Committee resolution passed on 7 October, Hua Guofeng had been nominated chairman of the Central Committee and chairman of the Military Affairs Commission. There is no record of a full Central Committee meeting having been held on that day; it was more than likely a Political Bureau decision, perhaps made in consultation with some of the Central Committee members available in Beijing. Rumours regarding the arrest of the 'gang of four' were circulating in the capital by 12 October. The news was officially released on 21 October, and a million people attended a victory rally in Tiananmen Square on 24 October. Around 50 million people in all are said to have been present at similar meetings throughout the country. All accounts of foreign observers agree that the downfall of the 'gang of four' was greeted universally with an authentic demonstration of joy and unalloyed relief. Moreover, at least a dozen sources repeat one identical story. Although the Chinese have always had the reputation of being rather moderate drinkers, all the liquor stores were emptied within a few hours of the news being released; it was really an occasion for celebrating to one's heart's content.

The 'cultural revolution' was over. Now, People's China had to face the infinitely complex problem of how to pick up the pieces and put the country back on the road to normal and sensible development.

PART THREE

Seek Truth from Facts
1976–86

CHAPTER TEN

Facing Up to the Past,
September 1976–December 1978

The leadership of the CCP was faced in the late autumn of 1976 with a bewilderingly complex set of problems if the attempt to rehabilitate the country, ravaged economically, politically and morally by the decade of the 'cultural revolution', was to be accomplished successfully.

Practically no reliable statistical data were published in the PRC in the decade 1966–76, and it was not possible then to delineate a true picture of the economic consequences of the 'cultural revolution'. Since 1982, however, the situation has improved greatly; much new material has been provided by Chinese sources, and a reconstruction of the main lines of economic development is now feasible.

The figures for steel output can be considered an indicator of the general level of industrial production. Having reached 15.3 million tons in 1966 (compared to 12.2 million in 1965), steel production sank to 10.2 million in 1967 and 9 million in 1968. This would tend to confirm the estimates that overall industrial production fell in 1967 by around 20 per cent and by at least 10 per cent in 1968. In 1969 steel output mounted to 13.3 million tons, rising to 17.7 million in 1970. It reached its highest level for the decade in 1973 at 25.2 million, sinking to 20.4 million in 1976.

Significant increases occurred in the oil and coal industry largely due to the utilization of reserves and a very high rate of investment, as well as the intensive work of those employed in these fields. Oil production increased from 14.5 million tons in 1966 to 87.1 million in 1976, while coal output rose from 252 million tons in 1966 to 483 million in 1976.

Grain production fell from 214 million tons in 1966 to 210 million in 1969. After this most turbulent period of the 'cultural revolution', production increased, as the 1981 Resolution notes, 'relatively steadily', from 239 million in 1970 to 286 million in 1976. However, it should be borne in mind that the population grew from 745 million in 1966 to 937 million in 1976, an increase of 192 million (the total population of Japan and France combined, as a Chinese economist pointed out). The increase in grain output barely kept ahead of demographic growth and grain rations remained at an almost unchanged level throughout the decade, as did pork rations. The allowance of edible vegetable oil, an indispensable ingredient in Chinese cooking and diet and already severely rationed, decreased still more. The situation was also unfavourable relative to the production of cotton, which fluctuated from 2.3 million tons in 1966, up to 2.5 million in 1973, down to 2 million in 1976. The skimpy ration of cotton cloth remained the same.

The policy throughout the decade consistently favoured capital accumulation; investment in productive capital construction was therefore much greater than in non-productive construction such as housing, schools, etc.

There is little doubt that the standard of living in the PRC during the 'cultural revolution' remained basically unchanged at its previous extremely low level. This was in part due to the 'tremendous losses' resulting from the disorganization of everyday life during the 'cultural revolution', especially in 1966–9. It is also ascribed to the activities of the Lin Biao and Jiang Qing cliques, since the interminable political campaigns they initiated and pursued had a disastrously disruptive effect on the normal functioning of the economy, a conclusion which is substantiated by the figures relating to the growth of national income.

The present CCP leadership maintains that some progress was made during this decade and some significant achievements attained. There was one field of production where the negative effects of the 'cultural revolution' were reduced as quickly as possible – atomic technology connected with national defence. Already in October 1964 the first atomic bomb had been tested successfully, with a second experiment taking place in 1965. The first hydrogen bomb was tested in June 1967 and the second one in September 1969. However, 'none of these successes can be attributed in any way to the "cultural revolution", without which far greater achievements could have been gained'. This appears to be a fully justified assessment, based on the facts, and buttressed by a comparison with the growth rates achieved in all fields in the years before and after the 'cultural revolution'.

The economic consequences of the 'cultural revolution' were dire enough. Some of the CCP leaders, Hua Guofeng for example, even maintained that by October 1976 the economy was 'on the brink of collapse'. But clearly the human cost was by far the greater tragedy. Hundreds of thousands of people died, countless numbers were imprisoned, innumerable families were broken; the litany of suffering which resulted directly from this artificially instigated catastrophe is endless and its effects on all those who lived through it must have been traumatic, to say the least. Yet the 1981 Resolution states that 'the Party . . . and Chinese society on the whole remained unchanged in nature' after going through this ordeal. This is highly debatable although the reasons for advancing the thesis can be understood: to preserve a semblance of continuity and to refurbish the Party's overall credibility. In discussing in 1977 one aspect of the problems which the Party faced, Deng Xiaoping noted that during these ten years the Party's standards of social conduct had become debased, 'things reached such a pass that many of our Party comrades dared not speak out, and, in particular, dared not tell the truth but resorted to pretence and deception'. If this was true of the country's political elite – and it is hard to say why Deng's evaluation should not be accepted – then surely Chinese society as a whole must have been no less affected. In other words, it did not emerge from the 'cultural revolution' unchanged. On the other hand, it is true to say that 'enormous vitality' was displayed not so much by the Party and the socialist system – as is claimed – but by the Chinese people, who have demonstrated this quality time and time again in their four millennia of unending struggle against oppression. It did take enormous vitality to survive this last horrible visitation of fate.

There had been a large degree of unanimity among the senior CCP leaders as to the advisability of ridding the Party and the country of the 'gang of four'. There was much less accord as to how the political future was to be shaped. Above all, opinions were sharply divided over two crucial issues: should the programme of the Great Proletarian Cultural Revolution, with all that this implied, be upheld, or should it be discarded and replaced with one which would correspond to the country's actual needs? The first choice had one immense advantage – it would seemingly make political continuity possible and those advocating it would be able to cloak themselves in the mantle of full legitimacy. The second course was hazardous indeed, for it implied submitting the 'cultural revolution' to a searching analysis and criticism, considered indispensable for clearing the road for the country's rehabilitation.

The second issue was bound up almost entirely with the personality cult. Mao Zedong's role during the years 1966–76 was clear to everyone; he was the author and prime mover of the Great Proletarian Cultural Revolution. A repudiation of it would automatically mean evaluating his position and activities. Could this be accomplished without irreparably shattering his image as the founder of People's China, and, perhaps still more important, without inflicting permanent damage on the prestige and credibility of the Party? A number of the top CCP leaders and especially Hua Guofeng, now ensconced as Mao's successor as chairman of the Central Committee, appeared to be convinced that there was only one possible answer to both these questions. The 'cultural revolution' should be appraised positively and the cult of Mao Zedong should be propagated much as in the past. These views were reflected at the very outset in the decision taken on 8 October 1976 to build a mausoleum for the departed leader and to entrust Hua with the editing and publishing of the next, fifth, volume of Mao Zedong's Selected Works. Moreover, within the next six months, this approach was to be expressed in what can be considered the basic ideological position of Hua Guofeng and some of his colleagues in the Political Bureau, such as Wang Dongxing. It was known as the 'two whatevers' stance. The expression comes from an editorial of 7 February, which reads: 'We will resolutely uphold whatever policy decisions Chairman Mao made, and unswervingly follow whatever instructions Chairman Mao gave.' Next month, during a Central Work Conference convened by the Central Committee, this became the principal leitmotif of Hua Guofeng's speech.

This approach was accompanied by the constant and quite conspicuous building up of a new cult – that of Hua Guofeng – which was to co-exist harmoniously with the old one of Mao Zedong. By March, the media were already beginning to refer to Hua as 'the wise leader', and on innumerable occasions portraits of the two men, identical in size, were displayed side by side. In part at least the propagation of the Hua cult was intended to remove doubts about the legitimacy of his succession since it was based on only two things – the Political Bureau decision of 7 October, as yet unconfirmed by a Central Committee meeting, and the cryptic written message he is said to have received from Mao Zedong: 'With you in charge, I am at ease.'

It should be noted as well that while the 'gang of four' were undoubtedly the principal political beneficiaries of the 'cultural revolution', they were by no means the sole ones. The members of what can be called the 'two whatevers' group had also done quite well, which perhaps explains their choice of policy in relation to the 'cultural revolution'.

Another group within the top leadership, while not really benefiting from the 'cultural revolution' and even at times opposing some of its excesses, had come through the decade relatively unscathed. The group included Ye Jianying and Li Xiannian, each of whom could probably refer to his experiences, at least partly, in a Chinese paraphrase of Abbé Sieyès's famous '*j'ai vécu*'. They would not be particularly averse to setting the record straight and giving, sooner or later, a correct appraisal of the 'cultural revolution', but would stress caution in view of the political consequences involved.

An urgent and troublesome political problem was posed from

211

the outset for Hua Guofeng and the Political Bureau by the case of Deng Xiaoping. It was clear that the now deposed 'gang of four' had been the principal initiators of the campaign against him, begun at the end of 1975, and especially of his removal from all posts in the aftermath of the Tiananmen incident, although these actions had been carried out with Mao Zedong's approval. The extent of support which Deng enjoyed among senior Party, PLA and state officials was well known, and his rehabilitation could be politically advantageous for the new leadership, apart from the fact that it would remedy an obvious injustice. However, the situation was not that simple. The campaign against Deng Xiaoping continued to be waged, albeit half-heartedly, until the end of 1976. Wang Dongxing and Wu De, the first secretary of the Beijing Party Committee and the city's mayor who had been actively involved in the suppression of the Tiananmen demonstration, as well as at least two other members of the Political Bureau strongly favoured its continuation and opposed Deng's return to the political arena. Hua Guofeng's stand was ambivalent. He was well aware that certainly one of the two posts he held – that of premier – had been gained by him only because of Deng's removal. Furthermore, if Deng were reinstated in a senior position, he would no doubt continue to advocate policies similar to those he had in 1975, which were implicitly critical of the 'cultural revolution' and opposed to the political line chosen by Hua. In view of these considerations, Hua played for time, expressing approval in principle for having the case re-examined, but adding a number of reservations to delay Deng's actual return.

In January it became clear that Deng's situation was much in the public mind. Posters went up in Beijing demanding his recall and also a revision of the evaluation of the Tiananmen incident, for the two issues were obviously linked. Both were discussed, particularly the case of Deng Xiaoping, during the lengthy Central Work Conference held by the Central Committee in March, and a decision was finally reached that Deng's reinstatement would be approved at the next plenum of the Central Committee.

In the meantime, Deng went back to Beijing and lost no time in attacking the views of the 'two whatevers' group, pointing to the illogical assumptions on which they were based. Infallibility did not exist; according to Deng, 'Mao Zedong himself said repeatedly that some of his own statements were wrong'. Thus the 'two whatevers' thesis was simply not in accord with reality or a materialist approach.

The long awaited Central Committee plenum promised by Hua Guofeng finally assembled during the summer on 16–21 July 1977. Of the three main resolutions passed, the one pertaining to Deng Xiaoping aroused the greatest interest. He was now fully rehabilitated and reinstated in the three key posts he had held before his second downfall in April 1976. In accordance with strict protocol, he was now shown as the third man in the supreme leadership, after Hua Guofeng and Ye Jianying. Deng's return was proclaimed by an editorial in the central media as conforming to the wish of the people. This was not propagandistic hyperbole; a reliable foreign observer reported that when the news of Deng's return was broadcast in Beijing 'the staccato clatter of firecrackers broke out from different parts of the city'. For the next two days, hundreds of thousands of people marched through Tiananmen; the celebrations were marked by genuine jubilation and a carnival atmosphere prevailed. Why? Primarily because Deng Xiaoping had become representative of an end to the turbulence of the 'cultural revolution' and hope for a better life.

In his speech at the plenum Deng dealt with a number of key topics, including the policies which should be pursued towards the intellectuals, and the proper approach to, and correct utilization of, Mao Zedong Thought. Deng also put forward one of the two fundamental guidelines which were to characterize his activities and policies in the years to come. He resurrected the four-character slogan which Mao Zedong had written in 1942 for the Central Party School in Yan'an – *shi shi qiu shi*, 'seek truth from facts' or, more fully, 'arrive at the truth by verifying the facts'. Deng Xiaoping maintained that this principle constituted the quintessence of Mao Zedong's philosophical thinking; the implications of applying it towards both the past and the present were far-reaching indeed.

At the July plenum Hua Guofeng's position as chairman of the Central Committee, which he had assumed nine months earlier, was officially confirmed. The action taken against the 'gang of four' was also approved, and all of them were expelled from the Party. A considerable part of the session was also probably devoted to discussing the formulation of the Party's political line in connection with the preparations for holding a new Party congress in the following month.

The Eleventh Congress convened in Beijing shortly after the Third Plenum, on 12–18 August. The 1510 delegates now represented a still larger Party, for the membership had increased by 7 million since 1973 to reach over 35 million; about half had entered the Party after 1966, a fact of considerable political significance.

The long political report, which took Hua Guofeng almost four hours to deliver, was the most important item on the agenda. Basically, it reflected the views of Hua and probably the majority of the senior leadership of the time that continuity with previous policies should be preserved. Much time was therefore devoted by Hua to a panegyric of Mao Zedong, 'the greatest Marxist of our time', the fulsome terms of which almost matched those employed at the height of the cult in the first stage of the 'cultural revolution'. All the victories won in the 'cultural revolution' were attributed to Mao's leadership; oddly enough, so was the success in eliminating the 'gang of four'. (The official ceremony inaugurating the Mao Zedong Memorial Hall on 9 September provided another occasion for demonstrating this determination to keep the personality cult very much alive.)

Although Hua proclaimed the termination of the 'cultural revolution', he stressed the necessity of continuing to implement a number of its main policies, including 'grasping the key link of class struggle'. He ascribed 'tremendous achievements and historical significance' to the 'cultural revolution' which he depicted as 'an event which will go down in the history of the dictatorship of the proletariat as a momentous innovation'. Such a definition of course precluded any critical analysis of it as a whole or of any event during it, with one crucial exception. The misdeeds of the 'gang of four' were dealt with by Hua Guofeng at length and in great detail, but as if somehow their actions were completely separate from the 'cultural revolution', as if they had not held the highest posts in the Party throughout the decade. Similarly, in dealing with the critical attitude which Mao Zedong is said to have demonstrated towards the Jiang Qing faction in the last two years of his life, Hua disregarded the fact that its members had been up to that time his closest collaborators. The same had been true, of course, of Lin Biao up to 1970. How far Hua succeeded in convincing his audience that Mao Zedong had no connection with the activities of the two 'counter-revolutionary cliques', thus preserving the credibility of both the 'cultural revolution' and its initiator, remains open to question.

The present CCP leadership's evaluation of the Eleventh Congress differs considerably from its appraisal of the preceding Ninth (1969) and Tenth (1973), which it dismisses almost out of hand as wrong in every respect. The Eleventh Congress, on the other hand, is praised in the 1981 Resolution – as is implicitly Hua Guofeng – for its 'positive role in exposing and repudiating the "gang of four" '. Certainly this task had been carried out with utmost thoroughness and zeal. The Eleventh Congress also receives an accolade for 'mobilizing the whole Party for building China into a powerful, modern socialist state'. It is not quite clear how one is to reconcile this with the statement that one of the Congress's shortcomings was that 'it reaffirmed the erroneous theories, policies and slogans of the "cultural revolution" instead of correcting them'. This accords with all the available material pertaining to the Congress, including Deng Xiaoping's closing speech which, not surprisingly, is not included in his Selected Works. So was the Party really mobilized on the basis of an erroneous programme? If it was, then all the considerable efforts directed in the next few years towards rectifying it would seem to have been redundant.

The failure to undertake a critical reassessment of the 'cultural revolution' at this time is attributed to two factors: 'the limitations imposed by the prevailing historical conditions' and the influence of Hua Guofeng's mistakes. If the first factor is to be understood as a reference to the monumental ideological and political confusion within the Party, then it is possible to appreciate that any jettisoning of the ballast of the 'cultural revolution' would have been a very difficult undertaking indeed, for the confusion was a direct result of the 'cultural revolution' decade and half the CCP's members had entered the Party in response to the 'cultural revolution's' slogans. Reappraisal called for careful preparation, especially ideological, and this was in fact the main content of political development up to the end of 1978. Nonetheless, it would seem that the CCP leadership at this time was divided between those who were satisfied with stopping at the stage reached at the Eleventh Congress, and those who wanted to progress towards removing all the obstacles created by the 'cultural revolution', which blocked a successful advance to a better future. As to Hua Guofeng's own role, the mistakes ascribed to him were primarily favouring and representing the position of the first of these groups.

At the end of the Eleventh Congress a new Central Committee was elected. Its composition differed markedly from that of its predecessor; 59 of the former 174 full members, and 51 of the former 123 alternates were not re-elected. Presumably a large number of them were considered to have been supporters of the 'gang of four'. Their places were on the whole taken by rehabilitated veteran cadres. A slightly larger Political Bureau was chosen (23 members and 3 alternates), with a number of veteran senior cadres, such as Nie Rongzhen, reappearing in it. The new Standing Committee of the Political Bureau was composed of the chairman and the four vice chairmen of the Central Committee – Hua Guofeng, Ye Jianying, Deng Xiaoping, Li Xiannian and Wang Dongxing. This in itself reflected the different tendencies within the leadership. However, the divergences remained largely an inner-Party affair, and outwardly a display of accord and unity was carefully maintained.

Although the Great Proletarian Cultural Revolution was still officially sacrosanct, Deng Xiaoping and his supporters saw no reason why its numerous victims should not be rehabilitated, even if this had to be done without publicity. A clear call for such action was voiced by the central Party press in October and the appointment of Hu Yaobang in December to the key post of head of the Central Committee's Organization Department signified, among other things, that the rehabilitation campaign would now be pursued with the vigour it deserved. Nonetheless, it turned out to be a lengthy, tortuous process which stretched out to the end of 1978. But during this time justice was done not only to the multitude of those repressed during the 'cultural revolution' but also to those victimized still earlier during the Anti-Rightist Campaign of 1957. In April 1978, a Central Committee decision called for the removal of the rightist 'label' from those unjustly persecuted twenty years earlier. Over 100,000 people, mostly intellectuals, some of them still in prison or exile, benefited from this amnesty.

There was a general consensus among the CCP leadership that economic development must be speeded up and that the Four Modernizations programme advanced by Zhou Enlai in 1975 must be implemented as soon as appropriate. The problem of future economic policies was among the most important discussed at the Second Plenum of the Central Committee on 18–23 February 1978. It approved the 'Outline of the Ten-Year Plan for the Development of the National Economy, 1976–1985'. The goals set in this document were quite ambitious; grain production was to increase from 295 million tons to 400 million by 1985, and the mechanization of agriculture was to reach 85 per cent. Steel output was to rise from around 30 million to 60 million tons, and the construction of 120 large-scale projects was planned. These aims were based on the premise that overall investment in capital construction for the last eight years of the plan would be equivalent to the total for the past twenty-eight years. However, there were no indications in the documents available, particularly in the speeches of Hua Guofeng, as to where the resources were to be found for this grandiose programme. And there was no sign of any serious intention to re-examine the basic economic policies implemented thus far or to consider whether extensive reform of the economic system, particularly in agriculture, obviously its weakest link, should not be put on the agenda. Instead, there were hackneyed slogans and appeals for continuous political mobilization. Hua paid much attention to continuing the mass movement of learning from Dazhai, the agricultural brigade in Shanxi, and from Daqing, the oil field in Heilongjiang. Both of these units had been highly praised in the 1960s and 1970s, and their methods of work had been recommended as an infallible model to be followed by agriculture and industry throughout the country. Later on, it was discovered that the authenticity of the reported experiences of the Dazhai brigade was dubious, to say the least, and the slogan 'Learn from Dazhai', which had been plastered all over the country, quietly faded into oblivion. Daqing, on the other hand, continues to be the PRC's most important oil field; its initial construction under extremely trying climatic and living conditions was without question the result of much hard and devoted work on the part of its constantly growing labour force.

The overall task of the Second Plenum was to make all the preparations for the Fifth National People's Congress to be held a few days later from 26 February to 5 March. There was no attempt to disguise the fact that every item raised at the NPC had been discussed and settled beforehand at the plenum. This included the Ten-Year Plan, the text of the newly revised PRC constitution (the third since 1949), and the entire list of new central government officials to be nominated by the NPC. Thus Hua Guofeng retained his post as premier. Since the office of chairman of the PRC had been abolished in January 1975, the role of formal head of state was to be played by Ye Jianying, now elected chairman of the NPC Standing Committee. In a move which symbolized, like a number of other measures of this period, a return to the practices of the 1950s, the Chinese People's Political Consultative Conference – the united front forum – was revived from its hibernation of over twelve years. Deng Xiaoping became chairman of its National Committee.

The consensus within the CCP leadership did not preclude distinct differences in the approach of individuals to economic development strategy as well as to numerous fundamental political problems. By 1978, divergent views about economic theories and the problems of socialist construction could be expressed, without immediately incurring the danger of being stigmatized as a capitalist roader, revisionist and so forth. Thus it can be assumed that Chen Yun, who had reappeared in the political arena and was the most experienced in economic matters of all the senior CCP leaders, was now able to present his views. At the end of 1978 he was to join the top leadership again.

The 'cultural revolution' had turned China into an intellectual and cultural desert, in which the only flag that was visibly flying was that of phrasemongering illiteracy. Now new possibilities were being created in this sphere too. A key role in the process of intellectual rejuvenation was played from 1977 on by the newly established Chinese Academy of Social Sciences, headed from March 1978 on by Hu Qiaomu. Among the eminent economists active in the academy, Sun Yefang (1908–83) deserves special attention, not only for his significant contribution to Chinese economic thought, but also because his life constitutes an illuminating example of the fate of some of the country's most prominent intellectuals. A Party member since 1924, Sun held the important post of director of the Institute of Economics in the 1950s. His critical appraisal of the Great Leap Forward – he called it a 'disruption of socialism' – stirred up trouble for him. From 1963 on, Sun was attacked as a 'revisionist', and a particularly vehement campaign against him was launched after the outbreak of the 'cultural revolution'. In 1968 he was imprisoned and kept in solitary confinement until April 1975. As he himself stated, he was not told why he was jailed nor why he was released. Sun spent these seven years on two projects: a profuse annotation of Marx's *Capital* – his copy of it is said to be quite unique – and the writing in his mind of a work of one million characters on the economic theory of socialism. After regaining freedom, Sun Yefang returned to his theoretical work; his views on the importance of the law of value and on the role of the market under socialism have had considerable influence on the economic policies formulated in the PRC since 1978.

The discussions on economic theory were further stimulated in 1978 by the work of Hu Qiaomu, whose lengthy report on this subject was delivered in July. In his comprehensive analysis of the economic tasks confronting the CCP, Hu stressed the need to observe economic laws. The laws, which possess an objective nature of their own, had been systematically ignored by those favouring only the concept of 'politics in command'. Failure to study and abide by economic laws led inevitably to stagnation and regress in economic development.

Hu Qiaomu admitted that so far socialism had not attained higher labour productivity than capitalism had. The two reasons for this – both valid for the PRC – were initial backwardness of the country and lack of experience. However, after thirty years, lack of experience could no longer be advanced as an excuse for failures. The record of the PRC was markedly uneven. Up to 1958 a high growth rate in labour productivity had been maintained, as it had in industrial output. After 1958 there was no further growth in labour productivity or in wages, and the increase in industrial output was achieved only by enlarging the number of workers. The existence of a socialist social system was no guarantee by itself that objective economic laws would be observed, or that economic development would proceed at a higher rate.

A summing up of China's positive and negative experiences was imperative, according to Hu, if the Four Modernizations were to be realized. For this purpose it was also necessary to study capitalist methods of economic management and to employ the advanced science and technology of capitalist countries. Without this type of learning there would be no advance and no building of socialism. In effect, Hu's theses formed the foundation stone of the new policies being advanced by Deng Xiaoping and his group, whose aim was to open the country to the world and reject the 'self-reliant' autarky favoured during the 'cultural revolution'.

Probably reflecting Sun Yefang's views, Hu Qiaomu emphasized the need to abide by the law of value – which he defined as the universal law of commodity economy – and by the law of planned and proportionate development. The lack of ability or the failure to act according to these laws manifested itself in slow technical progress, high costs and low labour productivity, thus resulting in a waste of manpower, material resources and money.

An improvement in the economy would be unattainable, according to Hu, if the material interests of all workers were not taken into consideration. Thus an end must be put to the policy of negating personal interests, propagated during the 'cultural revolution', and the principle of 'to each according to his work' must be strictly observed. Hu made the trenchant point that if the CCP could not work for the interest of the majority, then such a party was not needed.

Hu Qiaomu did not attempt to disguise the serious conditions of Chinese agriculture, marked by a sluggish rate of advance. The problems here rested in a pricing policy which in most areas had resulted in little or no increase in the peasants' income since 1949. Hu envisaged reforms in the functioning of the communes, but in this case the measures taken since 1978 have far exceeded his recommendations. However, most of Hu's concepts were accepted by the CCP leadership and constituted the theoretical basis for the economic policies pursued since 1979.

The Ten-Year Economic Plan had stressed the importance of the development of science and technology. Even greater emphasis was placed on this in the course of the well-publicized National Science Conference held in March 1978 and attended by the top CCP leaders – the triumvirate, as it was called by foreign observers, of Hua Guofeng, Ye Jianying and Deng Xiaoping. The National Plan for Science and Technology for the years 1978–85, discussed at the conference, was based on a realistic assessment of the backwardness of the PRC, which lagged behind the advanced countries by fifteen to twenty years in many fields, and more in some areas. The policies and measures proposed for the elimination of this gap were ambitious, but not unattainable. It can be assumed that they reflected, above all, the ideas of Deng Xiaoping and his associates, since in the customary division of responsibility among the communist leadership, Deng had been assigned the fields of science, technology and education.

There was practically no area in the life of the PRC affected as adversely by the 'cultural revolution' as education, particularly higher education, and no stratum of the population as repressed and discriminated against as the intellectuals. The urgent need to repair step by step the damage inflicted had been recognized by Deng Xiaoping in 1975, but implementation of the directives for future development prepared under his auspices had been frustrated by his removal from office in April 1976. It was only after July 1977 that Deng and his followers were able to recommence their important work in this field.

One of the prime tasks was to eliminate the pernicious influence of the anti-intellectual concepts propagated during the 'cultural revolution', particularly by the 'gang of four'. According to them the vast majority of intellectuals were basically bourgeois in outlook; the intelligentsia as a whole had been stigmatized as 'the stinking number nine' – the ninth category of 'enemies of the people', after landlords, rich peasants, counter-revolutionaries, bad elements, rightists, renegades, enemy agents and capitalist roaders. These views negated all the educational achievements of People's China up to 1966, since the bulk of Chinese intellectuals had been educated in the seventeen years since 1949. By the late 1970s the overwhelming majority of intellectuals had become, according to Deng Xiaoping, an integral part of the working people; no antagonism existed or could exist between those engaged in mental and manual labour, and hence between the intellectuals and the working class. Moreover, Deng maintained that politically and ideologically the great majority of Chinese intellectuals were revolutionary and favoured socialism; thus they were a force on which the CCP could and should rely.

The urgency of adopting a correct approach to the intelligentsia was, of course, closely linked with the overall goal of implementing the Four Modernizations programme, since one of the most obvious manifestations of China's backwardness was the lack of scientific researchers. Deng illustrated this by comparing China's 200,000 research personnel with the United States' 1,200,000 and the Soviet Union's 900,000. The figures spoke for themselves.

The pseudo-egalitarian practices and policies pursued during the 'cultural revolution' in higher education, when universities finally resumed functioning in 1970 and 1971, had produced sorrowful results. Through no fault of their own, a large majority of the students admitted were inadequately prepared, and much of the education they received was garbled and incomplete. When they graduated, many of them did not have the necessary knowledge and skills to continue work in their fields. Few of them could be regarded as 'illiterate hooligans', but according to Deng Xiaoping this would have been the ultimate result of the educational policies favoured and implemented by the 'gang of four'. From 1977 higher education was gradually returned to the standards that had existed before 1966. The reintroduction of entrance examinations in October 1977 was one of the first crucial measures taken.

In the late spring of 1978 Deng Xiaoping and his colleagues inaugurated the second of their key philosophical and ideological debates, which played such an important part in breaking the intellectual atrophy and confusion created by the 'cultural revolution' and its concomitant personality cult. Following on from the thesis 'seek truth from facts', the debate put forward the role of practice as the sole criterion for verifying truth. This approach signified the launch of an assault on the dogmatism and sectarianism which had characterized the thinking of the ultra-left and had dominated the CCP since 1958, particularly during the decade of the 'cultural revolution'. Politically, it was directed against the 'two whatevers' faction, whose attitude to the past and present epitomized sectarian dogmatism.

The debate was initiated on 11 May by a lengthy polemical article in one of the central newspapers. Its authors stressed that Marx, Lenin, and Mao Zedong as well 'did not think that their

223

theories embodied absolute truth or were free from verification by practice, nor did they think that the conclusions of their theories and theses were unchangeable. They always used practice to verify their own theories, theses and directives.' Hence, Marxism 'is not a heap of stark and inflexible dogmas. It must continuously absorb new opinions and conclusions and discard those that no longer fit the new situation.' Thus, the conclusion was that 'all ideas and theories must always be verified by practice without exception'. It might appear odd that such prosaic and common-sense ideas could have created the storm they did, but the personality cult and interminable political campaigns had converted Marxism, and especially the works of Mao Zedong, into Holy Writ. It was permitted to use approved quotations from it, but not to employ it as the theoretical basis for independent and creative thinking.

The issues raised in this supremely important debate were developed further by Deng Xiaoping in his speech on 2 June at the All Army Conference on Political Work. Deng noted that some people 'maintain that those that persist in seeking truth from facts, proceeding from reality and integrating theory with practice, are guilty of a heinous crime. In essence, their view is that one need only parrot what was said by Marx, Lenin and Comrade Mao Zedong – that it is enough to reproduce their words mechanically.' Furthermore, Deng, a consistent practitioner of the principle that 'politics is the art of the possible', took great pains to illustrate by proper reference to Mao's works that the latter himself had steadfastly maintained that correct ideas 'come from social practice and from it alone', and that 'there is no other way of testing truth'. What Deng forgot to add, for transparently obvious reasons, was that from 1958 on Mao had started to neglect the observance of this fundamental and salutary principle, and had abandoned it entirely during the last decade of his life.

An important editorial in the *People's Daily* on 24 June continued the polemic by stressing the need for the criterion of truth to be practice and for the relationship between theory and practice to be based on theory verified by practice, and not practice 'tailored' by theory. A week later, on 1 July, a speech delivered by Mao Zedong on 30 January 1962 at the famous 7000 Cadres Conference was published officially for the first time (earlier it had been known only from a slightly different version which appeared in the Red Guard press). The significance of this event rested in the fact that this rambling, lengthy and at moments fascinating discourse contained not only some very pertinent remarks on the indispensability of democracy and collective leadership within the Party, but also Mao's self-criticism for errors committed during the Great Leap Forward. The key passage reads as follows: 'For shortcomings and mistakes in our work in the last few years, the responsibility rests first with the Central Committee, and in the Central Committee, with me.' He also made an admonition that his mistakes must not be kept hidden from the Party. Thus, Mao's own words were now used to chip away at the legend of his omniscience and infallibility so painstakingly constructed, with his own approval, during the preceding two decades.

By the autumn of 1978, the criterion of truth debate had developed into a national political campaign, for the subject was taken up for discussion by Party committees on all levels. There seems to be little doubt that it created considerable controversy, for the 'two whatevers' faction fought back against the activities and programme of what could be called Deng Xiaoping's 'practice faction' with all the still extensive means at its disposal. It had, after all, representatives not only in the top Party authorities (Wang Dongxing and other Political Bureau members) but also throughout the Party and state apparatus. The decades of dogmatic indoctrination in the personality cult had undoubtedly produced tangible results. The possibility that a critical reappraisal of the past, and especially of individual behaviour and actions during the 'cultural revolution', could become a real threat to their position made many middle and lower echelon cadres apprehensive of the consequences should the 'practice faction' win victory. However, it is also possible that quite a large number of officials did not adhere to either of these contending groups, but simply favoured what was referred to in the lively polemics of this period as the 'wind faction'. It was said to be composed primarily of careerists and opportunists who 'trim their sails according to the wind . . and with necks on ball bearings . . . change colour as they scent what the wind brings them'. Again this was hardly a specifically Chinese phenomenon, and it can be safely assumed, judging from events in other countries, that most of the members of this group did manage to switch to the winning side at the appropriate moment.

According to the present CCP leadership there was one very prominent individual who had tried to suppress the discussions referred to above. This was none other than the chairman of the Central Committee himself, Hua Guofeng. He is also charged with having promoted the 'two whatevers' policy in the first place, with obstructing the rehabilitation and reinstatement of veteran cadres and the redressing of injustices left over from the past. Deng Xiaoping and his associates had by now come to the conclusion that under Hua's leadership it would be impossible to correct the errors within the Party. Their decision to remove Hua Guofeng from his key posts was probably made by the late autumn of 1978. It was to be realized in a slow and undramatic fashion, without recourse to the drastic measures previously employed in inner-Party conflicts.

The numerous controversial issues raised in the preceding two years became the subject of prolonged and no doubt heated discussions during the course of the Central Committee Work Conference which took place in Beijing from 9 November to 13 December 1978. The forces represented by Deng Xiaoping emerged victorious from this political confrontation, probably due in part to the support given to Deng by the veteran cadres now in the process of being reinstated. These experienced and authentic revolutionaries were his logical constituency. Like him, they had been cast aside for following the more sensible and pragmatic policies of the first seventeen years of the PRC. As one writer has put it so aptly, they still believed in these policies, which Deng was reintroducing. This was their second and last chance to make them work.

On 18–23 December, within a few days of the closing of the

Work Conference, the Third Plenum of the Central Committee was held in Beijing, one of the most momentous meetings of the Party leadership in the entire post-liberation era. In the opinion of the present writer it deserves the accolade it received in the 1981 Resolution which describes it as a 'crucial turning point of far-reaching significance'. A number of fundamental issues were dealt with decisively during the plenum.

The ideological underpinning of the programme adopted by the plenum was a positive evaluation of the debate on practice as the sole criterion for the verification of truth, in line with Deng Xiaoping's affirmation that this had been in reality a 'debate about the ideological line, about politics, about the future and the destiny' of the Party and the nation. Moreover, it accepted Deng's formulation that one of the primary tasks facing the Party was emancipating the mind, making use of the brain and seeking truth from facts. Such an approach signified, of course, a total and explicit rejection of the 'two whatevers' position.

One of the most important decisions taken at the plenum was to discard the slogan 'take class struggle as the key link', now deemed to have become unsuitable in a socialist society. It had been the foundation stone of the policies advocated by the ultra-leftists, especially during the 'cultural revolution' decade. The explicit implication of this was that the Party would cease to devote its main efforts to the interminable political campaigns which had been characteristic of the past, and focus them instead on the crucial problem of socialist modernization. This shift of emphasis has shaped the basic policies implemented by the CCP from 1978 to the present.

The burning issue of redressing the multitude of injustices perpetrated during the 'cultural revolution' – and earlier – was not avoided by the plenum, although it was resolved only partially. Peng Dehuai, Tao Zhu, Bo Yibo, Yang Shangkun, and a number of less well-known veteran cadres were fully exonerated. Memorial meetings were held for Peng and Tao. However, the case of Liu Shaoqi was passed over in silence, although it was obvious that this most flagrant individual instance of rank injustice would have to be taken up sooner or later. In passing, it should be noted that up to the end of 1978, Hua Guofeng and some other leaders still referred approvingly to the elimination of Liu. Deng Xiaoping, biding his time, simply avoided mentioning Liu's name.

The failure to rehabilitate Liu Shaoqi at this time may well be connected with the decision taken by the plenum to delay taking a stand on the two most controversial, troublesome and quite inseparable political issues facing the Party – an honest, accurate and definitive assessment of the 'cultural revolution' and of the historic role and place of Mao Zedong. The second of these problems, approached most gingerly, was pushed aside on the grounds that 'it would not be Marxist to demand that a revolutionary leader be free of all shortcomings and errors'. As far as the 'shortcomings and mistakes' of the 'cultural revolution' were concerned, 'they should be summed up at the appropriate time . . . however, there should be no haste about this'. It was stated that 'shelving this problem' would not prevent the 'solving of all other problems left over from past history'. This assertion was untenable, as future developments were soon to demonstrate. It is more than likely that this 'shelving' was conceived of as a compromise measure, intended to alleviate to some degree the acrimonious inner-Party strife on these issues.

There was one issue which Deng Xiaoping and his supporters did not want shelved; in fact they had raised and solved it already during the Work Conference. This was the reversal of the verdict on the famous Tiananmen incident of 1976, which had also resulted in Deng's dismissal. On 16 November, the Beijing Municipal Committee of the CCP declared that the mass actions honouring the memory of Zhou Enlai had been 'completely revolutionary' and all those persecuted should be rehabilitated; most of those who had been arrested were now finally released from prison. The repercussions of this decision, confirmed by the Third Plenum, were far-reaching, as they also affected those still in the CCP leadership, not excluding Hua Guofeng, who had taken an active part in suppressing the Tiananmen demonstration. A special two-volume edition of the Tiananmen poems was quickly readied for publication and on

18 November the central press carried photographs of the book's title inscribed in Hua Guofeng's own calligraphy. In view of his position in April 1976 as acting premier and minister of public security, this act of blatant hypocrisy revolted some of the participants in the demonstration.

Among the organizational measures taken at the Third Plenum, the elevation to Political Bureau membership of Hu Yaobang, Deng Yingzhao and Wang Zhen – all close collaborators and friends of Deng Xiaoping – was especially significant, as was the assumption by Chen Yun of the position of vice chairman of the Central Committee and hence member of the Standing Committee of the Political Bureau. Chen also became chairman of the newly created Discipline Inspection Commission, whose role in cleansing the Party of members considered unreliable politically and morally was to be important.

The political significance of the Third Plenum rested in particular in the fact that from this moment on Deng Xiaoping and his associates, enjoying the support of a majority in the Political Bureau and the Central Committee, were in command of the key posts in the central Party apparatus. Henceforth, Deng, while *primus inter pares*, became ever more obviously the dominant personality in the CCP leadership. However, and undoubtedly in accord with his own wishes, no trace of a cult of his personality has so far appeared. Both in 1983 and 1986 not a single picture of him could be found displayed in any of the customary places.

It is maintained by the present leadership that the overall importance of the Third Plenum rested in its 're-establishing the correct line of Marxism, ideologically, politically and organizationally', which has enabled the Party to tackle successfully the many problems left over since 1949 as well as the new ones arising after 1978. This is a somewhat sweeping assertion, and difficult to verify on the basis of facts. But it is possible to look at how much progress the CCP did achieve during the eight years from 1978 to 1986 in overcoming some of the most negative legacies of the past.

Two historical influences stood out with special prominence.

The first was three millennia of bureaucratic despotism combined with local and lord rule which affected every domain of
Chinese life, not least the autocratic style of politics, the authoritarian mode of exercising power, and thus the behaviour of
both the rulers and the ruled. Building a democratic pattern of
life in a country where little had previously existed was
immensely complex and difficult. The second influence had
affected all China's actions since 1949 – the use of the Soviet
Union as a model for socialism in all areas of society, which in
practice had meant imposing the Stalinist system on a largely
semi-feudal and patriarchal society. The undesirable consequences of this dual heritage had been compounded by Mao
Zedong's adamant refusal to draw almost any of the obvious and
necessary conclusions from the tragic experiences of the Soviet
people in the years 1932–53. While the CCP documents of the
late 1970s and early 1980s show a growing consciousness of the
problems emanating from China's past, there are practically no
signs of any awareness of the lingering adverse ideological and
political effects of the Stalinist model. On the contrary, in the
1981 Resolution Stalin is still referred to – along with Marx,
Engels and Lenin – as one 'whose scientific works' are 'a guide to
action'. If Stalin's grotesque distortion of Marxism is regarded
in such a fashion, then doubts must arise as to the aptness of the
phrase 'correct line of Marxism' employed by the CCP in 1981.

Another problem comes to mind almost automatically. The
Chinese communist leaders were honest enough to admit in
1981 that the Party's prestige had been 'grievously damaged
during the "cultural revolution" '. Undoubtedly true. However,
it had already suffered a severe blow as a result of the Great Leap
Forward, but had managed to recover from it. Is it possible to
restore the Party's prestige fully without also tackling, on an
equal basis, both of the elements in China's dual heritage? For
the time being, this question must remain open.

The principal line of PRC foreign policy established in the
early 1970s, especially after the 1972 Nixon visit, and the attitude set then towards both the Soviet Union and the United
States remained basically unaltered during the last years of Mao

Zedong's life. By 1974 Mao is said to have developed an analysis of the international situation known as the Three Worlds theory. According to this, the world was composed of the two superpowers, the developed capitalist and socialist states, and the developing countries of, primarily, Asia and Africa. China was placed in the third category. This theory was enunciated by Deng Xiaoping in April 1974 in his speech at a special United Nations session. In the same speech Deng announced the demise of the socialist camp, which simply meant that any reconciliation between the Soviet Union and the PRC could not be expected in the foreseeable future.

There was no abatement in the mutual hostility between Moscow and Beijing; in Chinese foreign policy statements and the media the Soviet Union was more frequently and bitterly attacked than the United States. However, Sino-Soviet negotiations on overall relations and the border question were continued, although the results were nil. Mao Zedong's death brought about a temporary, one-sided pause in the barrage of mutual venom, for the Soviet media suspended their attacks from September 1976 till May 1977. Thereafter, both sides returned to the fray, with the Chinese attacks on Soviet 'social imperialism' becoming even more intense.

The situation in Indochina in the aftermath of the Vietnam War in the spring of 1975 and the victory of the Khmer Rouges in Kampuchea increased the antagonism between the Soviet Union and the PRC. Sino-Vietnamese relations deteriorated too, partly as a result of the growing rapprochement between Vietnam and the Soviet Union. The Vietnamese communists had performed for long years a miraculous balancing act in face of the growing Sino-Soviet conflict, which they bitterly resented since it went against the interests of their own struggle. But from 1976 they began to draw nearer to the Soviet Union, which culminated in November 1978 with the signing of a twenty-five-year Soviet-Vietnamese treaty of friendship and alliance.

In the meantime, the poor relations between Vietnam and Kampuchea entered a critical stage in October 1977 when border incidents became endemic. Beijing initially sought to preserve a neutral stand towards this conflict, but it was clear that its sympathy lay with Phnom Penh. The reasons for this rested not so much in admiration for the genocidal actions of the Pol Pot clique – which had been quite close to the 'gang of four' – but in what seemed to be a facile interpretation of China's national interests, perilously close to the banal adage 'my enemy's enemy is my friend': the rapprochement between Vietnam and the Soviet Union made Kampuchea automatically deserving of Beijing's support.

This seemingly harsh evaluation of the PRC's foreign policy is not based solely on the question of Indochina. In August 1977, Tito was given a rapturous reception in Beijing; Yugoslavia was now once again a socialist country, according to the Chinese media. While this could be considered part of a belated and quite correct attempt to remedy two decades of vilification, the place of improved relations with Yugoslavia within the larger framework of the Sino-Soviet confrontation was obvious to all concerned. The implications of Hua Guofeng's visit in August 1978 to Rumania and Yugoslavia were similar. This was highlighted still more by the not particularly fortunate decision to end his tour with a stay in Tehran, in the twilight months of Pahlavi's reign.

A more positive, and certainly less controversial, achievement of Chinese foreign policy, and in line with the marked strengthening of its international position which had been progressing steadily since the mid-1970s, was the signing in August 1978 of the treaty of peace and friendship with Japan. Three years of complex and arduous negotiations had been necessary to achieve this goal, which reflected the ever closer economic relations between the two countries. It was clear that Japan was destined to play a significant role in China's modernization. The miracle of Japan's post-Second World War economic development must have given rise to some bitter reflections among the Chinese, emerging from the ravages of the 'cultural revolution'. An atmosphere of cordial Sino-Japanese amity and accord prevailed during Deng Xiaoping's visit to Japan in October 1978. Bygones were bygones, but this did not signify, as events in 1985 were to show, that the Chinese had forgotten completely what had happened in their country in the years 1937–45.

In the spring of 1978, Sino-American negotiations towards full normalization of relations between them began to advance significantly. This was due primarily to the willingness of the Carter administration to acknowledge finally some of the demands of Beijing in relation to the Taiwan issue. Washington was now ready to terminate diplomatic relations with the KMT regime in Taipei, abrogate the 1954 US–Taiwan defence treaty and withdraw all American forces from the island. On 15 December Carter and Hua Guofeng announced that diplomatic relations would be established on 1 January 1979.

Both sides felt, not unjustifiably, that each had markedly improved its position vis-à-vis the Soviet Union; there were few serious attempts by either the American or Chinese governments to disguise that this had been one of the principal motives for the entire undertaking. This point was made particularly clear by the Chinese side during Deng Xiaoping's highly publicized visit to the United States from 29 January to 4 February. This new stage in Sino-American relations had, of course, other important aspects as well, for it facilitated to a considerable extent the future development of contacts in many fields, especially the economic. Deng Xiaoping and his colleagues had already stressed that their economic development strategy urgently required the acquisition of modern technology from abroad. The recently signed treaty with Japan had this goal very much in mind; it was hoped that the new relations with the United States would ultimately bring similar results. Both undertakings were part and parcel of the policy of opening up the PRC to the world.

Just as the new phase of Sino-American relations was being celebrated, the situation in Indochina took a drastic turn for the worse. Against a background of constant border incidents, the Vietnamese had organized a Kampuchean National Liberation Front composed of anti-Pol Pot elements. Then they assembled their own forces, well trained and supplied with largely American military equipment either lost in battle or abandoned, for a decisive confrontation. On 25 December 1978, up to a dozen Vietnamese divisions crossed the border. Meeting with practically no resistance, they captured Phnom Penh on 7 January 1979, and within two weeks were masters of almost the entire country.

The action of the Vietnamese was vigorously denounced by the PRC from the very beginning. It was described as flagrant aggression, and Deng Xiaoping himself spoke of the Vietnamese leaders as agents of Soviet 'social imperialism'. However, it was soon decided in Beijing that a propaganda barrage, even of mighty proportions, was by itself an insufficiently strong response. Incidents on the border between China and Vietnam had taken place as early as April 1978. The situation was further exacerbated by the campaign conducted by the Vietnamese authorities against the large Chinese community, over one million strong, in Vietnam. By the end of May close to 90,000 Vietnamese of Chinese origin had fled Vietnam to take refuge in Guangxi and Yunnan. By January 1979 the number had increased to 160,000. A vituperative propaganda campaign of mutual recrimination ensued, with both sides accusing each other of responsibility for having created the refugee problem and for provoking further border incidents. In addition, the Chinese charged the Soviet Union with supporting and instigating both Vietnam's war against Kampuchea and its hostility towards the PRC.

Thus, with the invasion of Kampuchea the stage was set for a particularly distressing armed confrontation between two countries, both claiming to be socialist, which had been allies – as close as lips and teeth, in the oft-repeated Chinese phrase – throughout the three decades of Vietnamese struggle against French and American imperialism.

On 17 February, PLA forces, estimated by foreign sources as 250,000 strong, crossed the Sino-Vietnamese border along a 450-mile front in what Beijing claimed to be a 'self-defensive counter-attack' undertaken as a response to two years of Vietnamese provocation. Furthermore, it was stated that no Vietnamese territory was wanted and that the ensuing military campaign would be a limited action analogous, by implication, to that undertaken by the PRC against India in 1962. However, history did not repeat itself; the PLA's advance into North Vietnam proved much slower than its lightning progress south of the Himalayas. It was also, due to stubborn Vietnamese resistance, much costlier, since the casualties, again based on foreign estimates, were considerable. After capturing on 5 March the provincial capital of Lang Son – razed to the ground in the fighting – the PLA commenced its promised withdrawal, completing it by 16 March. On 1 March the Chinese had proposed negotiations to end the border conflict. The Vietnamese accepted the proposal and, after the Chinese completed the withdrawal of all their forces, talks finally began. Both sides claimed complete victory. All that is certain is that socialist internationalism had suffered one more devastating and debilitating blow.

CHAPTER ELEVEN

*The Establishment of
New Guidelines,
1979–82*

The far-reaching significance of the policies adopted by the Third Plenum has already been discussed. The deep-set ideological and political divergences within the CCP at all levels did not, of course, disappear immediately. Nor did the great debate in 1978 resolve the issue of the criterion of truth and eliminate sectarian and dogmatic thinking. On the contrary, Deng Xiaoping and his supporters were faced with the necessity of continuing to conduct a complex ideological and political struggle against still numerous, well-placed and by no means powerless antagonists.

The opposition to the newly formulated Party policies was composed of various elements, but those referred to as the 'two whatevers' faction constituted its core. They attacked the political line established at the Third Plenum as a manifestation of right opportunism and a betrayal of Mao Zedong Thought. These ideas found considerable support within the Party and state apparatus, especially among the young officials who had been the beneficiaries of the 'cultural revolution' and now saw their vested interests and future careers seriously endangered. Some of them stated cynically that they could afford to wait ten to fifteen years for the older revolutionary generation to die off; then they would have the chance to make their comeback.

It was this situation which brought about the renewal in the summer of 1979 both of the debate on the criterion of truth and of the criticism of the adherents of the 'two whatevers' group.

The campaign, conducted province by province, was intense, with the 'two whatevers' group accused of practising factionalism, of clinging to the ideas of the Lin Biao clique and the 'gang of four', and of seeking to reintroduce chaos.

At the end of March 1979 Deng Xiaoping formulated his views on the Four Principles considered to be indispensable for implementing the main task of the Party – the Four Modernizations. The advance towards this goal had been made possible in the first instance by 'smashing the feudal fascism of the "gang of four" ' and unmasking its 'phony, ultra-left socialism' which actually meant universal poverty. Now, to advance further, four cardinal principles had to be observed.

The first principle was keeping to the socialist road; according to Deng, sixty years' experience had shown that only socialism could save China and any deviation from it would lead inevitably back to semi-feudal and semi-colonial conditions. Moreover, despite the errors committed, the progress made in the PRC during the past three decades was on a scale 'which old China could not achieve in hundreds or even thousands of years'.

In the second principle Deng called for upholding the dictatorship of the proletariat, presented by him as a socialist democracy, 'the broadest democracy that has ever existed in history'. This factor was of quintessential importance since 'without democracy there can be no socialism and no socialist modernization'. While arguing for the need to exercise dictatorship over forces hostile to socialism, Deng maintained that the CCP was 'opposed to broadening the scope of class struggle', that it did not believe that 'there is a bourgeoisie within the Party' (the words are those attributed to Mao Zedong) nor that 'under a socialist system a bourgeoisie or any other exploiting class will re-emerge'.

Deng Xiaoping's third principle was upholding the leadership of the Communist Party, which rested on the premise that the Party was indispensable. 'Without the Chinese Communist Party there would be no socialist new China' is an assertion with which it is impossible to argue, since it is so obviously in accord with the historical record. However, whether the conclusion which Deng drew from this undeniable statement – that 'in reality, without the Chinese Communist Party, who would organize the socialist economy, politics, military affairs and culture of China, and who would organize the Four Modernizations?' – follows completely logically is another matter. Of course, the Party did play the role which Deng ascribed to it, but whether it should perform it exactly as it had in the past, as the only actor on the stage, often completely unresponsive to its audience, is a subject which today is the source of much controversy.

Finally, Deng advocated the necessity of upholding Marxism–Leninism and Mao Zedong Thought, viewed as a scientific system whose recent falsification and distortion during the 'cultural revolution' had now been successfully overcome. Deng used the occasion to put forward a new definition of Mao Zedong Thought, which became a key element in the coming reassessment of the 'cultural revolution' and the role of Mao Zedong. Mao Zedong Thought was now interpreted as representing not his thought alone, but also that 'of his comrades in arms, the Party and the people', and hence it was viewed as 'the crystallization of the experiences of the Chinese people's revolutionary struggle over half of a century'. In this fashion a significant step had been taken towards eliminating some of the more absurd excrescences of the personality cult.

There is no reason to assume that Deng Xiaoping and his closest colleagues – all veteran communists – did not attach much importance to what they believed to be the intrinsic merits of the Four Principles. However, there were also at least two tactical reasons why the propagation of them at this stage was thought to be politically advantageous. In the face of attacks from the 'two whatevers' faction, the Four Principles could serve as a counter-argument intended to prove that the political line represented by the Deng Xiaoping group was not an abandonment of Marxism–Leninism and Mao Zedong Thought – as their opponents claimed – but, on the contrary, its correct interpretation and adaptation to present needs, the restoration of its original nature.

A degree of permissiveness had been displayed by the authorities, especially in Beijing, in the autumn of 1978 towards the continued activities of the unofficial press and the relatively uninhibited wall-poster campaign, referred to by Western journalists as the democracy movement. The toleration shown up to the spring of 1979 might well be explained by the fact that a good part of the material displayed and published concentrated its attacks on the most prominent members of the 'two whatevers' faction, such as Wang Dongxing and Wu De. However, the Four Principles were also plainly intended to define the limits of unofficial activity, in preparation for ultimately restricting and eliminating it altogether. In the speech in which he announced the Four Principles, Deng Xiaoping made it quite clear that any activities deemed to run counter to them would not be tolerated for any length of time. Strict regulations concerning the putting up of posters in Beijing were introduced in March, and were followed by arrests and trials of some of the more active participants in the uncontrolled press. By the end of 1979, this form of what was presumably regarded – whether correctly or not is another matter – as a source of potential opposition had practically ceased to exist.

At the beginning of 1979 it was apparent that the economic plans advanced by Hua Guofeng in 1977, and especially the Ten-Year Plan presented in February 1978, were unfeasible; they were too grandiose and had failed to take account of the country's actual conditions. In fact, they resembled to a certain extent the economic policies of the Great Leap Forward, but in this instance steps were taken in time to prevent consequences as disastrous as those of the 1959–62 period.

The new approach to current economic development was the main subject considered at the Central Committee Work Conference held on 5–28 April 1979. It was decided that a 'sober appraisal' of the economy, which was obviously suffering from serious imbalances inherited from the 'cultural revolution' decade, was imperative. Moreover, a partial retreat would have to be executed and a new general policy stressing the needs of the economy – readjustment, restructuring, consolidation and

239

improvement – should be introduced immediately, starting with the plan for 1979 and continuing for the next two years. This would create the basis for subsequently tackling the tasks of the Four Modernizations. Readjustment was taken to mean rectifying serious imbalances, improving co-ordination and maintaining a proper ratio between accumulation and production. Restructuring implied an overall reform of economic management which would observe economic laws. Consolidation was defined as an effective shake-up of enterprises, aimed at increasing their efficiency and productivity, while improvement was to involve raising the level of production, technology and management.

The introduction of these new economic policies involved also some painful readjustments of the overly ambitious investment plan, particularly in heavy industry. A large number of already negotiated foreign contracts, especially with Japan, had to be scrapped, and the compensation paid out was a heavy drain on the limited reserves of foreign exchange. However, the conditions for further economic development were not unfavourable in 1979; the results achieved in the preceding two years were quite impressive. Grain production had increased from 288 million tons in 1976 to 304 million in 1978; steel output had risen from 20.4 million tons to 31.7 million; coal output went up from 483 million tons to 618 million; oil production increased from 87 million tons to 104 million.

These figures formed the basis for the more realistic targets set in the 1979 plan which was submitted to the Second Session of the Fifth NPC on 18 June–1 July. The report on the plan, delivered on 21 June by Vice Premier Yu Qiuli, contained an unusually encouraging wealth of data, a truly welcome change from the self-centred, secretive practices pursued earlier, especially during the 'cultural revolution' decade. It thus became possible to acquire a deeper insight into the aspirations of the CCP leadership in every important domain of the economy. An even fuller source of information was provided on 27 June by the communiqué of the State Statistical Bureau which gave the economic results achieved in 1978, as contrasted with the figures for 1977. The policy of publishing economic statistics in a candid and straightforward fashion has continued ever since.

The lengthy process of redressing earlier injustices, inaugurated in October 1976, continued, albeit inexplicably slowly in some instances. In January 1979, the reappearance in Beijing of three prominent victims of the 'cultural revolution' was noted – Peng Zhen, Lu Dingyi and Wang Guangmei. In the case of Liu Shaoqi's widow, it is maintained that she was not released from prison until 1978. In February 1979, the Central Committee finally ordered a formal investigation into the charges made against Liu Shaoqi in 1968.

Deng Xiaoping stated that 'according to incomplete statistics, 2.9 million people were rehabilitated, as were an even greater number whose cases were not included among those needing special inquiries'. During the course of investigations into the immense number of innocent people persecuted during the 'cultural revolution', a more accurate assessment of the role in this period of two prominent senior CCP leaders was arrived at. Although in August 1977 Kang Sheng was still being eulogized by Hua Guofeng, undeniable proof of his malevolent and destructive activities, and those of his close accomplice Xie Fuzhi, accumulated rapidly. In December 1978 the Discipline Inspection Commission under Chen Yun was entrusted with investigating the actions of both these men. In July 1980 at a memorial meeting for one of his victims, Kang Sheng was bitterly denounced by Hu Yaobang. On 31 October 1980, the Central Committee announced an unprecedented decision to expel Kang and Xie posthumously from the Party. The principal charge was their direct participation in the criminal activities of the Lin Biao and Jiang Qing cliques.

It is small wonder that after the experiences of the 'cultural revolution' the present CCP leadership decided to pay attention also to the problem of a sound socialist legal system which involved, among other things, drawing up a proper code of criminal law and procedure. This had not been accomplished in the first three decades of the PRC, although repeated efforts had been made and more than thirty drafts of the criminal code prepared. Appropriately enough, it was Peng Zhen who was placed in charge of the preparatory work in this field; he presented the draft projects to the NPC in June 1979, and they were then enacted into law.

Anniversaries, especially in round numbers, can be troublesome sometimes, and the thirtieth anniversary of the establishment of the PRC, due to be celebrated on 1 October 1979, was obviously too important an occasion to be fobbed off with routine phrases. A further step in assessing the past had to be undertaken, even if earlier Party decisions, including those taken at the historic meeting in December 1978, called for caution and slowness. Thus, the Fourth Plenum of the Central Committee was convened on 25–28 September primarily for the purpose of discussing and approving the text of the anniversary address to be delivered by Ye Jianying.

It seems clear from Ye's speech that the Party leadership had decided that a partially self-critical analysis of the three decades of PRC history was called for, and that an initial evaluation of the ten years of the 'cultural revolution' could not be postponed any longer. It was admitted that these years had brought calamity to the extent that China suffered its most severe reversal since 1949; in short, it was 'an appalling catastrophe'. But there the matter rested. A truly thorough analysis of the 'cultural revolution' had not yet been made and the key question of responsibility for it had been left in abeyance.

By the beginning of 1980 Deng Xiaoping and his closest associates were inclined to believe that considerable political progress had been attained. In a review of the preceding three years, Deng pointed to what he characterized as the main achievements of this period. They included the settling of accounts with the 'gang of four' and its supporters; the restoration and strengthening of democratic life within the Party and the country; the righting of wrongs on the immense scale already mentioned; the termination of discrimination against intellectuals and former members of the propertied classes; the re-examination of the experiences and lessons of the thirty years of the PRC – although this process was by no means completed; the restora-

242

tion of a correct interpretation of Mao Zedong Thought and hence of an appropriate ideological line; and the beginning of a return to normality in education, science and culture as well as in other fields. Deng Xiaoping thought that all these attainments deserved to be recognized as a tremendous success. A vast amount had indeed been accomplished in a very short time and under conditions complicated by many factors, including that of deeply rooted divergences within the Party itself at all levels.

It was with such an evaluation of the political situation in mind that the decision to call a meeting of the Central Committee for the purpose of carrying out a number of far-reaching organizational measures was undertaken at this time. Thus, the Fifth Plenum which took place on 23–29 February 1980 approved the restoration of the Secretariat, composed of eleven members. It would be in charge of the day-to-day activities of the Central Committee, in accord with the instructions and decisions of the Political Bureau's Standing Committee. Within this new body Hu Yaobang took up the post of general secretary, once held by Deng Xiaoping in the 1960s. Simultaneously, Hu and Zhao Ziyang were elected to the Standing Committee of the Political Bureau; the other members of this supreme policy- and decision-making body were now Ye Jianying, Deng Xiaoping, Chen Yun, Li Xiannian and Hua Guofeng. Although Hua still formally held two of the highest Party posts – that of chairman of the Central Committee and of the Military Affairs Commission – and was still premier, his political importance had in fact ended. His role was increasingly that of a figurehead, until his complete removal could be quietly and gradually accomplished. Four former Political Bureau members – Wang Dongxing, Wu De, Chen Xilian and Ji Dengkui – were dismissed from their leading Party and state posts; all of them had been considered principal supporters of the 'two whatevers' faction and of Hua Guofeng.

The plenum also decided that the next Party Congress was to be held earlier than the statutory requirement, and recommended that delegates to it be elected by November 1980. In the event the Twelfth Congress did not convene until September

1982. No official explanation has ever been given for this incon-
sistency, but it can be assumed that the time necessary for
appropriate ideological and political preparation had been very
much underestimated.

Finally, the 'biggest frame-up' in the history of the CCP – the
case of Liu Shaoqi – was dealt with. The plenum now ascertained that Liu had been 'loyal to the Party and the people at all
times over the past decades, and devoted all his energy to the
revolutionary cause of the proletariat . . . Lin Biao, the "gang of
four" and company [had] concocted false evidence and deliberately subjected Comrade Liu Shaoqi to political frame-up and
physical persecution.' Hence, it was decided 'to remove the
labels of renegade, traitor and scab' which had been put on Liu,
'to cancel the erroneous resolution expelling him from the
Party' and to 'clear the name of Comrade Liu Shaoqi as a great
Marxist and proletarian revolutionary and one of the principal
leaders of the Party and the State'.

Although the public had been partially prepared beforehand
by the media for this event, the news of Liu Shaoqi's rehabilitation came nonetheless as a shock. For ten years, all still fresh in
everyone's memory, Liu had been reviled unceasingly and systematically on every possible occasion; practically every book,
article, speech – even information provided by a production brigade leader – had to contain the obligatory ritual condemnation
of the man and all his deeds. Now it turned out that it was all a
lie. The blow to the CCP's credibility was severe indeed. The
Party tried to mitigate the effect by taking credit for the rehabilitation as an action which demonstrated that it 'is a serious, earn-
est, open and above-board Marxist revolutionary party that
seeks truth from facts and corrects its mistakes whenever they
are found'. It was also claimed that Liu's rehabilitation was
carried out 'not only for his own sake, but in order that the Party
and the people will for ever remember this bitter lesson'. The
injunction was superfluous; the lesson would not easily be forgotten. The damage had been done, and not only to the Party,
but to the image of its erstwhile leader as well, since – in spite of
all the efforts to gloss over this matter in the resolution

announcing Liu's rehabilitation – everyone remembered Mao Zedong's role in bringing about the downfall of Liu Shaoqi. Deng Xiaoping had this clearly in mind when, in March 1980, he spoke of the 'considerable ideological confusion' resulting from Liu's rehabilitation. On 17 May, a memorial meeting was held for Liu in Beijing; fittingly, Deng, who had been the moving force in the campaign to restore Liu's honour and good name, delivered the eulogy.

Against such a background the need to proceed with the task of evaluating the past three decades of CCP history was now more urgent than ever before. However, the preparation of the fundamental document, whose full title was the 'Resolution on Certain Questions in the History of Our Party Since the Founding of the People's Republic of China' – referred to already so many times by the present writer – proved to be an extraordinarily complex, arduous and time-consuming task. The work on this project was probably begun in March 1980 by a drafting group headed by Hu Qiaomu, under the direct supervision of the Political Bureau and the Secretariat and, personally, of Deng Xiaoping and Hu Yaobang. The original draft was revised many times and in October 1980, 4000 senior Party members took part in a discussion of it. The Resolution was finally completed in the spring of 1981 and submitted for adoption that June.

One reason why the final version took so long to formulate was probably the desire first to see justice finally done with regard to the Lin Biao and Jiang Qing cliques. The trial of the surviving 'principal culprits' of the two factions lasted for over a month, from 20 November to 29 December 1980, and the verdicts were finally announced on 25 January 1981.

Although the fifty-page indictment spoke of sixteen 'principal culprits', only ten of them were in the dock: the 'gang of four' – Jiang Qing, Zhang Chunqiao, Yao Wenyuan, Wang Hongwen; five members of the Lin Biao faction – Huang Yongsheng, Wu Faxian, Li Zuopeng, Qiu Huizuo, Jian Tengjiao; and, in a category all of his own, Chen Boda. The other six – Lin Biao, his wife Ye Qun, his son Lin Liguo, his collaborator Zhou Yuchi, as well as Kang Sheng and Xie Fuzhi – were all already dead.

245

The indictment is a dreary, depressing document; it sets out with a wealth of detail the multitude of crimes which the defendants were charged with committing during the 1966–76 decade, as well as the fate of many of their victims. Even so, what was revealed and corroborated during the trial was only a minute part of the sufferings inflicted on millions of Chinese in these years. It should nonetheless be required reading for all the myopic Western admirers of the 'cultural revolution' who may then reflect on how much truth there was in the fairy stories they parroted after returning from their guided tours.

The main charges against the accused, of conducting the 'frame-up and persecution of Party and state leaders', of 'the persecution and suppression of large numbers of cadres and masses', as well as of planning to seize supreme power, were substantiated by the evidence and testimony given at the trial. But much more important to the current CCP leadership than proving the guilt of the ten defendants was separating the crimes perpetrated by them – and by many thousands of others – during the 'cultural revolution' from the political errors committed during this same period by the Party and, in particular, by its supreme leader. The trial provided a forum for a strenuous attempt to bolster the tarnished image of the Party's foremost leader by disassociating Mao Zedong completely from the top leaders of the two cliques. Since they had been his closest chosen collaborators, the difficulties involved in achieving this aim are obvious; only the Chinese can answer the key question as to what degree of success was attained. The political motives of the CCP leadership to seek by all means possible to repair the image of the Party and the founder of the PRC are understandable. There were equally comprehensible personal motives, for all the members of the Standing Committee of the Political Bureau had themselves been for decades close followers of Mao Zedong, although their experiences and actions during the 'cultural revolution' differed considerably.

An attentive reading of the trial documents gives rise to a number of other questions. How is it that the enormities documented could have been committed with practically complete immunity – in one case up to 1971, in the other up to 1976 – in a country which claimed to be socialist? The words 'feudal fascism', used by Deng Xiaoping himself, come to mind once again, but if feudal fascism is to be accepted as an answer – and the present writer is inclined to do so – then a further question arises. How could the superstructure of a country which had public ownership of the means of production and supposedly socialist relations of production – the customarily advanced although quite incomplete definition of socialism – be distorted into what was surely its opposite? After all, while the conspiracies and plots were the accused's own work, most of the crimes perpetrated were not carried out directly by them, but by the state apparatus which followed their orders. Only an analysis of the shortcomings and faults of this apparatus, and of the Party as well, can resolve the question. And this in turn can probably only be accomplished if full consideration is given to the truly fundamental issue – the dual heritage of feudalism and Stalinism, the real albatross weighing on the neck of the Chinese people. The price of failing to confront this problem – or even to acknowledge its existence – in the 1950s and 1960s was a heavy one indeed. Whether it has been dealt with effectively since 1978, and if not, whether it will be in the foreseeable future, must remain an open question.

The sentences pronounced at the end of the trial were not unexpected. Jiang Qing and Zhang Chunqiao were sentenced to death with a two-year reprieve. This has since been changed to life imprisonment, the punishment received by Wang Hongwen. The others, all of them over sixty except for Yao Wenyuan, received sentences of from sixteen to twenty years. A tragic chapter in the history of the PRC appeared to have been closed but, in reality, the memory of the horrors of the 'cultural revolution' will remain alive until the generations which experienced them have passed away.

In the autumn of 1980 the draft of the Resolution on Party History was submitted to the members of the Political Bureau for discussion and appraisal. It has been stated – but there is no documentary proof available – that Hua Guofeng objected strenuously to the way in which the criticism of Mao Zedong and the condemnation of the 'cultural revolution' were formulated in the document. The confrontation continued during a series of nine meetings of the Political Bureau from 10 November to 5 December. A majority of its members accepted the view of the Resolution, and questioned the advisability of having Hua continue to hold the post of the Party's principal leader. It is also maintained that as a result of the above controversy Hua Guofeng resigned on 13 November from his two key posts of chairman of both the Central Committee and the Military Affairs Commission.

By this time Hua had already been stripped of his premiership and replaced by Zhao Ziyang. Zhao had been transferred to Beijing from Sichuan in early 1980 and made vice premier in charge of the day-to-day work of the State Council. As first secretary in Sichuan since 1975 he had earned a considerable reputation for his administrative skill and innovative approach to economic reform, helping to bring about a recovery of the potentially very rich province, which had been devastated during the 'cultural revolution'. In September 1980 Zhao was promoted to premier in place of Hua Guofeng. The move reflected the need to press on with new economic measures. A new Five-Year Plan had to be prepared for the years 1981–5, which would take into account that while some further successes in increasing agricultural and industrial production had been attained, the overall economic situation had not improved as much as had been expected. The imbalances in the economy still persisted, over-investment in capital construction had continued, resulting in a ten billion yuan deficit for 1980. The policy of readjustment would have to continue at least up to 1983, and a number of significant reforms would have to be implemented in the economic field, commencing with agriculture.

Information about the mistakes made by Hua Guofeng since October 1976 (which were specified in detail in the Resolution on Party History) was published in a circular and distributed within the Party following the November–December meetings of the Political Bureau. The circular also recorded the decision taken during these meetings to propose to the coming Sixth Plenum of the Central Committee that Hua Guofeng's resignation be accepted and that Hu Yaobang be elected chairman of the Central Committee and Deng Xiaoping chairman of the Military Affairs Commission. Thus, four years after Mao Zedong's death, having failed to consolidate his potentially immensely strong political position, the man supposedly chosen by Mao as his successor was quietly but firmly deposed from power.

Six months later the Central Committee met in a short plenary session on 27–29 June. In line with the Political Bureau's proposals, Hua Guofeng's resignation was accepted and Hu Yaobang and Deng Xiaoping were formally elected to the two posts vacated by him. Hua was permitted, however, to remain as one of the vice chairmen of the Central Committee, whose composition thus remained unchanged. At last, the Resolution on Party History was passed and now made available to the 39 million members of the CCP and their 900 million fellow citizens. It was – and remains – a remarkable document and its political significance was of the first order, since it was intended to shape the views of the Chinese on their country's recent past, the present and the future.

The 1981 Resolution is a composite work of 35,000 words in which the authors undertook the ambitious task of writing a synthesis of sixty years of the Party's history, with the major part devoted to its years in power after 1949. It was clearly written with great care and, on the whole, is cogently reasoned, if one accepts the premises on which the reasoning is based. It is not unfair to state that it represents, above all, the views of Deng Xiaoping himself; this would be a reasonable assumption given that his position of dominance in the leadership had been firmly established and was basically unchallenged by the time of the document's completion, but it emerges also from the many illuminating commentaries he made in the course of its long gestation.

Three tasks had been set for the authors: the Resolution was to affirm the historic role of Mao Zedong and to explain the need for continuing to uphold Mao Zedong Thought; to analyse the rights and wrongs in the thirty years' history of the PRC; and to present a synthesis of the past work of the Party on which a consensus could be reached. All this was to be carried out in the spirit of seeking truth from facts. A formidable assignment indeed.

The central and most troublesome issue was how to assess the role of Mao Zedong. There was one clear and obligatory directive given by Deng Xiaoping: 'We will not do to Chairman Mao what Khrushchev did to Stalin' (the phrase comes from an extraordinarily candid interview granted by Deng in August 1980 to Oriana Fallaci, which contains much other interesting material as well). However, this injunction only conveys the desire to avoid a simplistic denunciation; the intention was obviously to give a balanced presentation of Mao's activities which would buttress the conclusions desired.

By adopting Chen Yun's suggestion to preface their account of the 1949–80 period with a brief, succinct and very skilfully written summary of the history of the CCP from 1921 to 1949, the authors were able to convey a much fuller picture of Mao Zedong's activities and one in which the proportion between merits and demerits becomes much more favourable than would have been the case if only the PRC era had been dealt with. However, Chen Yun's concept, wise as it was, especially insofar as casting a favourable light on the overall record of the Party is concerned, does lead to another problem, for it is possible to draw the conclusion that there were many more successes during the struggle for power than there were after power was attained. This was a daunting issue which the authors of the Resolution did not, understandably, choose to pursue. But in all fairness it should be stated that they did not juggle the facts and seek to whitewash the basic mistakes committed in the post-1949 period.

The account of the revolutionary struggles up to 1949 – happily free of the earlier hagiographic falsifications – portrays Mao Zedong as 'the most prominent' among 'the many outstanding leaders of the Party' – an evaluation which corresponds with the historical facts. And as such 'his contributions to the Chinese

Revolution far outweigh his mistakes', and his 'immense contributions are immortal'. Having settled this fundamental point – primarily, it should be repeated, on the basis of Mao's undeniable pre-1949 achievements in helping to bring about the victory of the Chinese Revolution – the authors felt that they had sufficient grounds to describe him as a 'great Marxist, great proletarian revolutionary, strategist and theorist'.

It should be noted that many veteran Chinese communists agree with the statement Chen Yun is said to have made that 'had Chairman Mao died in 1956 there would have been no doubt that he was a great leader of the Chinese people. . . .' But he did not, and therefore the situation becomes infinitely more complicated. Achievements are said to outweigh errors up to 1957 (the anti-rightist movement) or to 1959 (the Lushan meeting and the attack on Peng Dehuai); they become more or less equal up to 1962, after which, from the launching of the 'cultural revolution' in 1966 on, the errors are dominant and there is no attempt to conceal their disastrous consequences. The cause of the errors is explained by pointing to the changes in Mao Zedong's style of work, the historical circumstances of the time and the failure of the Party to prevent their growth. Thus, while the main responsibility, both for the Great Leap Forward and especially for the 'cultural revolution', is unequivocally assigned to Mao Zedong, it is also partially placed on other senior leaders.

Since its adoption, the Resolution on Party History has been regarded as the official authoritative interpretation of CCP history for the PRC era, binding on all Party members. The desire to achieve unanimity of opinion within the ranks of the Party was what motivated its sponsors – the current leadership – and its capable authors, and so far none of its basic conclusions has been either criticized or challenged officially, as far as is known. On the contrary, it appears that the Resolution is regarded as a final, definitive verdict – for the time being at least. A tumultuous and complex chapter of history could now be closed and attention focused on present and future tasks.

The above impression is confirmed by, for example, the commemoration in December 1983 of the ninetieth anniversary of

251

Mao's birth in accordance with the conclusions arrived at in the Resolution. In his speech on this occasion Hu Yaobang maintained that 'Mao's position and role in the CCP and the Chinese Revolution were unparalleled' and described him as 'the greatest and most outstanding figure China has had in the past century or more'. Incidentally, and most interestingly, Hu also revealed some of the arguments which had taken place within the communist leadership in connection with the assessment of Mao. Some senior members had argued that 'having followed him for decades, they could not overcome their emotional barriers enough to criticize him'. Hu himself has given a very emotional account of his personal contacts with Mao from the period of the anti-Japanese war. Others 'worried that open exposure of his mistakes would throw the Party into confusion and cause a crisis of confidence'. Hu Yaobang then hastened to point out that these sentiments were set aside and instead the Party went on to make what, in his opinion, was a comprehensive appraisal of Mao Zedong.

Similarly, in September 1986, on the tenth anniversary of Mao Zedong's death, the Chinese media took great pains to feature prominently various statements by Deng Xiaoping regarding Mao which had, in fact, served as guidelines for drawing up the Resolution. In this fashion the attempts to preserve the image of the Party's most important leader and the founder of the PRC in the most favourable light possible were consistently pursued.

In the Resolution much effort was concentrated on drawing a distinction between the mistakes made by Mao in his later years and Mao Zedong Thought. The definition of the latter as 'the crystallization of the collective wisdom of the CCP' is employed here as well, although it is clearly intended to convey the idea that Mao's own contributions to it were the most significant. This is accomplished by enumerating those works of his which are considered to be fundamental to a large number of topics. Mao Zedong Thought is defined as a 'major contribution to the development of Marxism', as a 'guiding ideology' which is a 'theoretical synthesis of China's unique experience in its protracted revolution'. In simpler terms, it is viewed as the sum of the Party's arduously acquired experiences; hence, the need to uphold it. The Thought should not be abandoned, for it was not the cause of such disasters as the 'cultural revolution'; these were brought about by Mao Zedong's mistakes which in essence were a negation and violation of the Thought.

The Resolution's evaluation of the 'cultural revolution' is unqualified. It was a 'comprehensive long drawn out and grave blunder' and a 'tremendous misfortune for the Party and the people'. The didactic intention of these assertions, and of many other parts of the Resolution, is unambiguous. The lessons from this catastrophe must be learned and a repetition of it prevented at all costs. A lengthy concluding section is devoted to a detailed exposition of the tasks facing the Party in accomplishing its fundamental objective of 'turning China step by step into a powerful socialist country with modern agriculture, industry, national defence and science and technology and with a high level of democracy and culture'. It is held that this can be done because, among other things, the CCP has both 'the courage to acknowledge and correct its mistakes and the determination and ability to prevent a repetition of the serious mistakes of the past'. The Resolution's basic political significance rests in the attempt to prove the veracity of the first part of the above assertion; only the future can show whether the second part is true.

The basic theses of the Resolution were fully reflected in the important speech delivered by Hu Yaobang on 1 July 1981, the sixtieth anniversary of the founding of the CCP. This was particularly so in respect to the evaluation of the 'cultural revolution' and the assessment of Mao Zedong's role. In fact the speech seemed to indicate an even greater resolve to eliminate some of the more undesirable effects of the personality cult and, in particular, of the previous portrayal of Mao as the demiurge of the victory of the Chinese Revolution. In an ingenious passage, to which obviously much thought and care had been devoted, Hu paid homage to a large number of deceased communist leaders. Some of them were referred to as great Marxists – Zhou Enlai, Liu Shaoqi and Zhu De. Others were 'outstanding leaders' who, together with Mao Zedong, 'made important contributions to the victorious Chinese Revolution and to the formation and development of Mao Zedong Thought'. This category includes Peng Dehuai, He Long, Tao Zhu, Zhang Wentian and others persecuted during the 'cultural revolution'. 'Prominent leaders' in the Party's formative years include such men as Li Lisan, driven to suicide in 1967, Qu Qiubai, executed by the Guomindang in 1935, whose posthumous disgrace entailed also the desecration of his grave, and Peng Pai, the real pioneer of the communist-led peasant movement in the 1920s, executed by the Guomindang in 1929, whose role was negated and his family cruelly persecuted during the 'cultural revolution'. Thus, the names of these revolutionaries were at last cleared, and a version of the history of the CCP was presented which was certainly much closer to the historical truth than the sorry distortions concocted during the heyday of the personality cult.

The period from the Third Plenum in December 1978 to the Sixth in June 1981 saw the establishment of what the current CCP leadership considered to be a correct political line and strategy, as well as organizational changes. But this by no means signified the resolution of numerous problems in many domains. The Chinese media and especially the pronouncements of the senior leaders provided much material which revealed the existence as well as the nature of these difficulties.

The situation within the Party itself clearly continued to be a matter for serious concern. The older generation of veteran communist leaders would soon be departing from active participation in the country's political life and the question of choosing successors became increasingly urgent. The process of selecting appropriate candidates was complicated by the negative effects of the 'cultural revolution' not only on the generation which had participated in it, but on others as well. Deng Xiaoping warned that particular care had to be exercised to avoid promoting those whose outlook revealed that they were still under the influence of the 'cultural revolution' concepts, or whose behaviour during the 'decade of havoc' – the expression is Hu Yaobang's – was completely inexcusable. Thus, it was actually advisable to show preference for those who had been attacked during this period, although 'bystanders' – and assuredly these had constituted the majority – could also be taken into consideration. There was no lack of potential candidates since there existed a large pool of over 600,000 people who by 1976 had acquired the higher education necessary for advancement in the Party and state establishment.

However, the process of introducing young and middle-aged cadres into the government apparatus was complicated by the practice of abiding by the seniority principle – for the older generation was considered politically the most reliable – and permitting lifelong tenure of posts, in particular at the top of the pyramid of power. Much thought was given to finding a proper solution to these two problems, since a failure to resolve them would mean that an ever less effective gerontocracy would soon be ruling the country.

These issues were linked to two other problems. There was no attempt to disguise the fact that the Party and state establishment of the PRC still displayed a 'grave propensity to bureaucratism', especially at its higher levels. Overstaffing had always been characteristic of it, but by the late 1970s the problem had reached alarming proportions, especially in central government. Moreover, the functions of the Party and state overlapped excessively. It was thought imperative to implement a reform of both the Party and state apparatus so that the tasks of the two would be clearly separated. The Party, while retaining its overall leading function, should concentrate on its political and ideological role and leave the supervision of government work, especially in the economic field, to the state administration, which would have to be reorganized accordingly and streamlined.

In April 1982 it was announced that the number of central ministries and commissions had been reduced from 52 to 41, while the number of ministers and deputy ministers had been cut from 505 to 157. This move, however, pertained only to the pinnacle of the over-expanded establishment, and it is open to doubt whether the general problem of a bloated and unwieldy bureaucracy and its inefficient functioning in the middle and lower levels was tackled to any serious extent. The CCP leaders were certainly not unaware of the fact that one of the main reasons for the sluggish performance of the Party and state apparatus was the unwillingness of its functionaries to assume any responsibility for decisions. This trait was the natural result of the turmoil of the preceding decades and of what many felt was insufficient current political stability to guarantee that their actions would not become the object of unwarranted future criticism.

On economic issues, further progress had been made since 1978 in the development both of agriculture and industry. In 1981 grain production amounted to 325 million tons compared to 304 million in 1978 (but 332 million in 1979), while cotton output had risen to 2.9 million tons from 2.16 million in 1978, and steel output to 35.6 million tons from 31.7 million. However, coal output had increased only to 620 million tons from 618 million, while oil production was down to 101 million tons from 104 million. Cement output rose to 84 million tons from 65 million in 1978, and electricity to 309 billion kwh from 256 billion. Chemical fertilizers increased to 12.4 million tons from 8.7 million.

The intention from 1978 on was to try to meet, at least in part, the immense demand for durable consumer goods, basically unsatisfied for decades and stimulated by increased urban wages and higher peasant incomes (urban incomes are said to have increased in the period 1978–81 by 25 per cent, rural incomes by 67 per cent). The demand was reflected in the figures for the production of: TV sets – 5.4 million (1978, 0.5 million); radios – 40.5 million; wrist watches – 28.7 million (1978, 13.5 million); washing machines – 1.28 million; sewing machines – 10.4 million (1978, 4.8 million); and bicycles – the principal mode of transport for the overwhelming majority of Chinese – 17.5 million (1978, 8.5 million). The basic material for clothing, cotton cloth, rose to 12.2 billion metres compared to 11 billion for 1978.

Nonetheless, the imbalances in the economy, noted earlier by the leadership, still remained troublesome and were reflected in inordinately large financial deficits – 17 billion yuan in 1979 and 12.7 billion in 1980. This brought a marked increase in the rate of inflation, something which had been on the whole avoided in the previous decades, although only at the price of freezing the standard of living at a very low level. By curtailing capital construction and limiting industrial production, the deficit in 1981 was reduced to 2.7 billion.

In spite of the advances made in economic development up to the end of 1981, which had made possible a moderate rise in the standard of living, a large number of grave problems remained. One of the most important was that of urban unemployment. The growth rate of the urban economy, primarily in industrial production, was not high enough to equal the annual increase in population. This was exacerbated by the mass return to the cities of the millions of educated youth who had been unceremoniously shipped out to the countryside after 1968. Administrative measures taken to handle the situation proved insufficient, which gave rise, especially in Shanghai, to many serious social problems, including a marked increase in the crime rate. One of the means used to alleviate the unemployment question was the sanctioning of individual economic activities, particularly in services, trade and handicrafts. The rapid increase in the number of those employed in these domains did begin to reduce the ranks of youth 'waiting for employment'; this was the euphemism employed by the Chinese media, too embarrassed to admit that the scourge supposedly only of capitalism could emerge in a socialist society which, moreover, did not provide unemployment insurance. The much greater problem of mass under-employment in the countryside was not ignored, but its solution was seen as an integral part of what was perhaps the most difficult of all the socio-economic problems – the reform and restructuring of the agrarian economy.

The overall problem of the economy preoccupied the Fourth Session of the Fifth NPC on 30 November–13 December 1981 and was almost the sole subject of the lengthy and detailed report delivered by Zhao Ziyang. Apart from reviewing the previous record and the results of 1981, Zhao devoted the bulk of his speech to presenting ten principles of further economic construction, which were to form the basis of the economic strategy of the Sixth Five-Year Plan (1981–5). The ten principles were based on the premise that the process of readjustment, restructuring, consolidation and improvement would take longer than had been foreseen in 1979 and would continue for the full five years of the new plan.

The first principle called for an acceleration in the development of agriculture through correct policies and science. It was clear that this point had top priority since steady development of the economy as a whole depended on an overall increase in agricultural production. The principal problem rested in the limited scope for increasing state investment in this domain. A range of specific measures was advanced, including ever-wider application in the rural areas of the responsibility system. There were high hopes of the system, and the near future was to prove that they were not without foundation.

Another principle dealt with developing the consumer-goods industry and adjusting the service orientation of heavy industry. The aim was to realize the immense potential in this field, which had been systematically ignored throughout most of the first three decades of the PRC. The principle also represented an important decision to 'radically change the long-standing one-sided emphasis on heavy industry'.

The need to raise the energy utilization ratio and promote the building of the energy industry and transport was the content of another principle. Here Zhao Ziyang was dealing with perhaps the weakest link and the most troublesome bottleneck in the Chinese economy, for performance in this field was critically low, characterized primarily by enormous waste. Hence, emphasis was placed on the proper use of fortunately abundant resources of oil and coal.

An especially interesting point is the emphasis placed in Zhao's report on the need to persist in opening China up to the outside world. The country's participation in the world market, expansion of foreign trade, the import of advanced technology, utilization of foreign capital and implementation of different forms of international economic and technological co-operation were all measures which were considered beneficial for further economic development. However, they were not to be understood as a departure from the policy of self-reliance, but as the relinquishing of the autarkic concepts followed previously. There was no attempt to minimize the difficulties, deriving largely from lack of adequate experience, involved in applying this policy.

It is clear that Deng Xiaoping and his principal associates attached great importance to a successful Party congress and sought to prepare it as carefully as possible. This may have been one of the reasons why the initial plan to convene the Congress in late 1980 or 1981 had been abandoned. Another cause was probably that 'bringing order out of chaos', especially in ideological matters – a task which was to be fulfilled by the 1981 Resolution on Party History – also proved to be more difficult and time-consuming than had been foreseen. The restoration of 'the Party's prestige, gravely damaged during the "cultural revolution" ' had proved to be a laborious process too. It is possible to assume that by the summer of 1982 the Party leadership considered that the results attained in these respects were now satisfactory and thus resolved to wait no longer. In any case, further delay could have been interpreted – correctly or not – as evidence of continuing instability within the Party and especially its leadership.

The decision to convene the Twelfth Congress was announced in advance in August – an interesting contrast to earlier practices, particularly those of the 1966–76 decade – and its meetings on 1–10 September 1982 were surrounded with infinitely less secrecy than some of its predecessors. There can be no doubt that the aim was to make this Congress a milestone in the history of the CCP, especially the post-1949 period. While Deng Xiaoping spoke favourably of the Eighth Congress, he noted that its correct line and views were not followed in practice due to the Party's inadequate ideological preparation for

259

socialist construction. Therefore he pointed to the Seventh Congress (1945) as the model to be emulated, a meeting capable of summing up previous experiences and formulating correct policies for the future. It is worth noting that in his opening speech Deng passed over in silence the Ninth (1969), Tenth (1974) and Eleventh (1977) Congresses, which clearly reflected his negative appraisal of the 1966–76 period. This deserves to be kept in mind in any attempt to draw up a balance sheet of PRC history.

In line with the basic premises of the Congress's tasks, Hu Yaobang started his lengthy political report, which constituted the main item on the agenda, with a summary of the past. But there was little new that could be stated here for this had already been done by the Resolution on Party History, viewed by him as the successful conclusion of the work 'in setting the Party's ideology to rights'. What Hu did add was a list of the various measures undertaken in the preceding six years to resolve the many problems inherited from the 'cultural revolution' decade in all domains, but especially those pertaining to the economy. It was the economy, its present stage and plans for the future, to which Hu devoted a large part of his report.

The most important single task advanced by Hu Yaobang was to push forward the socialist modernization of China's economy. Only this would make it possible to attain the objective set by him for economic development, which was far-reaching indeed. It called for the quadrupling of the annual value of industrial and agricultural production from 710 billion yuan in 1980 to 2800 billion yuan in the year 2000. Deng Xiaoping had expressed this same idea in terms of raising individual annual income from US $280 to $800 in the same period. The achievement of such a goal would obviously transform China. However, the difficulties involved were clearly immense; three adjectives, often used by Deng Xiaoping when describing the problem, come to mind: 'big', 'huge', and 'weak'. A big country with a huge population and a weak economy – a situation aggravated still more by the growth of this huge population and the decrease in arable land. There was full awareness of these aspects in Hu's report and, in particular, of the demographic problem. It was stressed that family planning was imperative and every effort must be exerted to keep the population within 1.2 billion by the end of the century.

Hu Yaobang placed much hope on the successful fulfilment of the two Five-Year Plans covering the 1980s which, in his view, could result in the building of a relatively solid basis for economic growth in the 1990s. He supplemented Zhao Ziyang's ten principles for economic construction with four more: concentrating funds on key development projects and continuing to improve living standards; upholding the leading position of the state economy and developing diverse economic forms; correctly implementing the leading role of the planned economy and the supplementary role of market regulation; and persevering in self-reliance while expanding economic and technological exchanges with foreign countries.

It was evident from Hu's elaboration of these principles that serious thought had been devoted to formulating a strategy of economic development which would correspond to the thesis advanced by Deng Xiaoping of building socialism with Chinese characteristics. It is too soon to draw conclusions regarding the degree of success attained in the overall implementation of this strategy, not least because up to 1985 the Chinese media reports on the advances made were so euphoric that the authorities themselves later criticized them.

The many factors involved in the no less important aim of building what is referred to as socialist spiritual civilization were also analysed by Hu Yaobang. He dealt with the negative features in the previous decades of neglecting the importance of education, science and culture and the discrimination against intellectuals, and enumerated the measures being taken to overcome these erroneous views and practices.

The changes in the international status of the PRC derived, according to Hu Yaobang, at least in part from the application of the principles of the foreign policy formulated by Mao Zedong and Zhou Enlai. The results included, among other things, a marked increase in prestige and in the development of relations with other countries, now totalling 125. The Five Principles of Peaceful Co-existence continued to be considered the valid basis for the PRC's foreign policy and Hu took obvious satisfaction in asserting that 'we do not station a single soldier abroad nor have we occupied a single inch of foreign land'. Unsurprisingly, nothing new appeared in his review of relations with Japan, the United States and the Soviet Union. In the case of the last, attention was focused on three factors which are portrayed to the present day as the obstacles hindering the normalization of Sino-Soviet relations: the stationing of massive Soviet armed forces along the Sino-Soviet and Sino-Mongolian borders; Soviet support for Vietnam's activities in Kampuchea; and Soviet action in Afghanistan. Much stress was also placed on China's role as a developing country of the Third World.

An important change in the policies of the CCP towards other communist parties, whether in power or not, could be noted in Hu Yaobang's speech. The guiding principles were now to be the recognition of independence, complete equality, mutual respect and non-interference in each other's internal affairs. The communist parties 'cannot be divided into superior and inferior parties'; the CCP 'had suffered from the attempt of a self-elevated paternal party to keep it under control'.

The presentation for adoption at the Twelfth Congress of a new, extensively revised Party constitution gave Hu Yaobang occasion to consider the Party's present overall situation as well as the troubles which had affected it during the three decades of the PRC. The principal problem had clearly been the personality cult which had caused the political life of the Party, and particularly of the Central Committee, to become more and more abnormal, 'leading eventually to the decade of domestic turmoil'. The efforts made since December 1978 had achieved a 'gradual return to the correct path, the path of Marxism', but still more was needed to restore the Party's functioning and particularly its style of work to a satisfactory level. In connection with this, Hu Yaobang announced plans for conducting a rectification and consolidation campaign, to begin in the second half of 1983. The campaign took place as scheduled, progressing from the top to the lower echelons of the Party. At the end of 1985 it was extended to the 22 million Party members in the rural areas, and was due to be completed in 1987. Unfortunately there are very few data – apart from vague generalities mentioned in the Chinese media – concerning its results and especially to what degree the anticipated consolidation of the Party has been achieved.

The revised Party constitution, adopted at the Twelfth Congress, revealed a highly ingenious solution to the problem of shifting at least some of the senior leaders from commanding posts and opening the road to advancement for the next generation. A Central Advisory Commission (CAC) was established, to 'act as a political assistant and consultant to the Central Committee'. Those serving on the CAC had to be Party members of forty years' standing or more – i.e. they had to have joined the movement before it came to power. The list of 172 members included some very distinguished veteran revolutionaries indeed. It was also stipulated that the chairman of the CAC must be a member of the Standing Committee of the Political Bureau, and Deng Xiaoping was elected to this post.

The Discipline Inspection Commission was enlarged to 132 members, thus enabling the number of senior officials on it to be increased. It continued to be headed by Chen Yun. In his speech at the Congress, Chen concentrated on the necessity of promoting young and middle-aged personnel, but firmly warned against the advancement of those who had risen to prominence during the 'cultural revolution', who were factionalist in their ideas and who had 'indulged in beating, smashing and looting'.

The Congress elected a somewhat larger Central Committee – 210 members and 138 alternates – of whom more than 60 per cent joined for the first time. Two-thirds of this new group were under sixty years old, thus providing an antidote to the problem of the ageing Party leadership. But there were fewer changes in the supreme bodies of the Party. The Political Bureau was slightly enlarged to 25 full members and 3 alternates. Here the seniority principle was still fully respected. Eighteen of the 28 members had participated in the 1934–5 Long March; 5 others had been active in the Party at the same time in other areas (north China and Shanghai), and only 5 had joined the movement in 1936 or later.

There was only one change in the most important body of all – the Standing Committee. Hua Guofeng was dropped from it – and from the Political Bureau – to remain only a Central Committee member. His political demise was now almost complete. The office of chairman, formerly held by Hua – and of course much more significantly by Mao Zedong – was abolished in the new Party constitution. Hence, the highest post became that of general secretary, to which the sixty-eight-year-old Hu Yaobang was elected.

CHAPTER TWELVE

The 'Second Revolution':
Socialism with Chinese Characteristics,
1982–6

The policy of opening to the world and the emphasis placed on the need for attracting foreign investment were two of the main factors which made a rational and peaceful solution of the future of Hong Kong an issue of far-reaching political importance. The role played by Hong Kong in the PRC's foreign trade and the potential value of its contribution to China's modernization are highly significant.

Talks between the PRC and UK governments on the future of Hong Kong began in 1983, and after twenty rounds of intricate negotiations full accord was reached; on 26 September 1984 a joint declaration was initialled by both sides. The formal signing of the document by the prime ministers of both countries took place in Beijing on 19 December 1984. Under the terms of the accord China will resume full sovereignty over the colony on 1 July 1997, the expiry date of the 'lease' on the greater part of Kowloon which forms the bulk of Hong Kong's territory. For fifty years thereafter the social and economic system of Hong Kong will be maintained without any fundamental changes to its status as a free port and an international centre for trade and finance. Politically, Hong Kong will be designated a special administrative region enjoying a high degree of autonomy.

Hong Kong was ceded to Britain under the terms of the Treaty of Nanjing, signed in 1842 at the conclusion of the First Opium War. Imposed by the British at gunpoint, the Treaty of Nanjing was the first of the 'unequal treaties' forced on the Chi-

265

nese during a century of humiliation and oppression at the hands of foreign powers. The peaceful restoration of China's sovereignty over Hong Kong will thus be an event of profound significance and satisfaction, particularly to the older generation of Chinese.

The 1984 accord on Hong Kong is based on the concept advanced by the Chinese of 'one country, two systems', which acknowledges that for half a century socialism and capitalism will co-exist within the PRC. Some sources maintain that Deng Xiaoping is the author of the concept; certainly no one else has spoken so much in favour of it. Deng has also exerted great effort to reassure representatives of Hong Kong that there is no reason to fear a future change in attitude by the Beijing government on this question. The idea is highly original and could be utilized for solving at some propitious time in the future another outstanding problem – Taiwan. This point has been made by Chinese leaders on numerous occasions ever since the signing of the Sino-British declaration on Hong Kong.

In 1978 the decision was made to begin the reform of agriculture; it appeared to be a simpler proposition than reforming the urban economy, and it would benefit the majority of the country's population, for 80 per cent lived in rural areas.

It is now maintained that the negative effects of the establishment of the commune system outweighed, over a period of time, its achievements. The peasants had become tired of the production team system, which deprived them of any initiative, responsibility or decision-making. Remuneration on the basis of work points also gave rise to dissatisfaction because its seemingly egalitarian character was actually unfair to those who made major contributions. At the same time, it created opportunities for corrupt practices. According to information published after 1978, the commune system appeared to have ended up in a blind alley; after more than twenty years it had done very little, if anything, to solve the problems of Chinese agriculture and create conditions for rapid growth.

After the Third Plenum in December 1978 the decision was taken to formulate a new agricultural policy and undertake experiments to find satisfactory forms of organization. The new measures included increasing the purchase price of agricultural products, which itself improved the peasants' economic position. Following a pattern applied often in the PRC, the search for new forms of organization was first conducted in a few chosen areas. In Sichuan, Zhao Ziyang took the lead in allowing the peasants to put forward their own proposals for changes. At the same time, sideline production was encouraged, and permission granted for the opening of rural markets. A similar set of policies was introduced in Anhui by Wan Li (now vice premier and Political Bureau member).

After an initial period of experimentation, the choice finally fell on contracting production to households – in other words, a partial return to individual farming. It goes without saying that in such a vast country, with its immense differences in conditions, the shift to household responsibility was incredibly complex. It was applied first to poorer regions, and then spread to the more prosperous. It seems clear that the momentum of its growth came largely from the peasants, who were eager to leave the production teams. It also seems certain that these changes were not at first favoured by the majority of the rural cadres, who feared criticism for permitting alterations which in the future might be characterized as a return to capitalism. However, by 1982 the majority of the rural cadres appeared to be convinced that the CCP leadership was intent on pursuing the reform, and they took an active part in hastening the development of the household contract system. Just as collectivization had been conducted at breakneck speed, the dismantling of a major feature of the collectives was now carried out at a similar pace. By 1984, household contracting had spread to well over 90 per cent of the rural areas. Furthermore, the Central Committee's directive on agriculture of January 1984 extended the length of the contract to fifteen years, to encourage stability and greater peasant investment. This caused some foreign observers to refer to the changes in Chinese agriculture since 1979 as 'a second land reform'.

Under the new system, each household has infinitely more

power to make its own decisions as to the economic activities it is to engage in. It still has to meet the government quotas, not only for grain but for other products as well. This is stipulated by contract, since the government monopoly on purchasing food has been eliminated. Each household pays taxes directly to the government and not by way of the production team; it can sell on the free market all its surplus and side products. Furthermore, it is claimed that mechanization has not been slowed down by the transition to the new system since the peasants have either contracted to use the machines still owned by the communes, or have bought them. In 1981, 380,000 tractors were bought; the figure went up to 1 million in 1982 and 2.1 million in 1983. By 1984, over 90 per cent of the country's tractors were in the hands of individual households. The economic function of the communes has been steadily decreasing since 1979, and their administrative role was abolished altogether with the reintroduction of district authorities.

Two issues have given rise to controversy in connection with the rapid spread of the household contracting system. Does it signify a complete decollectivization? The official position is that only the forms of management have changed. Since the land is still owned by the collective and not by the individual farmers, the new system is not a departure from collective farming. The second issue concerns the obvious discrepancies now arising in the income of individual households. The new policies are estimated to have resulted in an average increase in both agricultural production and peasant incomes of close to 100 per cent for the period 1979–84. However, the distribution of this increased wealth is another matter. While some households, especially the increasing number now specializing in a particular product, have markedly improved their standard of living, progress in the case of the poorer households and the more backward farming areas has been slower.

The reforms in agriculture have also contributed to a considerable growth in rural industries, which by the end of 1985 accounted for 66 per cent of the value of rural output. Fifty million of the rural labour force, 20 per cent of the total, found employment in this field. A large part of rural industry is concerned with food processing but, increasingly, it includes less complicated manufacture, particularly of component parts which are assembled in larger urban factories. The development of rural industry has given rise to the growth of small towns, a subject which has been placed on the agenda for review by the authorities.

The simultaneous development of agriculture, sideline production, and work in industry was not a planned phenomenon; it was primarily the result of the peasants' own initiative. What is particularly striking is that this process of industrialization in China departs from the customary pattern, since the majority of those employed in rural and small-town industrial plants continue to live in their villages. One of its important results is the increased prosperity of the rural towns, which had stagnated throughout most of the period following full collectivization.

The development of rural industries has been studied by the noted sociologist Fei Xiaotong, primarily in relation to his own native province, Jiangsu, which it should be noted is one of the most economically developed parts of China. Rural industrialization here, as elsewhere, has derived largely from agricultural improvements, as well as over-population. The surplus labour force of the countryside will only grow as agriculture continues to be mechanized. According to some sources, the problem will reach immense proportions within the not too distant future, with around 100 million people abandoning farming. But if rural industrialization can provide work for redundant farm workers, this should stem the constant drift to the cities, which are already greatly over-populated, and where all efforts are being made to stop the influx of more people.

Other accounts dealing with rural industries support the view that their development will undoubtedly give rise to a number of problems as far as the overall direction of the economy's development is concerned. According to a well-known economist, Xue Muqiao, considerably higher wages prevail in rural industries established by the peasant collectives than in their state-owned city counterparts, although the technical capacity of the rural plants is lower than that of urban factories. Co-operation exists between them, with rural plants not only providing components for the larger-scale urban industry but also taking up lines of production abandoned in the cities. The price of goods produced in the country is not subject to any regulation and is much more flexible as well as often lower than the state-owned factories'. The success of rural industry in spite of this price difference reveals the almost insatiable demand for the wide variety of consumer products it can provide.

The complexities involved in formulating a satisfactory agricultural policy are also demonstrated by what appears to be a conflict of interest between the positive results of the responsibility system and a proper solution to the population problem. The increase in agricultural output and therefore in peasant income could well mean that farming families might wish to increase their labour power by having more children than is recommended by the government programme for population control.

According to the last census, held in July 1982, the population of the PRC had grown to 1008 million, an increase of 310 million since 1964. (The population in 1953 was 583 million.) This immense growth has meant that available arable land has gone down from 3 mu per capita in 1949 to 1.5 mu in 1983 (15 mu = 1 hectare). As a result, the authorities are advocating rigorous observance of the population control programme which calls for restricting the number of children per family to no more than two, with the one-child family recommended as the proper and ideal model. If this programme is not adhered to and the rate of population growth recorded for 1981 continues, then by the year 2000 the total population will reach 1.3 billion, 100 million more than the figure planned for.

The lower level of literacy in the countryside is another factor which creates a problem in successfully implementing population control. According to the 1982 census, the number of illiterates and semi-literates amounted to 235 million (31 per cent of the population). While this is still a substantial proportion of the population, it did denote an improvement: the figure for

1964 was 52 per cent. However, the problem rests in the fact that the percentage of illiteracy is much higher in the rural areas, and proportionately higher still among rural women, where it reaches 45 per cent. One can therefore understand the claim of those who maintain that only further intensive growth of rural education can safeguard implementation of the population control programme.

The measures introduced in the first years of the Sixth Five-Year Plan proved successful; by the end of 1985 the plan's targets had not only been fulfilled but overfulfilled in a number of fields. Perhaps the greatest successes were in agriculture, due to the introduction of the responsibility system; for the first time in the history of the PRC the country became completely self-sufficient in grain and more than self-sufficient in cotton. Thus the problem of feeding and clothing a billion people – 22 per cent of the world's population – while cultivating only 7 per cent of the world's arable land had been basically solved. It is difficult to overstate the significance of such an achievement.

At the same time, the standard of living rose by 20 per cent per capita in urban areas and 80 per cent in the countryside, with 35 million people being given employment in the urban areas. The huge financial deficits which had marked the first years of the plan were also eliminated by 1985. The value of industrial output rose by 10.6 per cent per annum, and in agriculture by 10.8 per cent. This contrasted with an average annual increase of 3.5 per cent during the years 1953–80.

The table below illustrates the growth rate in a number of selected fields. The durable consumer goods listed are all high-priced articles very much in demand and, in many cases, quite difficult to obtain. Rationing of one indispensable item, cotton cloth, finally ceased on 1 December 1983. The information comes from the annual communiqués of the State Statistical Bureau, and should be compared with the figures for 1978 and 1981 given on page 256. It should be noted that the increase in the production of some of these goods – and others not listed, such as motorcycles – is partly due to the shifting of numerous defence enterprises to civilian production, which in 1985

271

PRODUCT	1982	1983	1984	1985
grain	353 m. tons	387 m.	407 m.	379 m.
cotton	3.5 m. tons	4.6 m.	6 m.	4.1 m.
coal	666 m. tons	715 m.	772 m.	850 m.
oil	102 m. tons	106 m.	114 m.	125 m.
steel	37 m. tons	40 m.	43.8 m.	46.6 m.
electricity	327 b. kwh	351 b.	374 b.	407 b.
cement	95 m. tons	108 m.	121 m.	142 m.
chemical fertilizers	12.7 m. tons	13.7 m.	14.8 m.	13.3 m.
cotton cloth	5.3 b. metres	14.8 b.	13.4 b.	14.3 b.
bicycles	24.2 m.	27.5 m.	28.5 m.	32.3 m.
wrist watches	33 m.	34.6 m.	36.4 m.	41.7 m.
radios	17.2 m.	19.9 m.	21.8 m.	n.a.
washing machines	2.5 m.	3.6 m.	5.7 m.	8.8 m.
TV sets	5.9 m.	6.8 m.	9.9 m.	16.2 m.
(colour)	0.28 m.	0.53 m.	1.5 m.	4.1 m.
sewing machines	12.8 m.	10.8 m.	9.3 m.	9.8 m.
refrigerators	n.a.	0.18 m.	0.53 m.	1.4 m.
cassette recorders	3.4 m.	4.9 m.	7.4 m.	12.7 m.

reached 40 per cent of their total output, compared to 10 per cent in 1979.

The successes obtained in agriculture undoubtedly facilitated the decision of the CCP leadership to grapple with the infinitely more complex issue of reform of the urban economy, to which much thought had been devoted since the end of 1978. On 20 October 1984 the Central Committee adopted a 'Decision on the Reform of the Economic Structure', which since then has been one of the blueprints of the Party's policies and activities in this field.

According to the noted Chinese economist Huan Xiang, the principal defect of the existing economic system was that it had become rigid and had ceased to correspond to the needs of socialist construction. No clear line of demarcation between the functioning of government and enterprises existed, thus stifling economic development. The government agencies' excessive control over enterprises left the latter with little or no autonomy. The overly bureaucratic direct planning from the top down failed to meet the needs of a complex economy. Furthermore, there existed a disregard for the role of commodity production, the law of value and the market, causing dislocation between supply and demand. The adherence to exaggerated egalitarianism in the distribution of income also adversely affected the functioning of the economic structure, which was anyhow irrational.

The common feature of the defects listed above is over-centralization, a characteristic of the PRC economic system which no doubt derives from its highly over-concentrated political structure. The possible political causes are not dealt with by Huan Xiang, but he does present a striking illustration, in the best tradition of Chinese chain reasoning, of the consequences of over-centralization: 'The more centralized, the more rigid; the more rigid the economy, the lazier the people; the lazier the people, the poorer they are; and the poorer the people are the greater the need for centralization, forming a vicious circle.' How to break out of this circle, how to obtain better economic results than those achieved in the years 1953–80, when 'the national income increased only four times and the actual standards of living only doubled', remains the fundamental question. Providing a positive answer is the aim of the reform programme finally formulated in 1984, which it is hoped will reproduce the successes attained in agriculture in the much more complex domain of urban industry.

The reforms, based on earlier experimentation, envisage increasing the autonomy of enterprises by enlarging their power to formulate production plans, market their products, set prices, use funds and regulate wages. The aim is to transform the enterprises into relatively independent socialist commodity producers. Moreover, various forms of the responsibility system have been, and are still to be, extended to industrial enterprises, while a corresponding reform of financial systems, including taxation, pricing and banking, is foreseen.

Ultimately, the basic aim of the economic reforms, according to Huan, is to give rise – after a relatively long period in which the centralized economy and a decentralized one will co-exist – to a new 'two-tiered' economic system which will keep the advantages of both and avoid the disadvantages of each. This may well prove to be the content of the oft-repeated concept of building socialism with Chinese characteristics.

The pressing need to approve the Seventh Five-Year Plan and implement the far-reaching proposals for changes to the composition of the leading bodies of the CCP led to the decision to convene a National Party Conference on 8–23 September 1985. On the eve of the conference, 64 members of the Central Committee, 37 of the Central Advisory Commission, and 30 of the Discipline Inspection Commission – a total of 131 – offered their resignations which the conference accepted. Some of the Central Committee members who resigned were among the fifty-six new members elected to the CAC. Their places on the Central Committee were filled by sixty-four new members, mostly in their forties and fifties. This was certainly a large-scale reshuffle of personnel, but its most spectacular aspect concerned the Political Bureau, ten of whose members resigned from the Central Committee. Six new members, all in their forties and fifties, replaced them.

In this fashion the policy of combining three echelons – veterans in their eighties, senior members in their sixties and seventies, and experienced officials in their forties and fifties – was now put into effect at all levels of the Party apparatus. It was claimed that the three echelons would ensure continuity in the implementation of the Party's programme and policies, while at the same time its leadership would be appropriately rejuvenated.

The comprehensive and detailed proposal for the Seventh Five-Year Plan (1986–90) approved at the conference was subsequently passed by the National People's Congress in the spring of 1986, at the very beginning of its time span. This was a wel-

274

come contrast to the fate of its predecessor, which had been adopted in December 1982, when two of its five years had already elapsed.

The new plan was summarized at the conference by Zhao Ziyang who began his report with an analysis of the achievements to date, asserting that a fundamental improvement in the country's financial and economic situation had been largely achieved and the economy had started to develop in a strong, stable and balanced way. Zhao considered the three main tasks of the new plan to be: (1) to create a sound environment for progress in structural reform; (2) to speed up the construction of key projects, the technological transformation of the country's industry, and intellectual development; and (3) to continue to improve living standards. Priority was assigned to the first point since without reform, stable development would prove impossible. According to Zhao, the two keys to solving the immensely complex problems involved were enhancing the economic efficiency of enterprises, and increasing their ability to earn more foreign exchange through export. The second key was obviously connected with the intention to expand the policy of opening to the outside world, on which Deng Xiaoping and his associates placed such great hopes. But as Deng Xiaoping's speech at the conference made clear, of supreme importance was the successful implementation of economic reforms, implying that this in its way would repair the damage inflicted on the country and its people up to 1976, and possibly 1978, when the CCP had 'neglected to develop the productive forces . . . after the socialist transformation of the ownership of the means of production had been basically accomplished'. If the reforms envisaged in the Seventh Five-Year Plan are carried out, then the ambitious goals set by the Party for the year 2000 can, in the opinion of its leadership, be attained.

The successful fulfilment of the Sixth Five-Year Plan signified that by 1985 a balance had been achieved between agriculture, heavy and light industry, with the share of each being more or less equal. However, economic instability was still evident in 1984 and 1985. The rate of industrial growth had in fact been excessive, leading to an over-heating of the economy, particularly in late 1984 and early 1985, which had to be dealt with drastically in the latter half of 1985. At the same time, the balance of trade was seriously disturbed, for the import of durable consumer goods, probably permitted in order to soak up excess consumer funds, had led to the serious depletion of scarce foreign exchange reserves. In 1984 the value of imports amounted to US $25.5 billion, while exports totalled $24.4 billion, thus creating a deficit of $1.1 billion. The situation in 1985 was still more serious. Imports increased to $33.4 billion, while exports amounted to only $25.8 billion, giving rise to a deficit of $7.6 billion. A large part of this deficit resulted from an unfavourable balance of trade with Japan. Over-investment in fixed assets and an excessive quantity of money in circulation also contributed to the instability. Control of the economy appeared to have been partially lost in the attempt to decentralize; to a non-specialist, the manifestations of this loss of control sometimes made very little sense. In particular, the removal of the chairman of the People's Bank of China, charged with responsibility for putting too much money into circulation, seems very odd indeed, for it is difficult to believe that he would have undertaken any basic decisions without first obtaining approval from the high officials in the Central Committee responsible for economic affairs.

China's economists maintained in the early 1980s that the price system was irrational and distorted. Partial reforms had been undertaken since 1983 but they resulted in a considerable rise in prices, particularly of vegetables and meat, which caused much dissatisfaction among the consumers. However, it is claimed that the increase in wages during 1981–5, which amounted to 68 per cent in urban areas, more than compensated for the price increases, estimated at close to 20 per cent. Thus, living standards did rise appreciably during this period, in line with what has been aptly formulated by Tian Jiyun (a vice premier and member of the Political Bureau since September 1985) as 'repaying the people for what should have been done for them'. This statement may be regarded as a self-critical admission of the failure of the CCP since coming to power to pay sufficient attention to raising standards of living.

It is clear that the rise in living standards was not equally spread. The rural households earning 10,000 yuan annually, to which the Chinese media devoted exaggerated attention, were few and far between. According to Tian, there were still millions of people in the countryside who did not have enough food and clothing. The newly created gaps in income were a serious problem although it is maintained that the question of polarization does not arise, since the means of production, and especially land, continues to be primarily in public ownership.

The results of the policy of opening to the outside world in the years 1981–5 were considered, on the whole, satisfactory by the CCP leadership. Up to the end of 1985 the four special economic zones which had been established earlier had witnessed considerable progress, and steps were taken to encourage foreign investment in the fourteen coastal cities which had been declared open. The principal aim in these areas was to import foreign technology, acquire managerial skills and attract foreign capital. By the end of 1985, close to US $20 billion had been invested, and 1800 joint ventures, over 3300 co-operative enterprises, and 109 foreign-owned plants had been put into operation. It should be noted that a major part of the foreign capital entering China came from overseas Chinese, particularly Hong Kong.

The policy of openness had more than just economic repercussions; it also involved the influx of what the Chinese authorities regarded as negative foreign influences which had to be resisted. Social problems were in fact created by the increased foreign contact, for it led to a significant rise in the scale of corruption, speculation, graft and other economic crimes. A prime example was the Hainan Island affair, in which a number of high Party and state officials took advantage of the open status of the island to import large quantities of automobiles and colour television sets for resale on the mainland at fabulous profits of from two to three hundred per cent. The Chinese authorities made no attempt to cover up the scandal, and measures have been taken to prevent such swindles in the future and deal with the problems involved nationally.

Among the many sad pages of PRC history one of the most tragic was the fate of the 'Double Hundred' policy – 'Let a Hundred Flowers Bloom and a Hundred Schools Contend' – which was drastically terminated in the summer of 1957, slightly more than a year after it was introduced. Thereafter, and particularly during the decade of havoc, it was regarded as the epitome of bourgeois liberalism. It was only under the radically changed political conditions prevailing after December 1978 that the 'Double Hundred' policy could re-emerge. Since then, it has become an integral part of the programme advocated by Deng Xiaoping and his associates, although undoubtedly considerable differences of opinion as to the degree to which it should be applied exist within the top CCP leadership, just as numerous divergences about other fundamental political and economic questions are present as well.

Nonetheless, it is now held that progress in many fields, particularly science and technology and hence the achievement of the Four Modernizations, is unthinkable without adherence to the 'Double Hundred' policy. It is clear, however, that its application to the arts – a subject purposely omitted in the present work – and the social sciences has given rise to much controversy on numerous occasions in the years since 1979. In the case of the latter one can note much progress in the advancing of innovative and creative concepts in numerous key domains – a welcome contrast to the intellectual sterility enforced during the 'cultural revolution'.

While the promise made by Deng Xiaoping to avoid a repetition of the strident, and often vicious and destructive political and ideological campaigns which characterized the pre-1976 era has on the whole been kept, some of the debates conducted in the early 1980s were uncomfortably shrill. The dispute on practice as the sole criterion for verifying truth certainly had very positive results, but it is not so easy to say the same about the discussions on alienation and humanism. And the debate held in late 1983 and early 1984 on 'spiritual pollution' – the supposedly negative consequence of the opening to the outside world – was particularly reminiscent of the decade of turmoil. But if the CCP leadership persists in its current efforts to implement the 'Double Hundred' policy fully in all domains, then it will not be necessary at some future date to bemoan the past once again and, in the words of an eminent social scientist, Yu Guangyuan, speaking in 1986, 'to wonder what heights the arts and sciences would have attained and how much the Chinese nation would have been freed of constant political suffering if the policy had been consistently followed'.

During this same period, the leadership of the CCP took considerable pains to demonstrate its continued full adherence to Marxism. On the centenary of Marx's death on 13 March 1983 Hu Yaobang acknowledged the debt of the Chinese communists by stating that 'without Marx's theory China could not possibly have become what she is today'.

Much effort has been devoted by Hu Yaobang and other theoreticians to seek to prove the continued relevance of Marxism, which had been a guide to revolution and still is, in their view, vital for the study of present-day problems. However, Marxism should be approached in line with the recommended emancipation of the mind, stressed so strongly since the end of 1978. To regard Marxism as the quintessence of knowledge is to facilitate the adoption of a correct attitude both to knowledge and to intellectuals. It follows that – in complete contrast to the ideas advanced during the 'cultural revolution' – respect for knowledge and the intellectuals is vital and urgent. Marxism, according to Hu Yaobang, is incompatible with any anti-intellectual tendencies; the more knowledge, the better. The CCP had paid a heavy price when it ignored these principles and when it failed, after 1949, to emphasize the need for having its own leadership acquire adequate knowledge and culture.

The proper application of Marxism to China's particular conditions deserves serious consideration, according to the noted historian Hu Sheng. This is particularly so since the legacy of China's past is a peculiar one; 'virtually nothing of what a capitalist society could have offered' was present when the Chinese

Revolution finally triumphed in 1949. True enough, but such a formulation inevitably gives rise to the paradoxical question as to whether such a triumph would have taken place had capitalism in China reached a fuller stage of development. Understandably, Hu Sheng does not take up this problem which belongs to the realm of historiosophic speculation. Hence, the difficulties and weaknesses of the PRC were largely due to the fact that Chinese socialist society evolved from semi-colonialism and semi-feudalism. This poses a vast number of questions regarding every phase of socio-economic development, which call for an appropriate Marxist explanation.

Since the Twelfth Congress of the CCP in September 1982, the PRC leadership has been very active in furthering foreign relations. The principal leaders, Zhao Ziyang, Hu Yaobang and Li Xiannian, have embarked on numerous trips abroad in the years up to 1986, between them covering every continent. There is little point in listing all the many heads of state who have visited China since 1979; those for 1984 give an indication: they included Nakasone, Reagan, Kohl and Thatcher. It is obvious that the purpose of the visits was more than simply to exchange views; they were intended to stimulate economic co-operation as well as scientific, technological and cultural exchange, as undoubtedly they have.

It should be noted that the policy of opening to the outside is at present interpreted as one which covers the entire world, and hence also the Soviet Union. The level of Sino-Soviet contacts has so far been comparatively low, but a senior vice premier, Arkhipov, did visit Beijing in December 1984. In September 1986, Deng Xiaoping, who has ceased to make foreign trips, expressed his willingness to meet Gorbachev in the Soviet Union, if the Soviet leader were to bring about the removal of what the Chinese consider the greatest obstacle to the normalization of Sino-Soviet relations – the presence of Vietnamese troops in Kampuchea. Relations between China and the Soviet Union have become noticeably less abrasive than at any time since the beginning of the great polemic in 1956. Trade between the two countries has developed considerably, and co-operation in science and technology has been renewed. It would seem that the Soviet Union is recognized once again as a socialist country, although its foreign policy is still subject to frequent criticism. As well as Kampuchea, Soviet action in Afghanistan and its heavy military presence along the Sino-Soviet and Sino-Mongolian borders continue to be the three impediments to fuller accord. The restoration of inter-Party relations between the CCP and the CPSU – the really important form of political dialogue – is still dependent, according to the Chinese, on the removal of all three obstacles. This is not the case in respect of the East European countries, with which the Chinese are willing to restore inter-Party relations. Visits were paid to Beijing by Jaruzelski in September 1986 and by Honecker in October the same year. Since the end of 1978 the Chinese Party has restored relations with a considerable number of non-ruling communist parties all over the world, having quietly abandoned its previous support for various splinter 'Marxist–Leninist' groups. Its contacts with the Italian and French communist parties in particular have taken on the nature of a working relationship.

Drawing up a balance sheet of the PRC's failures and achievements continues to be something which only the Chinese themselves are really entitled to do. It should be obvious from the preceding narrative that this is precisely what, to a large extent, the communist leadership has been trying to accomplish ever since the truly historic Third Plenum in December 1978. Whether this has been done with sufficient accuracy and clarity, and whether all the relevant conclusions have been made is another matter. This question can only be answered by applying the criterion of practice to what has been accomplished since 1978; the achievements to date would seem to indicate that the answer is in the affirmative. Nonetheless, a full evaluation will have to await the end of the present century, for only then will it be possible to ascertain whether the complex reform programme – the 'Second Revolution', in Deng Xiaoping's words – has been completed successfully and the goals of modernization set for the year 2000 attained.

The 1976–86 decade is still far too close for a proper perspective, but the indications are that the current Chinese leadership has learned indispensable and obvious lessons from the past, particularly from the appallingly catastrophic decade of havoc. A truly high price was paid for them in terms of human suffering. Whether the undeniable achievements of the PRC in many domains are commensurate to the price paid is again a query which only the Chinese can answer, for only they really know what the actual price was. In the last few years it has been possible to note a tendency to gloss over some of the bitter experiences of the past which might well derive from an understandable and commendable desire to focus attention on the present and even more on the future. It might well come also from the wish to let the deep and still painful wounds finally heal over completely, and from the feeling that scratching the scabs is anyway ultimately futile. Nevertheless, it can be hoped that a people as historically minded as the Chinese are not likely to turn their backs lightheartedly on the tragic ordeals undergone in the recent past. The stress placed for decades on the necessity and advisability of learning by negative example must also have some effect; there are more than enough such examples in the annals of the CCP, the CPSU and the international communist movement. Current visitors to the PRC have been greatly impressed by the determination of the Chinese, especially the intellectuals of the older generation, to pick up the pieces, to make up by their ambitious endeavours the time so unforgivably lost, and to hand over to their successors the knowledge and experience they have acquired.

As the leaders of the CCP – which is and will remain for the foreseeable future the dominant policy- and decision-making body in China – prepared for their Thirteenth Congress in October 1987, they faced tasks of formidable and unparalleled complexity. The completion of the reform of the urban economy is in itself an undertaking calling for immense effort and infinite ingenuity. Moreover, the problem of political reform seems to be of yet greater importance and intricacy. While it has been definitely placed on the agenda, its outlines are still nebulous. It is obvious, however, that the cardinal question relates to a further, significant and far-reaching democratization of political life, affecting both the Party and the nation and involving ever increasing popular participation. The student demonstrations of December 1986 with their call for speeding up significantly the process of democratization have shown the urgency of these issues. All of this implies facing up to the major problems of bureaucracy, over-concentration of power, patriarchal methods and privileges – all mentioned by Deng Xiaoping already in 1980. These have to be solved if the credibility and efficacy of the Party and the vitality and prestige of Marxism are to be restored to the desired level. It is only in this fashion that – assuming success in economic development – a resurgence of dogmatism and sectarianism with its disastrous consequences can be effectively prevented. It follows also that much thought will have to be given to a re-evaluation and restatement of the role and position of the CCP itself. The resignation of Hu Yaobang in January 1987 shows, however, that full unanimity on this and probably a number of other crucial issues does not exist among the top CCP leadership. It is clear that only a successful implementation of the economic and political reform programme will provide the Chinese communists with a chance to prove whether they are capable of making good their bold pledge of 1981 of 'turning China step by step into a modern socialist country which is highly democratic and highly cultured'.

Select Bibliography

Only books in English, pertaining in almost all cases exclusively to the post-1949 period, are listed below. Works in Chinese and the very extensive Soviet literature on contemporary China are not included. It should be noted that a wealth of material is to be found in specialist periodicals; the most useful of these is the *China Quarterly* (London, 1960–). The principal source of official Chinese documentation in English has been the weekly *People's China* (1950–8), superseded in March 1958 by the *Peking Review* (the *Beijing Review* since January 1979).

ADLER, Solomon *The Chinese Economy*. London: Routledge & Kegan Paul, 1957.

ANDORS, Stephen *China's Industrial Revolution: Politics, Planning, and Management, 1949 to the Present*. New York: Pantheon Books, 1977.

ARKUSH, R. David *Fei Xiaotong and Sociology in Revolutionary China*. Cambridge, Mass.: Council on East Asian Studies, Harvard University, 1981.

BACHMAN, David M. *Chen Yun and the Chinese Political System*. Berkeley: University of California Press, 1985.

BARNETT, A. Doak *Communist China: The Early Years, 1949–1955*. New York: Praeger, 1964.

—— *Uncertain Passage: China's Transition to the post-Mao Era*. Washington, DC: The Brookings Institution, 1974.

BAUM, Richard *Prelude to Revolution: Mao, the Party and the Peasant Question*. New York: Columbia University Press, 1975.

——, ed. *China in Ferment: Perspectives on the Cultural Revolution*. Englewood Cliffs, N.J.: Prentice-Hall, 1971.

——, ed. *China's Four Modernizations: The Technological*

Revolution. Boulder, Colo.: Westview, 1980.

—— and TEIWES, Frederick C. *Ssu-Ch'ing: The Socialist Education Movement of 1962–66.* Berkeley: University of California Press, 1968.

BERNSTEIN, Richard *From the Center of the Earth: The Search for the Truth about China.* Boston: Little, Brown, 1982.

BERNSTEIN, Thomas P. *Up to the Mountains and Down to the Villages: The Transfer of Youth from Urban to Rural China.* New Haven: Yale University Press, 1977.

BODDE, Derk *Peking Diary: 1948–1949, A Year of Revolution.* New York: Abelard-Schuman, 1950.

BONAVIA, David *The Chinese.* New York: Lippincott & Crowell, 1980.

—— *Verdict in Peking: The Trial of the Gang of Four.* London: Burnett Books, 1984.

BOORMAN, Howard L. and HOWARD, Richard C., eds. *Biographical Dictionary of Republican China.* New York: Columbia University Press, 4 vols, 1967–71. Index vol., 1979.

BORG, Dorothy and HEINRICHS, Waldo, eds. *Uncertain Years: Chinese–American Relations, 1947–1950.* New York: Columbia University Press, 1980.

BOWIE, Robert and FAIRBANK, John K., eds. *Communist China 1955–1959: Policy Documents with Analysis.* Cambridge, Mass.: Harvard University Press, 1962.

BRUGGER, Bill *China: Liberation and Transformation 1942–1962.* London: Croom Helm, 1981.

—— *China: Radicalism to Revisionism 1962–1979.* London: Croom Helm, 1981.

——, ed. *Chinese Marxism in Flux, 1978–84.* Beckenham: Croom Helm, 1985.

CHANG, Parris H. *Power and Policy in China.* University Park: Pennsylvania State University Press, 1978.

CHAO Kang *Agricultural Production in Communist China, 1949–1965.* Madison: University of Wisconsin Press, 1970.

CHAO Kuo-chün *Agrarian Policy of the Chinese Communist*

Party, 1921–1959. New Delhi: Asia Publishing House, 1960.

CHESNEAUX, Jean *et al. China: The People's Republic, 1949–1976*. New York: Pantheon Books, 1979.

CLAYRE, Alasdair *The Heart of the Dragon*. London: Collins, 1984.

CROLL, Elisabeth *The Politics of Marriage in Contemporary China*. Cambridge: Cambridge University Press, 1981.

—— *Feminism and Socialism in China*. London: Routledge & Kegan Paul, 1978.

DAUBIER, Jean *A History of the Cultural Revolution*. New York: Vintage, 1974.

DENG Xiaoping *Selected Works (1975–1982)*. Beijing: Foreign Languages Press, 1984.

—— *Build Socialism with Chinese Characteristics*. Beijing: Foreign Languages Press, 2nd edn 1987.

DERNBERGER, Robert, ed. *China's Development Experience in Comparative Perspective*. Cambridge, Mass.: Harvard University Press, 1981.

DITTMER, Lowell *Liu Shao-ch'i and the Chinese Cultural Revolution: The Politics of Mass Criticism*. Berkeley: University of California Press, 1974.

DOMES, Jürgen *The Internal Politics of Communist China, 1949–1972*. London: C. Hurst, 1973.

—— *Socialism in the Chinese Countryside*. London: C. Hurst, 1980.

DONNITHORNE, Audrey *China's Economic System*. London: Allen & Unwin, 1967.

ECKSTEIN, Alexander *China's Economic Revolution*. Cambridge: Cambridge University Press, 1977.

—— *et al.*, eds. *Economic Trends in Communist China*. Chicago: Aldine, 1968.

The Eighth National Congress of the Communist Party of China (Documents). Beijing: Foreign Languages Press, 1956.

ELLISON, Herbert J., ed. *The Sino-Soviet Conflict: A Global Perspective*. Seattle: University of Washington Press, 1982.

EPSTEIN, Israel *Tibet Transformed.* Beijing: New World Press, 1983.

ESMEIN, Jean *The Chinese Cultural Revolution.* New York: Anchor Books, 1973.

FAIRBANK, John K. *China Perceived: Images and Policies in Chinese–American Relations.* New York: Knopf, 1974.

FAN, K., ed. *Mao Tse-tung and Lin Piao: Post-revolutionary Writings.* Garden City, N.Y.: Anchor Books, 1972.

FANG, P. J. and FANG, L. G. *Zhou Enlai – A Profile.* Beijing: Foreign Languages Press, 1986.

FEI Hsiao Tung *Towards a People's Anthropology.* Beijing: New World Press, 1981.

FEUCHTWANG, Stephan and HUSSAIN, Athar, eds. *The Chinese Economic Reform.* Beckenham: Croom Helm, 1983.

FEUERWERKER, Albert, ed. *History in Communist China.* Cambridge, Mass.: MIT Press, 1968.

FOKKEMA, D. W. *Literary Doctrine in China and Soviet Influence, 1956–1960.* The Hague: Mouton, 1965.

—— *Report from Peking.* London: C. Hurst, 1971.

FRASER, John *The Chinese: Portrait of a People.* London: Collins, 1981.

GARDNER, John *Chinese Politics and the Succession to Mao.* London: Macmillan, 1982.

GARSIDE, Roger *Coming Alive! China after Mao.* London: Deutsch, 1981.

GINNEKAN, Jaap van *The Rise and Fall of Lin Piao.* New York: Avon Books, 1977.

GITTINGS, John *The Role of the Chinese Army.* London: Oxford University Press, 1968.

—— *Survey of the Sino-Soviet Dispute, 1963–1967.* London: Oxford University Press, 1968.

—— *The World and China, 1922–1972.* New York: Harper & Row, 1974.

GOLDMAN, Merle *Literary Dissent in Communist China.* Cambridge, Mass.: Harvard University Press, 1967.

—— *China's Intellectuals: Advise and Dissent.* Cambridge,

Mass.: Harvard University Press, 1981.

GRAY, Jack and WHITE, Gordon, eds. *China's New Developmental Strategy.* London: Academic Press, 1982.

A Great Trial in Chinese History. Beijing: New World Press, 1981.

GRIFFITH, William E. *The Sino-Soviet Rift.* London: Allen & Unwin, 1964.

GUILLERMAZ, Jacques *The Chinese Communist Party in Power, 1949–1976.* Folkestone: Dawson, 1976.

GURLEY, John G. *China's Economy and the Maoist Strategy.* New York: Monthly Review Press, 1976.

HARDING, Harry *Organizing China: The Problem of Bureaucracy, 1949–1976.* Stanford: Stanford University Press, 1981.

HARRISON, James P. *The Long March to Power: A History of the Chinese Communist Party, 1921–72.* New York: Praeger, 1972.

HINTON, Harold C. *An Introduction to Chinese Politics.* New York: Praeger, 1973.

HINTON, William *Fanshen: A Documentary of Revolution in a Chinese Village.* New York: Vintage, 1966.

—— *Hundred Day War: The Cultural Revolution at Tsinghua University.* New York: Monthly Review Press, 1972.

—— *Shenfan: The Continuing Revolution in a Chinese Village.* New York: Random House, 1983.

HO Ping-ti and TSOU Tang, eds. *China in Crisis.* 3 vols. Chicago: University of Chicago Press, 1968.

HOWE, Christopher *Employment and Economic Growth in Urban China, 1949–57.* Cambridge: Cambridge University Press, 1971.

——, ed. *Shanghai: Revolution and Development in an Asian Metropolis.* Cambridge: Cambridge University Press, 1981.

HSIAO, Katharine Huang *Money and Monetary Policy in Communist China.* New York: Columbia University Press, 1971.

HSIUNG, James C. *Ideology and Practice: The Evolution of Chinese Communism.* New York: Praeger, 1970.

289

HSÜ, Immanuel C. Y. *China without Mao: The Search for a New Order.* Oxford: Oxford University Press, 1983.

HSU Kai-yu, ed. *Literature of the People's Republic of China.* Bloomington: Indiana University Press, 1980.

HUNTER, Neale *Shanghai Journal.* New York: Praeger, 1969.

JOFFE, Ellis *Party and Army: Professionalism and Political Control of the Chinese Officer Corps.* Cambridge, Mass.: Harvard University Press, 1965.

JOHNSON, Chalmers, ed. *Ideology and Politics in Contemporary China.* Seattle: University of Washington Press, 1973.

JOSEPH, William A. *The Critique of Ultra-leftism in China, 1958–1981.* Stanford: Stanford University Press, 1984.

KARNOW, Stanley *Mao and China: From Revolution to Revolution.* New York: Viking, 1972.

KLEIN, Donald W. and CLARK, Ann B., eds. *Biographical Dictionary of Chinese Communism.* Cambridge, Mass.: Harvard University Press, 1971.

KRAUS, Richard C. *Class Conflict in Chinese Socialism.* New York: Columbia University Press, 1981.

LARDY, Nicholas *Agriculture in China's Modern Economic Development.* Cambridge: Cambridge University Press, 1983.

LEE, Hong Yung *The Politics of the Chinese Cultural Revolution.* Berkeley: University of California Press, 1978.

LEWIS, John W., ed. *The City in Communist China.* Stanford: Stanford University Press, 1971.

——, ed. *Party Leadership and Revolutionary Power in China.* Cambridge: Cambridge University Press, 1970.

LEYS, Simon *Chinese Shadows.* New York: Viking, 1977.

LIANG Heng and SHAPIRO, Judith *Son of the Revolution.* London: Chatto & Windus, 1983.

LIEBERTHAL, Kenneth *Revolution and Tradition in Tientsin, 1949–1952.* Stanford: Stanford University Press, 1980.

LINDBECK, John, ed. *China: Management of a Revolutionary Society.* Seattle: University of Washington Press, 1971.

MacFarquhar, Roderick *The Origins of the Cultural Revolution.* vol. 1: *Contradictions Among the People.* London: Oxford University Press, 1974. vol. 2: *The Great Leap Forward, 1958–1960.* Oxford University Press, 1983.

——, ed. *China under Mao: Politics Takes Command.* Cambridge, Mass.: MIT Press, 1966.

——, ed. *The Hundred Flowers Campaign and the Chinese Intellectuals.* New York: Praeger, 1960.

McMillen, Donald H. *Chinese Power and Policy in Xinjiang, 1949–77.* Boulder, Colo.: Westview, 1979.

Mancall, Mark *China at the Center.* New York: The Free Press, 1984.

Mao Tsetung *Selected Works*, vol. V. Beijing: Foreign Languages Press, 1977.

Maxwell, Neville *India's China War.* New York: Anchor Books, 1972.

—— and McFarlane, Bruce, eds. *China's Changed Road to Development.* Oxford: Pergamon, 1984.

Meisner, Maurice *Mao's China and After: A History of the People's Republic.* New York: The Free Press, 1986.

—— *Marxism, Maoism and Utopianism.* Madison: University of Wisconsin Press, 1982.

Moody, Peter R. *Chinese Politics after Mao: Development and Liberalization, 1976 to 1983.* New York: Praeger, 1983.

Myrdal, Jan *Report from a Chinese Village.* New York: Pantheon Books, 1965.

—— *Return to a Chinese Village.* New York: Pantheon Books, 1984.

Nee, Victor *The Cultural Revolution at Peking University.* New York: Monthly Review Press, 1969.

—— and Mozingo, David, eds. *State and Society in Contemporary China.* Ithaca, N.Y.: Cornell University Press, 1983.

Oksenberg, Michel, ed. *China's Developmental Experience.* New York: Praeger, 1973.

ORLEANS, Leo A., ed. *Science in Contemporary China.* Stanford: Stanford University Press, 1981.

PARISH, William L., ed. *Chinese Rural Development: The Great Transformation.* Armonk, N.Y.: M. E. Sharpe, 1985.

PENG Dehuai *Memoirs of a Chinese Marshal.* Beijing: Foreign Languages Press, 1984.

PERKINS, Dwight H., ed. *China's Modern Economy in Historical Perspective.* Stanford: Stanford University Press, 1975.

——, ed. *Rural Small-Scale Industry in the People's Republic of China.* Berkeley: University of California Press, 1977.

PERRY, Elisabeth J. and WONG, Christine, eds. *The Political Economy of Reform in Post-Mao China.* Cambridge, Mass.: Harvard University Press, 1985.

Resolution on Certain Questions in the History of Our Party since the Founding of the People's Republic. Beijing: Foreign Languages Press, 1981.

RICE, Edward E. *Mao's Way.* Berkeley: University of California Press, 1972.

ROBINSON, Joan *The Cultural Revolution in China.* Harmondsworth: Penguin, 1969.

ROBINSON, Thomas W., ed. *The Cultural Revolution in China.* Berkeley: University of California Press, 1971.

ROSEN, Stanley *Red Guard Factionalism and the Cultural Revolution in Guangzhou.* Boulder, Colo.: Westview, 1982.

ROZMAN, Gilbert, ed. *The Modernization of China.* New York: The Free Press, 1981.

—— *A Mirror for Socialism: Soviet Criticism of China.* Princeton: Princeton University Press, 1985.

SAICH, Tony *China: Politics and Government.* London: Macmillan, 1981.

SALISBURY, Harrison E. *The Long March.* New York: Harper & Row, 1985.

SCALAPINO, Robert A., ed. *Elites in the People's Republic of China.* Seattle: University of Washington Press, 1972.

SCHRAM, Stuart R. *Ideology and Policy in China since the Third Plenum, 1978–1984.* London: SOAS, 1984.

——, ed. *Authority, Participation and Cultural Change in China.* Cambridge: Cambridge University Press, 1973.

——, ed. *Mao Tse-tung Unrehearsed: Talks and Letters, 1956–71.* Harmondsworth: Penguin, 1974.

SCHRAN, Peter *The Development of Chinese Agriculture, 1950–1959.* Urbana: University of Illinois Press, 1969.

SCHURMANN, Franz *Ideology and Organization in Communist China.* Berkeley: University of California Press, 2nd rev. edn 1968.

—— and SCHELL, Orville, eds. *The China Reader: Communist China.* New York: Vintage, 1967.

SCHWARTZ, Benjamin I. *Communism in China: Ideology in Flux.* Cambridge, Mass.: Harvard University Press, 1968.

SELDEN, Mark, ed. *The People's Republic of China: A Documentary History of Revolutionary Change.* New York: Monthly Review Press, 1979.

—— and LIPPIT, Victor, eds. *The Transition to Socialism in China.* London: Croom Helm, 1982.

SEYBOLT, Peter J., ed. *The Rustification of Urban Youth in China.* White Plains, N.Y.: M. E. Sharpe, 1977.

SHABAD, Theodore *China's Changing Map: A Political and Economic Geography of the Chinese People's Republic.* London: Methuen, 1956.

SHORT, Philip *The Dragon and the Bear: Inside China and Russia Today.* London: Abacus, 1982.

SHUE, Vivienne *Peasant China in Transition: The Dynamics of Development Toward Socialism.* Berkeley: University of California Press, 1980.

SIMMONS, Robert R. *The Strained Alliance: Peking, P'yongyang, Moscow and the Politics of the Korean Civil War.* New York: The Free Press, 1975.

SNOW, Edgar *Red China Today: The Other Side of the River.* New York: Random House, 1970.

—— *The Long Revolution.* New York: Random House, 1972.

SOLOMON, Richard H. *Mao's Revolution and the Chinese Political*

293

Culture. Berkeley: University of California Press, 1971.

STARR, John B. *Continuing the Revolution: The Political Thought of Mao.* Princeton: Princeton University Press, 1979.

SU Shaozhi, ed. *Selected Studies on Marxism.* Beijing: Chinese Academy of Social Sciences, 1985.

TEIWES, Frederick C. *Politics and Purges in China.* Folkestone: Dawson, 1979.

—— *Leadership, Legitimacy and Conflict in China.* London: Macmillan, 1984.

TOPPING, Seymour *Journey Between Two Chinas.* New York: Harper & Row, 1972.

The Twelfth National Congress of the CPC. Beijing: Foreign Languages Press, 1982.

VAN SLYKE, Lyman P. *Enemies and Friends: The United Front in Chinese Communist History.* Stanford: Stanford University Press, 1967.

VOGEL, Ezra F. *Canton under Communism: Programs and Politics in a Provincial Capital, 1949–1968.* Cambridge, Mass.: Harvard University Press, 1969.

WAKEMAN, Frederic, Jr. *History and Will: Philosophical Perspectives of Mao Tse-tung's Thought.* Berkeley: University of California Press, 1973.

WALKER, Kenneth R. *Food Grain Procurement and Consumption in China.* Cambridge: Cambridge University Press, 1984.

WELCH, Holmes *Buddhism under Mao.* Cambridge, Mass.: Harvard University Press, 1972.

WHITING, Allen S. *China Crosses the Yalu: The Decision to Enter the Korean War.* New York: Macmillan, 1960.

WHITSON, William W. with HUANG Chen-hsia *The Chinese High Command: A History of Communist Military Politics, 1927–71.* New York: Praeger, 1973.

Who's Who in Communist China. 2 vols. Hong Kong: Union Research Institute, 2nd rev. edn 1969–70.

WILSON, Dick, ed. *Mao Tse-tung in the Scales of History.*

Cambridge: Cambridge University Press, 1977.

WITKE, Roxane *Comrade Chiang Ch'ing.* Boston: Little, Brown, 1977.

WU Yuan-li, ed. *China: A Handbook.* New York: Praeger, 1973.

XUE Muqiao *China's Socialist Economy.* Beijing: Foreign Languages Press, 2nd edn 1986.

YAHUDA, Michael *Towards the End of Isolationism: China's Foreign Policy after Mao.* London: Macmillan, 1983.
—— *China's Role in World Affairs.* London: Croom Helm, 1978.

YANG, C. K. *Chinese Communist Society: The Family and the Village.* Cambridge, Mass.: MIT Press, 1965.

YU Guangyuan, ed. *China's Socialist Modernization.* Beijing: Foreign Languages Press, 1984.

YUE Daiyun and WAKEMAN, Carolyn *To the Storm: The Odyssey of a Revolutionary Chinese Woman.* Berkeley: University of California Press, 1985.

ZAGORIA, Donald S. *The Sino-Soviet Conflict, 1956–1961.* Princeton: Princeton University Press, 1962.

Index

Afghanistan 262, 281
Africa 39, 157, 159, 231
Agrarian Reform Law 20
agrarian revolution *see* Land Reform
agriculture 18–21, 31–2, 34–5, 55, 60, 62–3, 65, 80, 84–5, 90, 94, 146, 192, 218, 221, 248, 253, 256–8, 266–73, 275
Albania 101–2, 121
All-China Federation of Labour 150
All-China Federation of Trade Unions 137
All Men Are Brothers 164
Analects 170
Anhui 136, 144, 267
Anti-Japanese War *see* War of Resistance
Anti-Rightist Canpaign 53–4, 124, 217, 251
Arkhipov, I. 280
Asia 39, 157, 159, 231
atomic technology 58, 75–6, 81, 145, 208
Australia 79
Autumn Harvest Uprising 145

Bandung Conference 39
Beidahe 181
Beijing 17, 25, 27, 30, 39–40, 42, 52, 73–4, 76, 84–5, 87–8, 101–2, 104, 110–11, 114, 120, 122, 124–7, 130–2, 134–6, 138–41, 144–9, 154, 157, 160–1, 163–4, 166, 168–9, 171–4, 180–1, 183–4, 186, 189, 195–9, 201–2, 212–14, 226–8, 231–4, 239, 241, 246, 266, 280–1
Beijing Aeronautical Institute 72, 121, 129
Beijing–Hankou Railway 30
Beijing University (Beida) 52, 56, 118–20, 122, 124
Belgium 144
Beria, L. P. 85, 156
Bhutto, Z. 200
Bo Yibo 154, 165, 227
Bolsheviks 174
bourgeoisie 16, 23, 45, 51, 92–3, 103, 106, 194, 197, 222, 237, 273, 278
Bucharest 100
Buddha 126

Bulganin, N. A. 40
Bulgaria 27
bureaucracy 22–3, 38, 45, 47, 51–2, 110, 255–6, 283
Byzantium 44

Camp David 76
Canada 79
Canton *see* Guangzhou
Canton Commune 136, 144, 146–7
Cao Diqiu 134
Capital 219
Carter, J. 233
cement production 90, 256, 272
census (1953) 47, 56
   (1982) 270
Central People's Government 17
Central Soviet Area 63, 143–4, 147, 150–1
Changsha 181
Chanqun Railway 27
chemical fertilizers 90, 256, 272
Chen Boda 82–3, 95, 118–19, 122–3, 156, 167, 177, 180, 245
Chen Duxiu 14
Chen Pixian 134
Chen Xilian 180, 201–3, 243
Chen Yi 15, 35, 141–3, 146, 151, 157–8, 170, 192
Chen Yonggui 188
Chen Yun 15, 48, 63, 81, 123, 141, 143, 148, 219, 229, 241, 243, 250–1, 263
Chen Zaidao 166
Chengdu 17, 129, 163
Chiang Kai-shek 17, 26–8, 84, 109, 142
Chinese Academy of Science 42, 71–2, 86, 193
Chinese Academy of Social Sciences 219
Chinese Communist Party (CCP) 13–28, 31, 34–54, 57–61, 63–4, 67–74, 76, 78–88, 92–6, 98–111, 113–4, 122–3, 128, 130–40, 142–58, 161–3, 167, 173–83, 185–93, 196–7, 199–200, 207–17, 219–23, 225–30, 236–8, 241–4, 246–56, 259, 262–3, 267, 272, 274–5, 277–83
Central Advisory Commission (CAC) 263, 274

Central Committee 34–6, 39–40, 42,
47–8, 51, 62, 66–8, 79, 84, 93, 107,
120, 122–3, 129, 132, 134, 136,
138, 142–7, 150, 154–5, 159, 165,
173, 175–9, 186–7, 191–2, 196,
198–9, 201, 203, 210, 212–14, 216–
17, 225–7, 229, 239–43, 248–9,
262–4, 267, 272, 274, 276
Congress: First (1921) 126; Seventh
(1945) 46, 142, 145, 150–1, 260;
Eighth (1956) 46–9, 63, 68, 92,
142, 144, 152, 173, 175, 193, 259;
Ninth (1969) 174–9, 182, 187, 215,
260; Tenth (1973) 186–90, 215,
260; Eleventh (1977) 214–6, 260;
Twelfth (1982) 243, 259, 262–3,
280; Thirteenth (1987) 282
Constitution 48, 123, 173, 175, 187,
262–3
Discipline Inspection Committee 229,
244, 263, 274
Military Affairs Commission (MAC)
95, 181, 191, 203, 243, 248
Political Bureau 18, 38–9, 63–4, 68–
70, 82, 84–5, 110–11, 114, 117–18,
139, 141–8, 150–1, 154–5, 165,
176–7, 179, 186, 188, 191, 196,
198, 201–3, 212, 216, 225, 229,
243, 245, 248–9, 263–4, 267, 274,
276
Standing Committee 48, 82, 111, 118,
123, 136, 139, 143, 155, 177, 188,
191, 216, 229, 243, 246, 263–4
Third Plenum (1981) 227, 236, 254,
266, 281
Chinese Eastern Railway 27
Chinese People's Political Consultative
Conference (CPPCC) 16–17, 218
Chinese People's Volunteers (CPV) 29–
30
Chinese Revolution 16, 25–6, 46, 61, 140,
148, 150–2, 156, 164, 174, 195, 199–
200, 251–4, 279–80
Chinese Revolution (1925–7) 15, 63, 69,
85, 142–3, 150–1, 164
Chongqing 38–9, 52, 163
class struggle 51, 86, 92–3, 106, 193–4,
199, 214, 227, 237
coal production 19, 55, 66, 90, 207, 256,
272
colonialism 237, 280
collectivization 21, 35–7, 42, 55, 60–1,
267, 269
Common Programme 16, 20

communes, people's 36, 63–4, 66, 75, 77,
79, 93, 221, 266, 268
Communist International 25, 104
Communist Movement, International 43,
50, 57–9, 99, 101–2, 104–5, 282
Communist Party of China *see* Chinese
Communist Party
Communist Party of the Soviet Union
(CPSU) 58–9, 73, 93, 98–105, 159,
183, 281–2
Twentieth Congress 41, 43, 46, 99
Twenty-second Congress 101
Communist Youth League (CYL) 22,
137–8
constitution (PRC) 16, 37–8, 180, 218
cooperatives, agricultural 34–7, 63–4
cooperativization 21, 34
Confucius 126, 170, 189–90
Confucianists 190
cotton production 56, 60, 66, 90, 208,
256, 271–2
Cuba 102
'cultural revolution' 21, 45, 49, 51, 68, 72,
85, 88, 90, 94, 96, 101, 106–7, 109,
114, 117, 119–20, 122–3, 126–30, 132–
3, 136–7, 139–41, 148–9, 153–63, 165,
167, 169, 172, 174–9, 182, 186, 188,
192–5, 198–200, 202–3, 206, 208–23,
225, 227–8, 230, 232, 236, 238–42,
246–8, 251, 253–4, 259–60, 263, 278–9
Cultural Revolution Group (CRG) 118,
120–3, 129, 131, 133, 135–6, 141, 143,
149, 153, 155–8, 161, 166–8, 170
culture 48, 92, 114, 119, 126, 237, 243,
261
Czechoslovakia 172

Dalien 27
Daqing 218
Dazhai 218
December Ninth Movement (1935) 52,
109, 118, 120, 150, 197
Democratic League 87
Democratic Party (US) 28
demography *see* population
Deng Pufang 128
Deng Tuo 87–9, 111
Deng Xiaoping 15, 48, 81, 86, 94, 101–2,
138, 148, 151–2, 168; during the 'cultural revolution' 125, 128–9, 133, 149,
152, 154, 174, 190–6, 198–9; policies
and activity, 1976–86, 209, 212–3,
216–8, 220–34, 236–9, 241–3, 245,
247, 249–50, 252, 254, 259–61, 263,

266, 275, 278, 280–1, 283
Deng Yingzhao 190, 229
Deng Zihui 35
Djilas, M. 52
dogmatism 46, 103–4, 223, 225, 236, 283
Dong Biwu 177, 188
Double Hundred *see* Hundred Flowers
Dubcek, A. 172
Dulles, J. F. 39

economy 13, 18, 22, 31–2, 34, 48, 56, 59–
    60, 62, 66–7, 74, 76, 80–1, 85, 92, 94,
    137, 187, 208–9, 217–20, 233, 237,
    239–40, 248, 256–61, 266, 268, 272–6,
    278, 283
education 24, 91, 222–3, 243, 255, 261
Eighth Route Army 69, 138, 145, 147,
    165, 199
Eisenhower, D. 76
electrical power 55, 91, 256, 272
Eliot, T. S. 68
Engels, F. 54, 170, 180, 230
Europe:
    Eastern 32, 37, 49–50, 56, 58, 75, 121,
        132, 160, 281
    Western 76, 160
Eyuwan Soviet 144, 146

Fallaci, O. 250
Fei Xiaotong 269
Feng Yuxiang 151
feudal fascism 73, 194–5, 237, 247
feudalism 20, 84, 130, 237, 247, 280
Field Army: First 165; Second 138, 144,
    151; Third 40, 142, 146; Fourth 82–3,
    169, 180; North China 145
Five-Year Plan: First (1953–7) 31–2, 35,
    55, 65; Second (1958–62) 48, 63; Sixth
    (1981–5) 248, 258, 261, 271, 275;
    Seventh (1986–90) 261, 274–5
Forbidden City 124
foreign policy 25, 230, 232, 261–2, 280
Four Families 22, 84
Four Olds 126
Four Pests 60
Four Principles 237–9
France 29, 141–4, 151, 160–1, 163, 208,
    234, 281
Fu Lei 127
Fu Tsong 127
Fujian 83–4, 145

'gang of four' 89, 136, 203, 210–12, 214–
    15, 222–3, 232, 237, 242, 244

Gansu 69
Gao Gang 39–40
Gate of Heavenly Peace *see* Tiananmen
Geneva 38
Germany 38, 104, 163
Gomulka, W. 49–50
Gorbachev, M. S. 280
grain production 18–19, 55, 60, 66, 77, 79,
    90, 208, 217, 240, 256, 271–2
Great Britain 28, 63, 161, 166, 265–6
Great Leap Forward 49, 62–70, 74–5, 78,
    80–1, 86–7, 90, 93, 98, 104, 108, 146,
    148, 219, 225, 230, 239, 251
Great Proletarian Cultural Revolution *see*
    'cultural revolution'
Green Gang 23
Guangdong 72, 136, 139, 144, 147–8
Guangxi 139, 151, 163, 171, 234
Guomindang (KMT) 13, 16–19, 21–2, 26,
    28–9, 39, 41, 52, 69, 74, 84–5, 138,
    142–7, 150, 154, 163, 165, 201, 233,
    254

Hai Rui 87, 112
Hai-lu-feng 146
Hainan 17, 277
Hakkas 147
Han dynasty 180
Hangzhou 112, 117, 181, 198
Hankou 165
Hanyang 165
He Long 15, 164–5, 168, 172, 191–2, 254
health 91
Heilungjiang 140, 218
Henan 64, 139, 144, 162, 170
Himalayas 235
Historical Records 86
Honecker, E. 281
Hong Kong 139, 161, 265–6, 277
Hongqi 84
Hopson, D. 161
How to Be a Good Communist 150
Hoxha, E. 121
Hu Feng 41–2
Hu Qiaomu 192, 219–21, 245
Hu Sheng 279–80
Hu Yaobang 138, 192, 217, 229, 241, 243,
    245, 249, 252–3, 255, 260–2, 264, 279–
    80, 283
Hua Guofeng 42, 188, 196, 197, 199,
    201–3, 209–18, 221, 226, 228–9, 232–
    3, 239, 241, 243, 248–9, 264
Huai-Hai Campaign 142, 146, 151
Huan Xiang 272–4

Huang Yongsheng 180, 245
Hubei 82, 143–4, 155, 170, 201
Humphrey, H. 75
Hunan 27, 69, 78, 87, 127, 136, 138, 143, 145, 150, 164, 170, 182, 196
Hundred Flowers and Hundred Schools 46, 51–3, 87, 278–9
Hungary 49–50, 110

I He Tuan 27
Imperial City 131
illiteracy 24, 60, 91, 270–1
Inchon 29
India 74, 76, 102, 235
Indochina 38–9, 231–3
industry 18–23, 31–3, 48, 55, 59–60, 62, 65, 70, 79–80, 192, 207, 218, 220, 240, 248, 253, 256–8, 268, 270–3, 275
industrialization 20, 31, 33, 35, 41, 48, 269
inflation 19, 257
intellectuals 14–15, 24–5, 41–3, 46–7, 51, 53, 69, 81, 110, 127, 185, 213, 217, 219, 222, 242, 261, 279, 282
Italy 281

Jacobins 54
Japan 15–16, 18, 26–7, 39, 41, 82, 85, 138, 142, 144–5, 147, 151, 154–5, 208, 232–3, 240, 261, 279, 282
Jaruzelski, W. 281
Ji Dengkui 188, 243
Jian Bozan 127
Jian Tengjiao 245
Jiang Qing 84, 111, 112, 114, 118, 122–3, 130, 133, 147, 155, 158, 164, 166–8, 173, 177, 179, 186, 189–97, 199, 201–2, 208, 215, 241, 245, 247
Jiangsu 92, 192, 269
Jiangxi 114, 142–5, 147, 150–1, 174, 190, 201
Jinggangshan 69, 121, 138, 142, 145

Kaifeng 174
Kampuchea 231–4, 262, 280–1
Kang Sheng 84–5, 97, 111, 118, 122–3, 155–6, 158, 167, 173, 177, 188, 201, 241, 245
Khmer Rouges 231
Khruschchev, N. S. 40, 43–4, 59, 74–6, 100–2, 104, 117–19, 159, 196, 250
Kissinger, H. 184
Ko-lao-hui 164
Kohl, H. 280

Korean War 21, 26, 28, 30, 38, 96
Kosygin, A. 183
Kowloon 265
Kuai Dafu 149, 172

Lan Ping *see* Jiang Qing
land reform 19–21, 33–4, 49, 93, 267
landlords 16, 18, 20, 93, 223
Lang Son 235
Lao She 127
Latin America 159
League of Left-wing Writers 88
Legalists 190
Lei Feng 95
Lenin, V. I. 160, 170, 224, 230
Li Da 126
Li Dazhao 14
Li Desheng 188
Li Fuchun 33, 141, 144
Li Lisan 254
Li Xiannian 15, 141, 143–4, 146, 155, 199, 202–3, 211, 216, 243, 280
Li Junhe *see* Jiang Qing
Li Zuopeng 180, 245
Liao Mosha 87–9
Liaoning 201
Liberated Areas 18–19, 21, 88, 150, 196
Liberation Daily 112, 114, 119
Lin Biao 15, 39, 71, 82, 83–4, 89, 95–7, 109, 112–14, 120–4, 127, 129, 131–2, 135–6, 140–1, 143, 153, 156, 158, 164–70, 174–5, 177, 179–82, 184, 186–8, 194–5, 208, 215, 237, 241, 244–5
Lin Linguo 180, 245
Lin Zhao 124
Little Red Book *see Quotations from Chairman Mao*
Liu Bang 180
Liu Bocheng 15, 144, 151, 170
Liu Shaoqi 15, 47–8, 67, 72, 78–81, 94, 98, 101, 106, 130, 132, 142, 148, 150–1, 152, 153; and the Great Leap Forward 78–9, 86; during the 'cultural revolution' 118, 120, 123, 125, 129, 133, 137, 149, 152, 154, 168, 173–4; rehabilitation of 227–8, 241, 244–5, 254
Liu Ying 72
Long March 15, 39, 68, 71–2, 82, 96, 111, 114, 138, 142–7, 150–1, 165, 188, 264
Lu Dingyi 42, 46, 114, 130, 136, 241
Lu Ping 118
Lu Xun 41
Lushan Conference (1959) 70–2, 75, 78, 82, 156, 251

Lushan Meeting (1970) 179–80
Luo Fu *see* Zhang Wentian
Luo Ruiqing 113–14, 130
Luoyang 162

Ma Yinchu 56
MacArthur, D. 29
Malraux, A. 109
Malthusianism 56
Manchus 127
Mao Anying 29
Mao Yuanxin 201
Mao Zedong 13, 15–16, 21, 26, 29, 33, 39,
    48, 50–1, 54–5, 57, 66, 68, 70, 72, 79,
    83–8, 92–3, 96, 102, 104, 106, 108,
    124, 126–7, 133, 142–3, 145–8, 150,
    152–3, 180, 200–1, 213, 224–5, 230,
    249, 252, 254, 261, 264; and collectivi-
    zation 21, 35–6; and 'cultural revolu-
    tion' 45, 94–5, 107, 110–2, 114, 117–9,
    121–3, 128–30, 135, 137, 139–40, 148–
    9, 159, 164, 166–8, 170, 172, 174–9,
    181–2, 185–90, 193–9, 202, 211–2,
    215, 231, 237, 244, 253; and economic
    policies 56, 59–60; and foreign policy
    25, 57–8; and Great Leap Forward
    60–2, 64–8, 81; and Hu Feng 41–2;
    and Hundred Flowers 46; and
    Kruschchev 74, 76, 100; and Peng
    Dehuai 69–71, 73, 81–2; personality
    cult of 48, 97–8, 109, 120, 123–4, 164,
    170, 175, 210, 214, 223–4, 238, 253–4,
    262; role and place in history 200,
    228, 238, 246, 248, 250–1; and the
    Soviet Union 43, 45, 74, 103, 105,
    159; and Stalin 43–5, 174
Mao Zedong Thought 48, 83, 95, 97, 119,
    128, 130, 140, 171, 175, 213, 236, 238,
    243, 250, 252–4
Marriage Law 24
Marx, K. 170, 180, 219, 224, 230, 279
Marxism 14, 37, 41, 52–3, 100, 104–5,
    127, 189, 196, 224, 228–30, 244, 251,
    253–4, 260, 279–80, 283
Marxism–Leninism 14–15, 44, 59, 75, 84,
    99, 104, 107, 238
May Fourth Movement (1919) 14, 52,
    109, 120, 197
May Seventh Cadre Schools 185
May Sixteenth group 166–7
mechanization (of agriculture) 21, 35, 63,
    217, 268–9
Ming dynasty 87
modernization 14, 21, 31, 48, 55, 197,

217, 220, 223, 227, 232, 240, 260, 265,
    281
Mongols 44
Mongolian People's Republic 181, 262,
    281
Moscow 26, 40, 49–50, 59, 73, 101–4, 144,
    147, 150–1, 159–60, 184, 231
Mussolini, B. 194

Nagy, I. 50, 198
Nakasone, Y. 280
Nanchang 138, 174, 181
Nanchang Uprising 82, 138, 142, 144, 164
Nanjing 138, 197–8
Nanjing Treaty 265
national minorities 20, 45
National People's Congress (NPC) 37,
    192, 218, 240, 242, 257, 274
National Revolutionary Army 142
nationalization 22, 32, 42, 61
Nazis 121
New Democratic Youth League 22, 138
New Fourth Army 40, 142, 144–5
New People's Study Society 143, 150
Nie Rongzhen 15, 144–5, 216
Nie Yuanzi 118–20, 134, 172
Nixon, R. 184, 230
Normandy 161
Northern Expedition 144, 147

October Revolution 14, 57, 170
oil production 90, 207, 240, 256, 272
Opium Wars 29, 265
Organic Law 17
'Outline of Project 571' 180–1

Pahlavi, M. 232
Pakistan 200
Paris Commune 135
peasants 14–16, 19–20, 22, 33–7, 45, 47,
    59, 62–4, 66, 78–80, 87, 92–3, 111,
    134, 138, 143–5, 150, 155, 164, 172,
    185, 196, 199, 201, 256, 266–70
Peng Dehuai 15, 29, 69, 70–3, 75, 81–2,
    88, 98, 112, 129, 147–8, 170, 191, 227,
    251, 254
Peng Pai 254
Peng Zhen 100–1, 111, 112–14, 117, 130,
    241–2
People's Daily 88, 95, 112, 119, 224
People's Liberation Army (PLA) 13, 17,
    20, 22, 26, 28–9, 38, 69, 71, 81–3, 95–
    7, 102, 106, 109, 113–4, 119–20, 124–
    5, 129, 132, 135–6, 138–40, 147, 151–

2, 159–61, 165–6, 169–72, 176, 182, 185, 188, 191, 199, 203, 212, 234–5
People's Militia 201
personality cult (Stalin's) 43–4, 48
Petőfi Club 110
Phnom Penh 232, 234
Pingxingguan 82
Pol Pot 232–3
Poland 49–50, 104
Polish United Workers Party 49
population 56, 59, 90, 208, 257, 260–1, 269–71
Port Arthur 27, 40
Poznan 75
practice criterion 223–5, 227, 236, 278, 281
production teams 79, 266–8
Proletariat *see* workers

Qian Xuesen 25
Qin Shihuang 180, 189, 190, 194
Qinghua University 120, 122, 149, 171
Qiu Huizuo 180, 245
Qu Qiubai 254
Qufu 126
Quemoy 74
Quotations from Chairman Mao Zedong 97, 121

Rao Shushi 39–40
Reagan, R. 280
Rectification Campaign (1942–4) 85, 150
Red Army, Chinese 69, 71, 82, 138, 141–2, 144–5, 147, 151, 165, 199, 201
Red Guards 120–34, 136–40, 146, 149–50, 153, 155, 158, 160–1, 165–6, 168–72, 192, 225
Red Star Over China 138
Republican Party (US) 28
Resolution on Party History (1945) 25
Resolution on Party History (1981) 54, 97, 107, 123–4, 161–3, 177, 181, 187, 194, 203, 208–9, 215, 230, 245, 247–53, 259–60
revisionism 59, 73, 92–3, 100–1, 103, 106–7, 110, 119, 126, 131, 158, 172, 195–6, 198, 219
Revolutionary Committee 136, 140, 161, 169, 171
Revolutionary Rebels 126, 129–30, 132–3, 137, 140, 153, 158, 161–3, 165, 171, 192
Rolland, R. 127
Rumania 100, 232

Russia, Tsarist 27, 31, 44, 183
Russians 45, 57
Russo–Japanese War (1905) 27

San-fan Campaign 23
Scarlet Guards 134
science 46, 192, 220–2, 243, 253, 258, 261, 278, 281
Scientific and Technological Commission 145
sectarianism 46, 51, 103–4, 223, 236, 283
'seek truth from facts' 213, 223–4, 227, 244, 250
Seoul 29
Shaanxi 39, 165
Shandong 84, 111
Shanghai 23–4, 41–2, 62, 85, 88, 95, 111–12, 117, 127, 133–6, 140, 142–3, 150–1, 184, 187, 189, 197, 201–2, 257
Shanxi 111, 140, 146, 154, 196, 218
Shehu, M. 121
Sichuan 17, 138, 141, 144, 146, 151, 162–3, 248, 267
Sieyes, E. T. 211
Sima Qian 86, 200
Sino–American relations 184, 233
Sino–Soviet relations 41, 58, 75–6, 81, 100, 102, 113, 152, 159–60, 173, 182–3, 232, 262, 280
Sino–Soviet Treaty (1950) 27
Sino–Vietnamese relations 231
Sixteenth May Circular 117–18
Sixteen Points Decision 123, 128, 137
Smedley, A. 141
Snow, E. 97, 107, 109, 138, 184
socialism 14, 25, 31–3, 35–8, 44–5, 48, 50, 52–3, 57–9, 61, 67, 73–4, 81, 86, 93, 99, 102–3, 105–6, 106, 118, 172, 187, 195, 197, 209, 215, 219–20, 222, 227, 230–2, 234–5, 237, 241, 247, 253, 257, 261, 266, 272, 280–3
Socialist Education Movement 93–4, 106, 111
Socialist Youth League 82, 150–1
Soviet Union 25–7, 30–2, 36–8, 40–1, 44–6, 49–50, 56–8, 74–6, 81, 85, 99–100, 102–5, 110, 114, 131, 156, 159, 161, 171–5, 183–5, 223, 230–4, 262, 280–1
Stalin, J. V. 12, 25–6, 36–7, 40–1, 43–5, 50, 59, 86, 97, 101, 104, 106, 170, 174, 250
Stalinism 44–5, 50, 86, 230, 247
State Administrative Council 17, 132, 248
State Planning Commission 39, 143

Index

State Statistical Bureau 66, 240, 271
Steel Campaign (1958) 64–6
steel production 19, 55, 65–6, 90, 203, 217, 240, 256, 272
students 52, 118, 120, 122, 127, 133, 136–9, 141–2, 150, 162, 165, 171, 223, 283
subjectivism 51, 68
Summer Palace 126
Sun Yefang 77–8, 219–20, 221
Suslov, M. 102

Taipei 233
Taiwan 17, 28–9, 184, 233, 266
Taiwan Straits 17, 29, 74
Tan Zhenlin 141, 143, 145–6
Tangshan 199
Tanzania–Zambia Railroad 157
Tao Zhu 136, 191, 227, 254
Tehran 232
Ten-Year Plan 217–18, 221, 239
Thatcher, M. 280
Tian Jiyun 276–7
Tiananmen movement 197–200, 212, 228–9
Tiananmen Square 124–5, 197, 213
Tibet 126
Tirana 121
Tito, J. 26, 73, 232
Tonkin Gulf 113
trade 22–3, 32–3, 257
trade unions 24, 137
transport 18, 65, 258
Truman, H. 28–9
Tsunyi 70
Twelve-Year Plan 60, 62
'two whatevers' group 211, 213, 223, 225–7, 236–9, 243

Uighurs 125
unemployment 257
United Nations 28, 184, 231
United States of America 26–9, 32, 39, 58, 74, 76, 83, 113, 139, 159, 175, 184–5, 223, 230, 234, 262
Urumqi 17
Ussuri 173, 182

Vietnam 113, 171, 231–5, 262, 280
Vietnam War 113, 159, 184, 231
Voroshilov, K. 57

Wan Li 267
Wang Dongxing 188, 201, 202–3, 211–12, 216, 225, 239, 243

Wang Guangmei 149, 155, 241
Wang Hongwen 134, 136, 187–8, 202, 245, 247
Wang Li 166
Wang Ming 25
Wang Zhen 229
War of Liberation (1946–9) 25, 39, 69, 82, 143, 145–7
War of Resistance (1939–45) 15–16, 18–19, 39, 41, 63, 69, 82, 84–5, 138, 142–5, 147, 150–1, 154, 165, 192, 252
warlords 14, 156
Warsaw 50
Warsaw Pact 50
Washington 113, 184, 233
Wei Guoqing 188
Whampoa Military Academy 82, 143–4, 146–7
White Paper on US–China policy 28
Women's Federation 24, 137
work teams 20, 94
workers 16, 18, 47, 51, 55, 63, 92, 119, 126, 133–4, 136–8, 162, 165, 171, 186, 222
Wu De 188, 212, 239, 243
Wu Faxian 180, 245
Wu Han 87–9, 111–12
Wuchang 165
Wu-fan Campaign 23
Wuhan 30, 66, 123, 140, 144, 165–6, 168, 181
Wuhan University 126
Wuxi 72

Xi'an Incident 38, 147
Xie Fuzhi 155, 156, 166–7, 173, 177, 241, 245
Xinjiang 41, 125, 139, 144, 146, 173, 183
Xu Shiyu 188
Xu Ziangjian 15, 141, 146–7
Xue Muqiao 269

Yagoda, G. G. 85
Yalu 29
Yan'an 15, 63, 83, 85, 111, 138, 150, 157, 192, 213
Yang Shangkun 114, 130, 201, 227
Yangtse 26, 82, 122, 131, 133, 163
Yao Wenyuan 112, 118, 133–5, 167, 175, 177, 202, 245, 247
Ye Jianying 15, 141, 147–8, 188, 199, 202, 211, 213, 216, 218, 221 242–3
Ye Qun 177, 180, 245
Yezhov, N. I. 85

303

Index

Young Communist League (YCL) 138-9
Yu Guangyuan 279
Yu Qiuli 240
Yugoslavia 26, 57, 59, 73, 93, 101, 232
Yunnan 139, 163, 324
Yunnan Military Academy 147

Zhang Chungiao 112, 133-5, 149, 167,
   175, 177, 188, 194, 202, 245, 247
Zhang Linzhi 130
Zhang Wentian 69-72, 254
Zhao Ziyang 139, 243, 248, 258, 261, 267,
   275, 280
Zhejiang 170

Zhengzhou 162, 198
Zhongnanhai 131, 152, 173-4
Zhou Enlai 15, 17, 29, 38-9, 47-8, 50, 81,
   98, 101, 104, 132, 142-4, 147-8, 151,
   157, 183-4, 195-7, 199, 228, 253, 261;
   and intellectuals 42-3, 46, 81; and the
   'cultural revolution' 123, 141, 146,
   158, 161, 166-8, 174, 177, 181, 186-8,
   190-2, 217
Zhou Yuchi 245
Zhu De 15, 48, 69, 82, 123, 138, 141-2,
   148, 177, 188, 199, 253
Zhu Yuanzhang 87, 180